Scriptless

*Jean —
I'm so grateful to you as neighbor

Have many great new scripts with your new knee

Aloha
Carol*

Scriptless
A Memoir

Carol McMillan

Sidekick Press
Bellingham, Washington

Copyright © 2023 by Carol McMillan

All rights reserved. No part of this publication may be reproduced, distributed, or transmitted in any form or by any means, including photocopying, recording, digital scanning, or other electronic or mechanical methods, without the prior written permission of the publisher, except in the case of brief quotations embodied in critical reviews and certain other noncommercial uses permitted by copyright law. For permission requests, please address Sidekick Press.

This memoir represents the author's recollection of her past. These true stories are faithfully composed based on memory, photographs, diary entries, and other supporting documents. Some names, places, and other identifying details have been changed to protect the privacy of those represented. Conversations between individuals are meant to reflect the essence, meaning, and spirit of the events described.

Published 2023
Printed in the United States of America
ISBN: 978-1-958808-10-8
LCCN: 2023901254

Sidekick Press
2950 Newmarket Street, Suite 101-329
Bellingham, Washington 98226
sidekickpress.com

Carol McMillan 1944-
Scriptless: A Memoir

Cover design by Andrea Gabriel

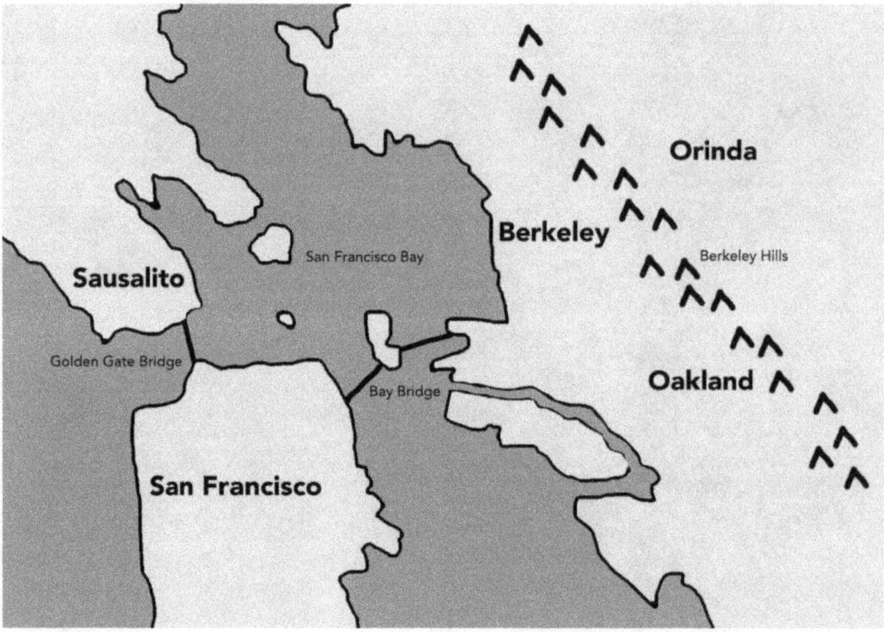
Orinda
Berkeley
San Francisco Bay
Berkeley Hills
Sausalito
Golden Gate Bridge
Bay Bridge
Oakland
San Francisco

PROLOGUE

Encouraged by island breezes, a thin layer of the Pacific Ocean rose up from its bed and slid eastward toward the hills of San Francisco. Invisible and unnoticed, it flowed on. Encountering the cold waters of a coastal current, the moisture's chilled droplets huddled together, startled into becoming a Fog. Unlike the usual fogs in this area, in the 1960s, The Fog of Change was forged by something mystical, carrying a purpose as it flowed through the Golden Gate to touch each human settlement that skirted the arms of San Francisco Bay.

The unique geography of the Bay isolates surrounding towns and cities, one from another. As with animal species that live on separate islands and evolve in different directions, so, too, the cities were evolving different cultures, each responding uniquely when touched by The Fog of Change.

Sausalito, north of the Golden Gate, housed many who became the Flower Children. Timothy Leary had recently told a generation to "turn on, tune in, and drop out," and the youth of Sausalito paid attention. The Fog of Change carried love, harmony, and connection to these young people as a new definition of life's purpose. Simon and Garfunkel sang the perfect lyrics, *feelin' groovy*, to be used for their theme song.

Moving south across the Golden Gate Bridge, The Fog rolled into San Francisco, urging it to become the place "where it's at." The Fog carried protests against the Vietnam War. Love-ins happened in the Haight-Ashbury and peace marchers strode their way up Geary Street. Friends began talking about Robin Williams, a young comedian playing in small clubs around the city. Concerts abounded: in Golden Gate Park with Janis Joplin and at the Avalon Ballroom or the Filmore West with Creedence

Clearwater Revival, the Grateful Dead, or Country Joe and the Fish. Joan Baez and Judy Collins lent their gentle voices to The Fog of Change enshrouding the city.

The billowing Fog of Change spread across the bay, watched by the dark eyes of Native Americans decolonizing the rock of Alcatraz Island, which was recently closed as a prison, then reclaimed by those who'd originally inhabited the land. The Natives planned to build centers of education, ecology, and culture in defiance of the state and federal governments who had claimed their land centuries before.

Flowing east from San Francisco, through steel "Xs" supporting the towers of the Oakland Bay Bridge, The Fog crossed the water, blanketing the border between two cities. With amoeboid dexterity, it streamed north, radicalizing most of Berkeley. The University of California campus became the intellectual hotbed of rebellion. Students occupied buildings with sit-ins, refusing to leave until the University met their demand to restore their right to organize peacefully on campus; Mario Savio stood on the steps of the administration building advocating the Free Speech Movement; and later, the People's Park was built on a neglected square of land.

When The Fog streamed south of Berkeley, it found the city of Oakland, the original terminus of the Transcontinental Railway, the primary port for commerce, and the site for many manufacturing plants. Largely blue-collar in the 1960s, the city's population was a patchwork of ethnicities mixed into a primarily African-American workforce. The Fog shrouded Black Panthers when they prowled the streets, shadowing cop cars in an effort to curb police brutality across the city. The Panthers organized to feed and clothe hungry children, and eventually they started their own schools to instill pride in their students and teach a history of the United States that California wasn't covering in its usual texts. The city grew an increasingly positive self-image with the rise of two sports teams: the Athletics baseball team moved to Oakland in 1968, and the Raiders football team got to the Super Bowl in the same year. Oakland became the "Raider Nation." Concerts held in the Oakland Coliseum tended to be edgier than those across the Bay: Jimi Hendrix, Ike and Tina Turner, and The Rolling Stones.

The Fog met its match, however, when forced to curl back upon itself as it vainly attempted to plow through the hills that define the eastern edge of Oakland and Berkeley. The Fog could not raise itself high enough to cross the Pacific Coast Range, where tiny, twisted roads wound their way through moneyed communities. Nor could The Fog squeeze itself small enough to follow Highway 24 east to emerge from the Caldecott Tunnel into affluent, suburban Orinda. Nestled in rolling hills, that town prided itself on creating excellent schools and being a safe place to raise light-skinned children. In the 1960s, the only people with darker skin were the gardeners and maids of the wealthy professionals who lived in ranch-style houses built on lots of an acre or more.

Eventually, The Fog shrank and flowed backward through the Golden Gate, passing the nesting birds of the Farallon Islands, merging once more with the waters of the Pacific Ocean where it had been birthed. But its mists had done their job; each city, each person, each culture that it touched had been forever changed.

ONE

In the fall of 1966, a light rain fell outside the San Francisco Airport where I stared uneasily out the window, immobilized by my deep-seated—admittedly irrational—fear of flying. Footsteps of hurrying passengers echoed around me while I contemplated the sole, dubious purpose of that massive edifice: to lift human beings off the terra firma of Mother Earth.

There's a reason they call it "thin air," I thought. No intelligent human could possibly believe that thin air could hold the tons of steel, aluminum, titanium, or whatever-it-was-made-of Boeing 707 lumbering toward the airport terminal. Despite having just witnessed its arrival, not one molecule of my twenty-one-year-old body believed such a behemoth could return to the skies and be held aloft by thin air.

Humans are land-dwelling mammals, I told myself, arguing with the pro-flight voice of reason in my head. My anthropology professors alleged that we had descended from tree-dwelling apes. Perhaps that is true, but my feet and yours are uniquely adapted now for standing, walking, and running on the solid surface of our planet. Homo sapiens are in no way adapted for flight. Pitiably, we have invented ridiculously heavy machines to compensate for our lack of feathered wings.

Images from John Wayne's 1954 movie, *The High and the Mighty*, began racing unchecked through my brain: humans barely saved from death as their plane hurtled toward Earth. At least their movie plane had propellers; the plane outside the airport window appeared to have no moving parts except wheels, nothing visible that could arguably keep it aloft.

Commercial passenger jets had been circling the globe for less than ten years, and I was about to trust one with my life. The thought was more than cringeworthy. Yet I was soon going to voluntarily, of my own free will, climb aboard that plane—or one of its cousins—and expect it to carry me several thousand miles to Florida.

I was headed to a Peace Corps' training camp in, of all places, Miami Beach. I squared my shoulders when my flight was called, and shuffled onto the waiting plane. After finding my seat, I fastened the fabric belt across my hips, scoffing at the futility of the gesture. Fat chance that would help when this plane plummeted out of the sky! Others in the seats around me read and chatted calmly, obviously not contemplating our probable demise when this plane attempted flight. Didn't it bother them that we were all aligned in neat little rows, quietly ignoring the fact that any one of a multitude of engine mishaps could send us spiraling to our deaths as human shrapnel? Turning to peer through the scratched window glass, I could not imagine how they accepted this situation as even remotely normal. It was clear to me that sailing through the air in an oversized tin can would lack any connection to a human biological imperative. "No wings, no flight" seemed a reasonable rule of thumb.

After a seemingly endless rolling rumble, far past the time when I knew the runway must surely be running out, defying all odds, the airplane did ascend off the tarmac. When it leveled off, I ordered a drink, planning to endure the flight by consuming more gin and tonics than I would care to have counted. After the alcohol had begun to weaken the steely grip of whatever faceless monster had its talons fastened around my stomach, I turned away from the window and distracted myself from the reality of this situation by considering what had put me on this uncharted course.

The life-script given little white girls in Post-WWII California had included, as its highest aspiration, living in a ranch-style home with a two-car garage and an Amana refrigerator, having a highlighted and dog-eared copy of *Betty Crocker's Cookbook*, being married to a well-employed husband who, at 5:30 each evening, would return home to our matched set of curly-haired children: a boy with a Red Rider air rifle and a girl with an ever-growing collection of storybook dolls. I was obviously not living up to that plan. When I was born, that starring role in our particular family's performance had already been cast, taken by my older sister. The part they'd hoped for me to play was the boy's role, and, although I did always covet the Daisy rifles advertised on the back of *Archie* comic books, I had not obliged the family by being born a boy.

Lesser roles had never been clearly defined. Dick and Jane's baby sister, Sally, toddled through our first-grade readers with no dialog and a unique ability to need guidance and rescue by her older siblings. I had floundered my way acceptably well through my own childhood, loving frilly party dresses but hating dolls; wishing for a horse with each puffy-cheeked exhale across my birthday candles, but never being taught, as my sister was, to create the perfect crusts with which my mother wrapped her Gravenstein apple pies. As a second daughter, just like Baby Sally, I, too, was largely scriptless.

When I graduated from the University of Colorado just three months before, I had not the slightest notion of what I would do with the rest of my life. I had skied my way through four years of college, only being lured from the powder-covered slopes when I discovered a love for anthropology. I became engaged once, but the relationship failed to follow through with the marriage-upon-graduation requirement written into that early 1960s script for women. With no fiancé hovering in the wings ready to sweep me into a Hollywood movie ending, I'd had no prescribed path to follow after the University president had handed me a diploma in June 1966.

Just before graduation, at a moment when the reality of my predicament was settling in, a voice on the radio suggested a solution to my plight. Boulder's KBCO disc jockey seemed to have heard my plea for guidance. "About to graduate? Have you thought about joining the Peace Corps? We're looking for volunteers to live in a Pacific Island paradise; could you be one?" A recruiter was coming to seek enthusiastic graduates for a special program involving ten thousand volunteers being placed in the United States' trusteeship of Micronesia.

I contemplated his proposal. *The Peace Corps?* President Kennedy had created the Corps four years earlier, just before his assassination. But Micronesia? I wasn't certain where it was, but it had to be a very long distance across the Pacific Ocean. I'd have to fly, and God, I hated flying! My shoulders had tensed just at the thought. But all in all, The Peace Corps might be a pretty good fit for an anthropology graduate who had no prospective plans for wifedom.

Now here I was, thirty thousand feet in the air, enduring this trial-by-angst. A highly questionable future was approaching me at six hundred miles an hour.

My teeth finally unclenched and my fists relaxed when our plane skimmed over the last of the palm trees and backyard pools, touching its wheels onto solid Florida earth. I breathed deeply, refilling my lungs with more air than I'd allowed into my body for several hours. The plane taxied to our arrival gate at the Miami airport and finally came to a stop.

Entering the building after we deplaned, I saw no one waving the "Peace Corps" sign I'd hoped would be there to welcome me. Surely someone had been sent to drive me to training camp! I spent twenty minutes in a futile search, then claimed my baggage, accepting the fact that I was on my own.

Thick humidity caused sweat to darken my cotton print dress, trickling down between my breasts. Still annoyed at the lack of a reception committee, I managed to make my way to the bus station. Signs offered many destinations, but none matched the address I'd been given for the motel grounds that would serve as our camp.

An older man, perhaps in his fifties, watched my struggle. "You look confused. May I help you?" Polite and slightly formal, he appeared harmless.

Nodding with a bit of relief, I held out the wilted paper with its now-smeared address.

"No problem! That's right on my way. Why don't you let me drop you there?"

Confused, grateful, slightly desperate, and probably still a bit drunk, I accepted, figuring he looked like a fatherly kind of man. When we got to his car, I smiled to see a red convertible with its top down. I would be arriving at the Peace Corps camp in style! He popped the trunk, lifting in my one bag. With a barely perceptible bow, he opened the passenger door, smiling at me when I climbed in. We chatted for a bit with introductions and small talk.

"As long as we don't have a deadline, why don't I show you a few of the sights of Miami Beach? I doubt you'll have much touring time once you're in camp."

"Sure." I felt anxious to get to camp, but I didn't want to be impolite. He was probably right; the Peace Corps wasn't going to supply us with tour guides during the three months of training camp.

He drove around Miami before heading out to an isolated sandy point. His original comment that the address I'd shown him would be "on his way" no longer seemed relevant. Parking the car on a strip of crushed coral, he turned sideways in his seat. A salty breeze moved the palm fronds above us, their rustling the only sound in the utter stillness.

"I'm a dentist here in Miami. My wife recently left me and I've been feeling pretty lonely lately."

At a loss as to how I should reply, I cleared my throat and merely nodded my head.

"I'd love to get to know you better. You seem like such a nice young woman," he continued, sliding a strongly muscled arm around my shoulders.

My neck went rigid. He clearly was older than my father: at least a thirty-year gap between our ages. Could this be one of those situations they warn young girls about? There were no other humans within shouting distance.

"Well, I just broke up with my boyfriend before I came here. I don't feel ready to see anyone else yet. Actually, I kind of hope we're not really broken up and that we'll get back together when I come home. And I'll just be in camp a short time, so I don't think seeing you would make sense anyway . . . but I'm sure you're a very nice man, and if circumstances were different . . ." I babbled, not caring what lie I was inventing.

When my voice petered out, he stared at me for a long minute. His look did not connote parental fondness. My back sweated under the weight of his arm, exacerbated by my increasing nervousness.

Maybe my naiveté helped switch him into a different mode, or maybe he merely took what I said at face value, but whatever process went on in his mind, he finally withdrew his arm and restarted the car. I exhaled the breath I'd been holding.

A stony silence replaced the friendly chatter of our drive during the ride back. A half-hour later, he delivered me to the Peace Corps camp. After winding through the thick tropical hedges that shielded it from the road, my ersatz chauffeur pulled to a stop in front of an aged motel. I quickly slid out of the red convertible, no longer caring about what sort of entry I made into camp. Thanking him politely for the ride, I wobbled on less-than-stable knees, grateful to have arrived safe and unmolested. For most of the day I'd been terrified on an airplane ride, but in reality, this may have been a far more dangerous situation. I walked away feeling naïve, stupid, and lucky.

Walls of tropical vegetation isolated the camp from the touristy culture of Miami Beach, allowing a fantasy of already having arrived in Micronesia. After checking into the office, I schlepped my bag into the clean-but-slightly-dilapidated former motel room assigned to me as my home for the next three months.

I imagine our camp routine mimicked military boot camp, but in a gentler way. Every moment of our daily routine was proscribed. For fourteen hours a day they attempted to morph us into ideal Peace Corps volunteers. The camp was supplied with tropical fruits, fishing boats, and six Micronesian men willing to teach us their language and customs.

"*Ran anim*," a well-muscled young islander greeted us while we took our seats in a small, dingy room.

"Ra-naa . . . min?" I ventured in reply, assuming we were expected to echo what he said.

He repeated his greeting and we answered several times before he went on.

"*Ifa usum?*" he said with a question in his voice.

"Ifausum." we repeated more confidently.

"Ngang me pechicum, kiniso, ng en, ifa usum?"

Well, that one stumped us. With gestures, he made us understand we were greeting each other and asking how we were. He gave us different possible answers, pantomiming happiness, sorrow, illness, exhaustion, and other states. For six hours each day, we listened and spoke. Nothing was translated into English for us, and I never saw the Chuukese language written. After studying Spanish for five years in high school and college, I could read and write the language fluently, but had always been a poor speaker of Spanish. I busily and consciously conjugated verbs in my head before they came out my mouth, during which time the conversation moved on without me. My Chuukese, however, became pitiful but fluent: no conscious cerebral involvement. I could easily say potentially useful phrases like *ua attau*: "we fish" and less useful phrases like *u sesine ifai ewe piong*: "I don't know where the hospital is." Some of the vowel sounds were tricky. Something similar to *Bwaapa ewe bwaupa mein bwuapa*, means "the happy turtle is pregnant." We had to be careful to get the right vowel sounds when we replied to a greeting by attempting to say, "I'm happy today."

My favorite phrase, which I still sometimes use when presented with a large and delicious meal, is *u mooga*; "I eat!" I always say it in my deepest voice. So satisfying! By the time we reached dinner in the mess tent each night, I was always more than ready to *mooga*. The results of our intensive language classes were impressive. We soon were babbling greetings and basic sentences to each other everywhere in camp.

I smiled while I crunched my way along the coral path between buildings. I had found a perfect place for me. Six Micronesians, ranging from handsome young men in their twenties to their fun-loving elder, Kasian, chipped away daily at our ethnocentric worldviews, helping us to begin seeing through the eyes of people who did not live in the hierarchy of a capitalistic society. Since homes and lifestyles differed little from family to family on the islands, the ability to establish and maintain good social relationships was valued far more than attaining material possessions. They taught us to build habitable structures from bamboo poles and coconut palm fronds. The U.S. government commandeered the fronds from the grounds of hotels up and down the Miami Beach strip. Soon we were weaving all types of useful items, thanks to the denuded palms of the rich and famous.

The Peace Corps camp was an anthropologist's dream, but one aspect irritated me. In line with what the Micronesians were teaching us, my college classes had ingrained in me the notion of cultural relativism: we ought not to judge other cultures through the lenses of our own. Each society holds valuable and unique knowledge. These precepts made me question our weekly required "American Education" sessions. Taught by a CIA guy sent from Washington every Friday, I chafed at the patriotic propaganda he fed us. Although I'd been raised in the midst of post–World War Two patriotism, putting *I Like Ike* stickers on cars in a Safeway parking lot, I was shocked at his nationalistic, ethnocentric lectures.

"While teaching them English, you will also be raising up their cultures from the primitive ways they live," he intoned with his steely gaze.

I strongly disliked the term "primitive."

"I wonder what we will be able to learn from them," I countered. "There must be countless concepts they have wisdom about that are missed by our lifestyles."

"If you consider weaving palm fronds a valuable art, you will be well educated there."

His utter disdain for the wit and intelligence of the Micronesians—qualities I already recognized from those living with us in camp—began to infuriate me. Every session I ended up arguing with him about the importance of preserving the cultures we'd be visiting and not merely attempting to turn the islanders into budding capitalists. After weeks of futility, I stopped attending the class.

Sundays offered the weekly great escapes. We did laundry and played with government toys. Miami's inland waterway, a strip of ocean separating Miami Beach from the Florida mainland, offered us a wet and wonderful playground. My favorite toy was a Sunfish, little more than a surfboard modified into a sailable craft. These were provided for us in the hope that we'd learn to sail before heading off to live for two years in a tropical lagoon.

One Sunday, several of us rowed a little dinghy back into the mangroves that lined the mainland side of the waterway. Crabs and giant spiders scuttled away as we twisted among the protruding mangrove roots and cypress knees. We were enjoying giving ourselves a mild case of the creeps when suddenly our craft began hanging up on the tangled tree roots that defined the channels. Having forgotten about tides, we analyzed our situation. No one wanted to spend the next twelve hours stranded there, prisoners waiting to be walked on and nibbled by the local creepy-crawlies. With no other options, we were forced to take turns abandoning ship, a la *The African Queen*, pushing the boat backward until we reached open water. None of us wanted to think about what lurked below, what might consider our toes to be tempting delicacies. I wondered if this kind of situation would be common in Micronesia. Would I become blasé about wading in murky waters where I couldn't see my feet? The thought seemed a bit icky.

Always looking for new ways to amuse himself and others, sandy-haired Marvin reported having found a genuine, old-fashioned ice cream parlor far down the Miami Beach strip. He convinced a bunch of us to hike several miles in search of frozen treats. After we'd walked over an hour in debilitating heat, I was fast becoming tired and cranky. I anticipated the taste of something cold and chocolaty.

Our waitress led us to a table, asking in a Spanish-accented voice filled with concern, "Are you from that Peace Corps camp?"

"Yes, we're going to Micronesia," a sunburned trainee proudly replied. "That's out in the Pacific, way past Hawai'i."

"There are clusters of islands, with people speaking different languages. Groups of trainees are learning each of the languages, so we can go to different islands," chimed in another, seemingly quite self-satisfied with how exotic our training sounded.

Sweat plastered my favorite University of Colorado T-shirt against my body. I feared we all smelled at least as bad as we looked. Handing us our menus, the woman gave me a compassionate look. "Are you all orphans?"

Startled, I looked up at the concern in her eyes. I'd expected a silent reprimand for our lack of presentability, but instead I saw empathy. "We all have families," I replied, somewhat defensively.

"Then why would you go so far away from them?" Her disbelief registered confusion and concern.

I don't remember how any of us responded then, but her question left me contemplating different worldviews. I thought of my sister. Jean would never consider going into the Peace Corps. Our hometown of Orinda was a perfect fit for her. I wasn't sure how that reflected on either one of us. Was I only going because I didn't fit in at home? Or could the Peace Corps offer me the comfortable life-script I'd never found?

The next day, we returned to our usual routine. Rolling out of bed at 6:00 a.m., I pulled on shorts and a T-shirt and jogged to an open area designated for calisthenics. After breakfast came three hours of immersion in the Chuukese language. There were classes in practical skills and cultural training, how to teach English as a second language, three more hours of language immersion, a seven-mile walk-run through the area, followed by our "free time" (more or less determined by the time one took to complete the run). Dinner was given to us in the mess tent, where minions of sand fleas feasted on our legs while we feasted on shrimp or some of their larger relatives. We'd conducted and participated in sand flea experiments: yes, some people are favored over others, more pleasantly flavored to sand fleas' tastes; yes, eating bananas makes one more sought after by the little biting machines; and, yes, eating lots of garlic keeps them at bay—along with most human friends.

Waiting in line for dinner that evening, I stood behind Marvin, the constant joker whose upbeat attitude I was coming to enjoy. Recognizing an opportunity for a bit of play, I grabbed a palm frond and whipped it around the head of my opponent-to-be. *"En garde!"*

Responding to my challenge, Marvin instantly dashed from the line to find his own weapon. Others backed away to allow us room for a full-fledged, palm-frond sword fight. We parried intensely for several minutes until I managed to flip Marvin's "sword" from his grasp. When I lunged at him, going in for the kill, my body rolled over my right ankle. A baseball-sized swelling immediately appeared. Friends flew into action, racing for Gretchen, the camp nurse. Stuffing me into a golf cart, Gretchen got me into her car and drove me to the Miami Dade Hospital. X-rays showed nothing broken, but I had a bad sprain and was not to walk on it for two weeks. As a young child, I'd broken the same leg, and been forced to use crutches for three months with no weight-bearing on my foot. As children do, I became proficient at crutching. I even went sledding, cracking my cast and forcing them to put on another. Fortunately, there had been no ill effects and my leg healed well. So, when the Miami doctors ordered two weeks on crutches, I felt undaunted by the sentence. Like riding a bicycle, using crutches is a skill best learned in childhood and seemingly never forgotten.

A few days later, I crutched my way off a bus into the heart of inner-city Miami. Although in Micronesia we'd be teaching English as a Second Language, here we were to observe regular elementary school classes. The goal was to learn classroom control and some basic teaching techniques. The program would last two weeks.

I saw mostly African American faces as I gimped several blocks along a sidewalk lined with concrete buildings. The school I arrived at looked to have been built in the 1930s and could have used a new coat of paint. When I struggled to pull open the heavy door, my stomach fluttered with excitement; I was going to be a teacher!

The master teacher assigned to me was friendly and encouraging, letting me observe at first, but later allowing me to take over the class for short periods. I practiced teaching some simple lessons. Inept at first, and sometimes losing control, I survived because the class was kind to me.

It's possible my injury served as a blessing in disguise, that the crutches helped me get by in the community of Miami's inner city. Crutching onto the bus each day, I accepted the help always offered to me. I think the students in my classroom behaved with more consideration; perhaps a disabled teacher evoked more sympathy than rebellion. These experiences left me feeling positive and hopeful for success on my own in a classroom, whatever that would look like. Thatched roof and open sides? I felt up to the challenge.

The effort to get myself miles into the city, teach for hours, and then come back to camp did prove exhausting. Each evening, our camp nurse greeted me with ice bags for my foot and subjected me to a bit of physical therapy, a jetted water bath being the most painful. One day when I was unable to suppress grimaces while she held my foot in the water, Gretchen asked, "Carol, why don't you just go home now, recover, and then join the next training group?"

Such a choice did not seem an option. In an unintentionally racist way, my mother often said, "I raised you girls to be chiefs, not Indians." Independence and self-sufficiency were family expectations. Children who were fledged did not return home in my culture. I continued crutching as my young body slowly healed itself.

Halfway through our three-month training, we faced an evaluation. The Peace Corps staff reviewed each of us to determine our fit for the program. At "mid-boards," I stared down at the white envelope our camp psychologist handed me, the contents of which would let me know if I would continue in the program or be sent home. I'd had no anxiety when our staff psychologist invited me into his office for our required meeting. I felt certain I'd be given a positive, high pass. Who better than an anthropologist could be sent out to live in a foreign culture? When I plopped into the wicker seat opposite his desk, Lenny leaned forward, propping his chin in his hands.

"We've classified you as a 'high-risk, high-gain person.'"

"A what?"

"The problem," he explained, his hands forming a teepee as he leaned back in his chair, "is with the American Education class. The instructor finds you difficult."

The American Education instructor? The ethnocentric idiot, blind to cultural relativism, had convinced the others to give me a questionable rating? I bit back a rant, swallowing the deluge of words that threatened to flood Lenny's office. I pursed my lips.

"Well, the envelope says I passed the mid-boards. Is there anything else?"

"No, but I recommend that you return to the classes."

Dismissed from his office, I walked away feeling angry at government stupidity. I knew they'd talked with anthropologists, one even lived in camp, so why didn't they hear what she had to say? At any rate, I was approved to continue. Maybe I even liked the fact that they found me a little risky.

The wool of Tom's Irish Fisherman sweater brushed my bare shoulder in the relatively cool evening air. I inhaled his smell while I contemplated the expensive loafers he always wore without socks. I still heard the echoes of expectations that I should be married by now, so I sought the company of this handsome Connecticut man who had already served in the Peace Corps in Turkey. I believed I could win him away from a girlfriend who had re-upped and was still there. Hanging out together, we'd reached a point where he was willing to let everyone assume we were a couple. However, our "relationship," while somewhat comfortable, was not progressing at an appreciable rate. More men than women lived in our camp, so I considered other possibilities while I looked over at his square jaw and long eyelashes. Alas, Tom certainly held the prize for best-looker, and that did hold more than a bit of sway for me.

On New Year's Eve, we all imbibed far too much alcohol at the camp party. In a last-ditch effort to seduce my handsome non-boyfriend, I had gotten him into someone's empty room. He plopped onto the bed and I settled beside him, gently stroking the back of his head. As I wet my lips, anticipating the long-awaited first kiss, Tom suddenly exploded with sobs. He crumpled forward, hiding his head in his lap.

"I'm Catholic. I can't sleep with anyone before I marry her. I still am in love with Victoria. I'm twenty-eight years old and I'm a virgin!"

I sat for a moment, continuing to stroke his hair. *Well, so much for the seduction of a potential husband*, I thought. The self-image that had suffered from what I had assumed to be his lack of sexual attraction for me felt slightly assuaged, but despite having hung out with him for two months, it was clear I didn't know this man at all. When the sobs subsided and his body lay still as if asleep, I left Tom to recover his dignity alone.

I carried my bruised ego out the door and into the darkness. Wandering the grounds, I let the garden's air soothe my jangled emotions. Passing between two dwarf palms, I nearly stumbled over the form of a man sitting with his head bent in his lap. I peered around to find that it was Kasian, sitting on a stone, quietly weeping. His liquid eyes held mine as I sank onto the rock beside him, not comprehending what could have put him into such a state. As the oldest of the Micronesians, Kasian held a position of honor for us. We all looked up to him as a bit of a father figure.

"They don't know. None of them."

I remained silent but held his gaze, waiting for more.

"They will come and kill our culture. The Japanese launched the attack on Pearl Harbor from Micronesia. Now the U.S. wants to own the Pacific." He looked down for a few minutes, but when I didn't respond, he sought my eyes again, wanting me to understand his thoughts. "People everywhere like Peace Corps volunteers much better than diplomats. Ten thousand of you, they say! All full of love and enthusiasm for capitalism. None of our cultures will survive you."

I thought about one trainee who spent his time developing a plan for fishermen on the islands; he wanted to help them build a canning plant and begin selling their catches to the Japanese. I understood the words I'd just heard were most probably correct. The Micronesians didn't need us, but we needed their land. Kasian confirmed the suspicions that had galled me during the American Education class. He wept as he foresaw the death of his culture. I shrank with helplessness at my inability to comprehend the depth of such grief.

After sitting with him for a time, I felt even more discouraged. Touching his hand for a moment as I got up, I wandered away from the buildings. My tears came then. Thinking of the Micronesian's words, I knew I could no longer go to Chuuk with a clear conscience. Reevaluating my lifelong Republican values overwhelmed me, challenging the postwar patriotism of apple pie, motherhood, and all the related flag-waving. "Stars and Stripes" forever. Was my government trying to use us to soften up a group of people so we could take them over? Given Kasian's insight and the propaganda apparent in the American Education classes, it seemed true that we were pawns in a larger plan. I felt disillusioned and speechless.

Moon shadows filtered by palm fronds danced on the sand. I picked a lingering jasmine flower, one of the last of its kind to bloom so late in the season, and held its fragrance under my nose, seeking some comfort for my confused emotions.

"I hope you don't mind that I followed you out here," came a masculine voice from behind me. Cute, short, usually humorous Marvin walked up and took my hand. "I heard what he said. Let's go walk on the beach," he suggested gently.

After our sword fight fiasco, Marvin had become solicitous of me, concerned with the progress of my recovery. We'd become good friends during the time I'd been pursuing Mister Twenty-Eight-Year-Old-Catholic Virgin. Marvin led me across the boulevard and down to the shore. A gentle Atlantic Ocean licked the sand as we lay down on our backs and looked to the rest of the Universe for consolation.

"It's not very noble, is it?" he stated more than asked.

"I can't go now, can I?" Also a statement more than a question.

"You see why I've decided not to go?"

I nodded, though he couldn't see it.

Still holding hands, we stayed silent. A little "ooh" escaped my lips when a shooting star flashed across the dome above us. We shared our concerns about the meaning of the program, then rambled on, deep thoughts interspersed with deeper silences.

Marvin began tracing one finger around the outline of my hand. Gently, slowly, up one finger and down its other side, lingering just a moment in the spaces between. We lay that way for the rest of the night, enjoying a warm, sexual arousal without acting on it.

Dawn sent us back across the highway to our separate rooms. The next day, we would all move out to an island in the middle of the Inland Waterway. We'd be expected to sustain ourselves with minimal Peace Corps' help. Each of the three groups had built traditional Micronesian homes to stay in for a week. Logs were lashed together, not nailed, and we'd learned how to *fau fau kiekies*, weave palm fronds, for the roof coverings. Marvin and I were in separate groups, and therefore, would stay in different longhouses. Since there wasn't room for all the volunteers in the thatched buildings, some of us were paired up in tents. My tentmate and I had just moved our things into our small shelter when Marvin appeared.

"Let's go to the married people's hut. We can stay there."

After the night on the beach, I needed no more prompting. Gathering up my meager gear, I followed Marvin to a large hut populated by the four married couples in our camp. They welcomed us with smiles. Such behavior was not openly accepted in the newly minted year of 1967, so we felt daring.

We spent a lively week on the island: fishing, swimming, laughing, and making too many pancakes from the flour, pineapple, and coconuts the Peace Corps gave us for supplies. Needless to say, Marvin and I enjoyed getting to know each other better every day. Marvin's sense of humor kept me smiling and focused on enjoying our current life on the island. Marvin took few things very seriously, including himself. We swam, fished, and sailed the week away, freed from classroom propaganda and greatly enjoying our time together.

On our last night before "final boards," Dr. O'Connor flew in from Washington, D.C. A large, serious man, he was all business. He chose—for some unknown reason, since he was by himself—to spend the night in the married trainees' hut. I can only assume we did not carry off our nightly exploits in total silence.

The next day was "final boards." Marvin and I met up back in camp, clutching our unopened white envelopes. Marvin opened his first.

"Deselected," read the message amid some consoling gobbledygook, along with a check for $150 for reentry into polite society. Neither of us was surprised, since he'd made no attempt during the last month to hide his disdain for the program.

I tore mine open, expecting a rave review accompanied by a statement welcoming me into the Peace Corps.

"Deselected," my letter read: the same as Marvin's. Icy shock. I had chosen to leave the Corps, but how could *they* possibly reject *me!* Reeling, I left Marvin and sought out our camp psychologist. Lenny welcomed me into his office.

"I was expecting you," he said. "You've read your report?"

I nodded numbly. "Why?"

"I was surprised too. It was Dr. O'Connor. We all expected you'd be going, but he vetoed it. Said you were indiscreet and needed to go home and grow up before you could represent the *U.S. of A.*"

Wow! I'd been rejected for "indiscretion." Wow! I took zombie steps back to find Marvin. Friends asked each other about our letters; everyone expressed appropriate amazement at what mine contained. Stating that I'd decided not to go anyway did nothing to lessen the blow to my self-esteem.

"You should come with me," Marvin put an arm around my shoulder. "We could go to New York and start everything fresh, or we could go back to my apartment in Sausalito."

On the following day, released by the Peace Corps with a combined total of $300 and two airline tickets to anywhere in the U.S., and with no other options I could think of, Marvin and I packed our belongings and boarded a nonstop flight. We both knew there was no prospect of marriage; Marvin's attractiveness stemmed partially from his indominable, free spirit. Our baggage tags read "San Francisco Airport." Once again, my future held not a single plan.

TWO

The Boeing 707 circled to the south, then glided toward the San Francisco Airport's infamous runways, notorious for extending far out into the bay. Landing was often further hampered by the city's numerous foggy days. Still hating to fly, I'd downed several gin-and-tonics to bolster my chances of surviving a trip across the country without beads of fear-induced sweat soaking my best outfit. As the whitecaps of south San Francisco Bay neared our plane's belly, I knew part of my anxiety stemmed from indecision over what to tell my parents about my return. But that concern currently held second place as it became increasingly apparent, despite the pilot's undoubtedly thorough training on how to land an aircraft, that he was about to settle our plane into the waves just short of the runway. A Japanese pilot had recently done exactly that in the same location.

It's okay, I told myself, *the bay is shallow here and no one died then; we'll probably be able to escape.* Just as the landing gear must surely have been getting wet with sea spray, asphalt appeared outside my window, and our plane touched down gently on solid ground. I mentally apologized to our pilot for my lack of faith.

When we made our way up the jetway and downstairs to claim our minimal luggage, Marvin called friends to meet us at the bus station across the Golden Gate Bridge in Sausalito, just north of San Francisco. I could have called my parents to come pick us up, but I still hadn't informed them of the previous week's events. I especially had no desire to let them know the reason for my "deselection." My mom and dad, Frank and Frances McMillan, had returned to California from an eight-year stay in New York. They were living once more in Orinda on the east side of the

San Francisco Bay area. They lived less than forty miles from Marvin's old apartment in Sausalito where we were now heading. No part of me wanted to go home to my parents under these circumstances, but I knew that, eventually, I'd have to let them know where I was. Figuring I might as well get it over with, I gathered up my courage to call them while Marvin and I waited for the bus.

I slid the glass door of the phone booth closed, picked up the large black receiver from where it hung on its cradle, and dropped a dime into the coin slot, listening to it clink into the heart of the phone before the dial tone came on. My index finger pressed the metal dial around as it found the first number. I listened to the whirr of its release before choosing the next. Nine whirrs later, their phone began to ring. I had three minutes to explain why and where I currently was, before I had to either add more coins or end the call. My dad answered and I gave him a brief synopsis as my mom picked up their other phone. They seemed quietly supportive and thankfully asked few questions, and I felt supremely grateful. I told them that the separation between the Peace Corps and me had been mutual, and that I'd be staying with a friend in Sausalito. They offered to come over the next weekend and bring me my car. I expressed gratitude and ended the call.

"That went surprisingly well," I told Marvin as I exited the booth. We schlepped our belongings out to the taxi area to await the right bus. My

Fran and Frank McMillan.

breath came more easily and my pulse began to slow as I realized that I'd crossed the first hurdle. It was true that I was returning "home," but I'd established a bit of independence and would be taking my life in a new direction. This was all right with me.

The next Saturday, my parents came to see me and deliver my little red Austin 850, the car they'd been keeping for me since my college graduation seven months earlier. Since Marvin's and my relationship hadn't progressed to living together, Marvin had decided to let me have his old apartment while he moved in with another friend for lower rent, but evidence of our joint arrival still filled the apartment. I hadn't thought about this until my parents knocked on the door. I realized that Marvin's clothes were hanging in the closet and his shoes screamed, "a male lives here" from the hall. Male toiletries sang the chorus to that song from the bathroom. As I hugged my parents and welcomed them into the apartment, their eyes lingered a bit too long on the shoes. In 1967, premarital cohabitation was definitely not the norm. We had polite conversation with my parents as they settled onto a sagging corduroy couch in the living room.

My handsome dad was a research chemist who worked on creating synthetic rubber during the Second World War. He had just retired from working for Shell Chemical where he was the head of the Plastics and Resins department, and where he had been credited with seven patents for new plastics. Leaning forward on the sofa, he pulled out his pipe, loaded it with Cherry Blend tobacco, and began to puff quietly. Although I loved the familiar, warm aroma of pipe-smoke, I'd figured out long ago that my dad filling his pipe served as a cover for the times he was uncertain about what to say.

"Do you plan to stay here in Sausalito?" He leaned back into the couch cushions, puffing his smooth-bowled Meerschaum pipe.

"You can always come home, you know. We had dinner last night with the Williams; I know they'd love to see you. And Lil Mika always asks after you." My diminutive mom, always the pretty, cheerful support for my charismatic father, began chattering away in her usual manner. Her sister held a PhD from the University of Michigan. During high school, I realized that my mother thought much deeper and more creative thoughts than her ditsy demeanor let on. Her chosen persona tended to grate on me; I wanted my mom to claim her brainpower and her status as an equal human in my parents' partnership.

"Thanks for bringing Sir Lancelot over." I'd named my car after the knight because we'd had many adventures together in Colorado, and he always brought me home safely. "Yes, I'll start looking for a job on Monday. Probably in the City. I bet I can find something there."

My dad nodded, if not in approval, at least in acceptance. After a bit more polite chatter—no one asked about the men's clothes and I didn't volunteer any explanation—we had a glass of wine each, a few slices of cheese, then went out to dinner at the Trident, a restaurant just down Bridgeway from the apartment. Before they headed back to Orinda, we had a short conversation about my finances and the ensuing job search. All in all, it had been an awkward, but acceptable, reunion.

THREE

The side windows of my Sausalito apartment overlooked a Hansel-and-Gretel-style cottage, seemingly made of hollyhocks and grapevines, nasturtiums, and pole beans.

"That's Hattie's house," Marvin stated with affection, leaning on the windowsill. He'd come over for dinner, despite the fact that he often reminded me there had been no commitment involved in our returning to California together.

"It's adorable. She must be an interesting person."

"She makes her own yogurt. She's in her seventies." Marvin's voice warmed with a caring and admiration I'd seldom heard from him. "You know," he continued, turning to look at me, "because you're an anthropologist and all, you think you know about different kinds of people. But you don't. You only know university kinds of people. You don't know people like Hattie." His voice had lost its warmth. His words flowed coolly but not unkindly. "Look, I'm not trying to put you down or anything, but you are kinda uptight. Everything's all intellectual and cerebral for you."

I didn't know what to make of what he was saying, but I knew this wasn't a compliment from Marvin's point of view. I cleared the dishes from the two-person wooden table, clattering them into the square, old kitchen sink with more energy than concern for their safety. Cramming a rubber stopper into the drain, I turned on the left faucet full blast, dribbling dish soap into its stream and watching bubbles pile up while I debated how to respond to Marvin. I took a deep breath to calm my annoyance. "It's important to think about everything. Science and our brains make sense out of the world. It bothers me when people just do things without thinking."

Marvin strode across the room and reached into the pocket of his Navy surplus jacket where it hung lopsidedly on the back of an oak chair. He took out a plastic baggie of dried green leaves and a yellow packet. "You need to try some of this." He opened the packet, pulling out a sheet of thin paper and pinching crumbly leaves in a line along its center.

I recognized that this was undoubtedly marijuana, not yet commonly used among white populations. A guy I'd dated my last year at Colorado had lived in a communal house. I knew everyone there smoked it, but I never had. I remembered one day my former boyfriend insisted I join his friends and listen to a new album, that "this guy's music was amazing." We'd hurried up the hill to the three-story white house where jagged notes squalled from open windows. The voice doing the singing rasped and grated. When I pointed out the obvious, my friend told me to listen to the words. We folded ourselves onto the weedy backyard lawn where his housemates were passing around a gnarly looking cigarette. I didn't take a puff, but I did listen carefully to the words of Bob Dylan's song.

When he belted out his anger, I figured out that Bob was decrying the injustice of farm labor, wailing that he ". . . wasn't gonna work on Maggie's farm no more." Rotten grammar aside, this song at least seemed novel, not about love or broken hearts or waiting for a guy to call, like most of the fifties' songs. But would I be drawn to play it over and over on my HiFi turntable like I did Pat Boone's hits or recordings of Broadway musicals? Not so much, I thought, wondering at the intent looks on the faces around me as they strained to grasp the lyrics. The next song lamented some man who played a tambourine and a clown chasing shadows, but I couldn't make heads or tails of what it meant. I hunkered there, weaving dandelions into a wreath, not quite pretending to see what they found so enthralling about this new music.

Now I watched Marvin carefully roll the marijuana into a funky-looking cigarette like those guys at Colorado had passed around. If you smoked one of these, would you understand what Bob Dylan's songs moaned about? And would that be a good thing?

Marvin pulled out a book of paper matches and lit the greenish cigarette, letting the match drop and sizzle into muddy dregs in the bottom of a coffee cup. "Try it. It won't hurt you. You've got to inhale and hold it in as long as possible." Marvin took a long, deep drag, held it in, and passed the cigarette—I remembered that people called them "joints"—across the table. A sweetish aroma of something akin to earth and dried leaves wafted toward me.

Inhaling, I immediately started coughing. I passed the joint back. Marvin sucked in another long breath. "Gently," he whispered, letting out as little air and smoke as possible. "Just a small hit," spoken through his tight lips.

I tried again, a smaller breath this time, and managed to hold it in. Marvin nodded his approval.

When we had smoked the joint down to its last half-inch, Marvin pinched it out, licked the end, and dropped it back into the baggie. "Well, I gotta go." He stood, grabbed his jacket, and headed for the door.

"You got me high, and you're leaving?"

"You'll be fine. See if you can turn down that brain of yours a bit. See ya," he added with a chaste kiss.

Mildly annoyed, but also curious, I finished the dishes, waiting to feel a bit drunk, but not finding any familiar buzz. I chose Beethoven's Seventh Symphony to put on my turntable. Straddling the seat of a straight-backed chair, I rested my chin on my folded arms and stared vacantly at the living room rug's peach-colored pile, waiting for something interesting to happen. Disappointment swirled in a muddy loop around my body. Nothing.

Minutes passed, and then more minutes. Miniature shadows wrapped themselves around the bases of the rug's erect fibers. My gaze wandered among them, seemingly in a forest of peach-colored tree stumps. I tuned into the music, listening to the violins for a while, then the horns, then appreciating how the drum's beat fit into the rhythm of the piece. I smiled at what the oboes were doing as my eyes wandered through the rosy forest of my carpet.

Suddenly I sat back, laughing. I'd never picked out individual instruments in a symphony before. And I didn't remember ever having wandered around feeling flea-sized in a carpet.

Okay, I grinned. *This is okay!*

The rest of Beethoven wound its way through my head that evening until I nestled my body between the silky coolness of my sheets and closed my eyes to await whatever drug-induced dreams might drop in.

The following week Marvin handed me a "lid" of marijuana, a sandwich bag partially filled with dried green weed. The story of my carpet concert had pleased him; his gift served as a prompt for similar explorations. In the following weeks, I made judicious use of his tribute, if periodic highs could ever be considered judicious.

Shadows had darkened my kitchen on a Friday evening when a phone call from one of Marvin's friends informed me that Super Spade, our Marin County hippie dealer, had received a shipment, including a pound or two of hashish, which I would be able to sample that evening at an address he delivered to me in the conversation. No one in Sausalito seemed to have much fear of being busted for the soft drugs they peddled and shared, but I felt satisfaction in knowing I had attained trustworthiness in this friendly little community.

Darkness found me winding my way up the hillside behind my apartment. Sausalito roads twisted through trees and bushes that threatened to swallow them the instant road crews ceased their constant vigilance. When parked cars blocked half the designated roadway, I knew the party house must be nearby. Music came from a large home overlooking the bay. I found the front door ajar, so I made my way inside, unsure if I'd know anybody there. Huge pillows slumped into colorful piles around the hardwood floors, some adorned with human bodies, others seemingly awaiting new arrivals. Several large hookahs exuded sweetish odors as I crossed toward a sparsely occupied corner. A man looked up from where he puffed on one of the water pipes. Gesturing with the hose he held between his fingers, he indicated that I should sit on the brocade pillow across from him. Kicking off my sandals, I complied. I leaned over my crossed legs and picked up a dangling, thin blue hose from the side of the hookah. Marijuana had proven to be a pleasant high, so I supposed I was ready for hashish, its concentrated extract. I peered at the shiny metal mouthpiece on the slender hose, wondering who had last used it and whether or not it would be cool to use the hem of my shirt to wipe it off. Deciding to risk both germs and an unknown experience, I held it to my lips and inhaled slowly. Hazy bubbles gurgled within the glass body of the pipe as smoke swirled through. Cooled and slightly minty—did they flavor the water?—the smoke slid more gently into my lungs than it had from Marvin's joint. I liked this way better.

A woman tiptoed across the floor to snuggle into the corner beside me. Mascaraed eyes peeked up from between strands of curly red hair. Painted fingernails reached for the hose I held out. No one seemed to be speaking, and music floated through the rooms, echoing soft and fluty. Candles flickered on small tables. As the girl and I passed the hookah hose back and forth, I stared at paisley patterns on the shirt of the man across from me. The pointed end of one golden teardrop curved against that of another as the fabric moved slowly outward when he inhaled. Circles inside of circles filled each shape, and more circles rolled around between them. The pattern looked fluid and beautiful.

Raising my head, I took in the rest of the high-ceilinged room. This didn't seem to be much of a party. No one was dancing. No groups chatted. No one even appeared to be flirting with anyone else. Nodding to my hookah-mates, I got up from my pillow and picked up my shoes. Stepping carefully along the straight grain of the wooden floorboards, appreciating its smooth polish on the soles of my feet, I traced my way back to the door. Following the flagstone path, I chose to walk on the damp moss between the stones, bending my feet around to fit their curving patterns. The night fog smelled of sea water and roses. I ran one finger along a fern's curving frond. Tiny droplets coalesced into a miniature stream that trickled down my wrist. I licked the moisture, tasting greenness.

My car looked small and friendly parked between the others. I wondered if Sir Lancelot had made friends with the VW bug in a neighbor's driveway. I thanked my car for waiting for me and not heading home without me. When I turned the key in the ignition, his gearshift began to vibrate in synch with the engine. My thumb traced a map of where to shift his gears, the white lines embossed on the round, dark knob at the end of the stick. Then I depressed the clutch and pushed Sir Lancelot's trembling rod into first gear. The smoothness of the clutch releasing as I pressed the accelerator with my other foot made it clear that Sir Lancelot was pleased that I'd returned, and that now he would be taking me home. My heart flooded with intense love for my little car, and it was obvious that he loved me back.

Winding our way down the hill, I began observing a miracle: I could move the entire road from side to side just by turning the steering wheel of my car! The steering wheel now controlled not the car but the road beneath it. The whole world must be pleased with me to have granted such powers. Enthralled, I continued to experiment for the entire drive home. If I headed toward the city, I wondered whether I'd be able to move the Golden Gate Bridge into place under Sir Lancelot, but decided not to risk it. Still, all the way down the hill, not once did the road fail to move directly underneath the wheels of my car whenever I rotated the wheel. Even an obliging curb moved right up beside my tires when I reached my apartment. Fascinating!

The humid air smelled of fabric softener and laundry soap as I folded a pair of lace undies and stacked them on top of a more utilitarian, cotton, polka-dot pair already nestled in the bottom of my wicker basket. Washing machines swished and dryers rumbled against the wall behind me as I contemplated the previous night's experience. While unquestionably pleasant, it seemed wise that I never repeat my drive home from such a scene. What would have happened if I'd met another car on the road? I had no detectable hangover, which seemed amazing considering how stoned I must have been, but my lack of judgement coming home told me I should stick to the mellower high of marijuana. Possibly no more hashish for this girl.

Folding the last of my T-shirts, I toted the laundry basket out to my car to head home. A passing blue Ford beeped at me and swung into the driveway ahead.

"We're going to the march in the city. Want to come?" a friend of Marvin's called to me from the driver's seat. I didn't recognize any of his three passengers.

"Sure, let me put my laundry in my car." I shoved the basket into Sir Lancelot's passenger seat and grabbed a sweatshirt from the back. Turning the key to lock the door, I realized that I'd parked in a two-hour zone and had been there more than an hour already. *What the heck*, I figured, and climbed in with the others.

A male voice rolled out of the car's radio, entreating me to "c'mon and light his fire." When he continued on to tell me that girl, we couldn't get much higher, I smiled. Had the singer been at the party last night?

"Worldwide! The protest is going on worldwide!" the guy riding shotgun exclaimed after we'd shared names. "There's supposed to be a huge march in New York City and another one in Paris."

My friends from Colorado opposed what was happening in Vietnam, the same friends who liked Bob Dylan's music. Their arguments had been fairly convincing, but I still had some concern about whether or not it would be safe to allow Vietnam to become a communistic country. Would that really have a domino effect across Asia, as some of our politicians had said? But, then again, I'd learned in the Peace Corps' training camp that the United States could have not-very-noble, imperialistic motives for some of its actions. At any rate, it seemed completely wrong to be killing people halfway around the world who weren't threatening our country in any way. And then there were the daily reports on how many Viet Cong had been killed versus how many of our soldiers. This method of scorekeeping seemed barbaric. Body counts as a measure of who was winning? *Crazy*.

"I heard that Martin Luther King came out against the war a few weeks ago." I wanted to contribute something that made me sound like I belonged in the car with them.

"He's supposed to be marching in New York today. Somebody said that his wife's gonna be here in San Francisco!"

"It's his passive-resistance example that we're using against the war. If we want peace, we can't be violent." Another voice: the other woman in the car. The tone of her words made me wonder if she was cautioning one of the men who might have argued for other tactics. Violence and combat, after all, had been a mainstay of the U.S.—from Westerns to old war movies, fistfights and gun battles had long been modeled as useful methods of dispute resolution. Roy Rogers and Gene Autry could knock out the bad guys with a single punch in the TV Westerns of my childhood. Audie Murphy blew up a whole German encampment single-handed in *To Hell and Back*. Newer tactics of nonviolent disobedience were borrowed from Mahatma Gandhi and used by King in the civil rights movement. Now, my generation was trying them out to protest the war.

"Yeah, even Muhammad Ali says he's against the war." This from the driver.

I pondered the irony of the heavyweight boxing champion of the world advocating peace. As someone said, maybe it was Bob Dylan: "The times, they are a-changin'."

The march poured through the city like an oversized football rally. In high school we used to tromp through the streets of Port Washington before every football game, shouting cheers for the team. Now we marched through the streets of San Francisco with an interesting conglomeration of protestors. The American Federation of Teachers carried a huge banner, as did the "Stanford Faculty and Staff." One group declared themselves to be the "ILWU," but I didn't know what that meant. Individuals carried banners asking that we "Bring the Troops Home" or proclaiming it to be a "Stupid War." One sign said that even "GIs Want Peace." At the rally inside Kezar Stadium, the speakers' platform carried a banner stating that "The Viet Cong Never Called Us Niggers." As we found seats and listened to impassioned testimonies, I realized that opposition to the war had become a major element of our evolving culture. My shoulders rose a little when I considered that I was now a part of it.

Later that evening, when my new friends dropped me back at my car, I found no ticket on the windshield. After seven-and-a-half hours parked illegally, I had been spared any fine. I laughed and figured that God or somebody must be on our side.

FOUR

Marvin and I had been drifting apart since we'd returned from the Peace Corps, though I still loved the way he cruised the world with his head thrown back and an endearing, duck-footed walk. His broad smile always hinted at a secret joke. But soon after I inherited the claw-footed tub and jungly back porch gracing the delightfully aged brownstone apartment building, his visits became increasingly scarce. Footloose and incorrigibly fancy-free, Marvin came and went.

A more serious form of potential involvement came to my Sausalito apartment unexpectedly one afternoon in the form of a fat beige envelope. Looking at the neatly crabbed writing, as familiar as the worn jeans I was wearing, I remembered that Steve was left-handed. As the ink spelling out my name and address began smearing under my moist hands, I reached for a knife. Wiping my damp palms on my pants, I tore open the flap. Even after four years, his well-known writing grabbed my chest like a friendly hug.

We'd first become a couple during the summer before our junior year when Steve and I spent two weeks at our church's youth camp. I was the California girl who began dating the tall, red-headed, Eastern boy. Although I'd moved to Long Island the year before, I hadn't become a New Yorker. Our opposite lifestyles from opposite coasts were a bone of contention between us. His mom never much liked me; I was the Westerner whose family did not belong to any country club. I was just too California for her taste.

Nevertheless, Steve and I became inseparable through our junior and senior years. There was little question that I'd follow Steve to college at Swarthmore, a bastion of East Coast intellectualism. Swarthmore had been a Bennett family tradition for three generations: both Steve's father and grandfather were alumni.

Swarthmore is a sophisticated institution. I still recall the exact moment when I knew I'd blown their entrance interview. At the end of a half-hour of successful questioning, I'd crossed my fingers on both hands and held them up, bouncing a bit as I told the woman that I "hope, hope, hoped they'd pick me!" I could tell by the instantaneous change in her expression that a moment's childishness had dissolved Steve's and my future together.

My second choice for college, the University of Colorado, actually fit my interests far better than Swarthmore would have, but it left Steve two-thirds of the way across the country. During our first year of college, envelopes like the one I now held had traveled from Pennsylvania to Colorado weekly, always bringing heartwarming messages. Steve and I tried to carry on a two-thousand-mile relationship from separate colleges, but one day I found Jim. Dark-eyed and handsome, seated comfortably on the back of a Colorado horse, Jim won my affections, causing me to break a mutually assumed engagement with Steve. But karma is a bitch. Two years later, Jim was the one who cancelled plans for our marriage.

Steve's inky blue writing squiggled in front of my eyes. His words informed me that he was in Berkeley getting his MBA from The University of California. Just across the bay. My Steve, my kind, faithful, handsome, loving-but-not-sufficiently-rebellious Steve, was living just across San Francisco Bay. Now, I felt certain, without asking my permission, he had come west for me.

Marvin and I had shared an acceptably gratifying physical relationship, but while I felt great affection for him, we had never shared the word "love." Now I faced a much more serious involvement, the possible renewal of a once passionate and still tender relationship. Steve and I had been each other's first real loves. I sat down at the table and reread the letter several times. My heart felt as if it held a captive bee. The world was twisting like a mobius strip and I felt dizzy from the wave.

A mere two days after his letter had crossed the bay, Steve followed. With the aid of a hand-painted hallway sign pointing "To the house of Tweedledee" and another further on pointing "to the House of Tweedledum," he now clanked the old brass knocker at my door. Blue-eyed and as familiar as my favorite warm sweatshirt, there stood Steve. His "Hi, Babe" found its way directly into a forgotten place I'd reserved somewhere above my diaphragm. Our hug was as clumsy as our greeting; both felt awkwardly intimate.

I invited him in, relishing the smell of him. Freshly ironed white Oxford cloth. Still Steve. Conversation flowed and stumbled, then regained momentum, only to falter again. I showed him around my little apartment, then suggested a walk.

The sun slid down the other side of the peninsula while San Francisco's lights twinkled across the bay. We strolled along Bridgeway, listening to waves lap at the seawall. He reached for my hand and looked at me with those blue eyes. "Lyle-style," he laughed. When we'd met at the youth camp in Lyle, New York, we'd bumbled trying to figure out how to hold hands and accommodate our almost one-foot height difference. Afterward it became a sweet joke whenever one of us reached for the other's hand. "Lyle-style" was our code for getting handholding right. As we walked side-by-side, I marveled at my hand feeling exactly right nestled inside his.

Darkness settled completely and a slice of moon rose over the water as our catch-up conversation stretched for hours. I learned about Steve's two-year-long relationship with Libby Miranda, another Bay Area transplant he'd met at Swarthmore.

We ambled on along the Sausalito waterfront, reunited with no definition of who we'd now be to each other but not minding being splashed on occasion. Steve's lengthy description of the girlfriend-who-came-after-me got a bit carried away. He informed me about a thing she had called her "rat," some kind of tube she used for rolling up her long brown hair.

I had little interest in a former girlfriend's hairstyle accessories, but tact had never been one of Steve's greatest strengths. The tradeoff was his total honesty. I could always believe what he told me. That night, when distant sounds drifted over the bay, he said their relationship had been over for almost two years. As we settled onto a railroad tie holding back the bay's dark waters, I decided that although Steve had shared possibly too much about Libby, I would not tell him a whole lot about Jim.

Strolling back to the house of Tweedledee and Tweedledum, Steve's arm hung a little too heavily around my shoulders. I noticed but didn't mention my discomfort. Images of past frustrations flitted through my awareness, but I dismissed them right away. Familiarity won out over nerves and my uncertain expectations. Sausalito now seemed a good place to be living, especially with sweet Steve being just across the bay. Our parting kiss felt perfect, a bit of restrained passion overridden with genuine affection. I remained outside on the curb, watching his red taillights shrink, then blink out around a curve.

On the Saturday following my reunion with Steve, he returned to Sausalito to take me dining at the little city's finest restaurant. I still owned one Saks Fifth Avenue dress Mom had bought me years before. I bent to pull on pantyhose before stepping into off-white heels. As the door knocker clacked, brass-on-brass, I scooped up a pair of opal earrings before opening the door. Steve and I shared a chaste peck. With classic New York manners, Steve held my coat as I slipped into the sleeves, remembering to point my elbows down. Unused to high heels, I picked my way carefully down the worn outside steps. Steve's hand felt strong gripping my elbow, guiding me across Bridgeway to the restaurant.

Warmed by candlelight and the prospect of Ondine's excellent French cuisine, we sat perched on a pier over the bay's shadowy waters. Steve's eyes matched his smile as we chatted, awaiting further service. As the patrons beside us finished their meal and departed, Steve reached over for their ice bucket, which held a half-finished bottle of wine. My eyes gaped, but he merely shrugged. So very Steve! We drank the wine.

When our food came, we lingered and talked. As I savored my final bite of warm grape from the fillet of sole Veronique, Steve asked if I wanted to go into the City. The music scene of San Francisco was beginning to attract global attention in 1967; we decided to investigate. After crossing the Golden Gate Bridge, we followed the trail of music pouring through from doorway of the Avalon Ballroom. As we made our way inside, blobs of colored light morphed across the walls and dance floor to the beat of Country Joe and the Fish's anti-war song.

The band was counting *one, two, three, four* and asking what we were fighting for. The crowd joined in, shouting that we didn't give a damn. The next stop would be Vietnam.

Steve and I shared a concerned look. Not about the lyrics, but about the inappropriateness of his blue necktie and my high heels. All around us, long skirts flowed beside fringed leather pants. Of one accord, Steve laid down his jacket and I kicked off my shoes. We stepped into the whirl of color. A girl with bells braided into her hair grabbed my hand and pulled us into the growing serpent-line of bodies, weaving through and among other dancers, laughing and chanting out the songs. Continuing to count, we celebrated the pearly gates and whooped that we were all gonna die.

We danced and danced, our bodies caught in the rhythms. The Chambers Brothers: *The Time Has Come Today*. On and on it went until Lester's clanging cow bell slowed, and we gasped for breath. Slower, slower, only one beat per second. Surely the song would end. But ever so gradually, the cow bell picked up the pace, and our feet surrendered. The tempo increased, and, breathless but laughing, we continued to dance. I cared nothing about the holes growing in my pantyhose or the sweat pouring into my best wool dress. No one stopped moving that night until the last note echoed through the ballroom.

Snuggling close felt perfect as Steve drove me home. A light flashed yellow at the intersection onto Bridgeway as he steered off the highway and down into Sausalito. He parked along the curb and walked me to my door. Steve's hands squeezed both of mine. Bodies pressed together; we understood the possible dangers if I invited him inside. At seventeen, we had shared our virginities, a bond gently lacing us for life. Now my body responded to all six-foot-three-inches of his, pleading "yes." I pulled slowly back. I'd already once broken the heart of possibly the dearest man on Earth; I didn't yet trust one of us not doing it again. We ended the evening with the first genuine, melding kiss of our rekindled alliance.

After our reunion, Steve's graduate studies at the University of California claimed much of his time. A full moon drifted in and out through layers of clouds one evening when an obviously troubled Steve arrived at my apartment. He suggested another walk along the bay.

"There's something I should have told you, but I hoped it wouldn't matter." Steve inhaled a deep breath and slowly let it out. With pain in his voice, he explained that the previous December, the same time I'd returned from Peace Corps training, his mom had invited Steve's one-after-me girlfriend Libby to join them on the family's Christmas ski vacation. Remembering Mrs. Bennett's less-than-positive opinion of me, I was not surprised to hear that she might have tried to distract Steve from seeing me in California. Although Libby was also a Westerner, at least she had been modified by four years at an Eastern college, making her a much more acceptable girlfriend. Steve claimed he hadn't known of his mother's plan beforehand, and, knowing Mrs. Bennett's methods, I believed him.

"I've gotten a letter," seriousness weighed in his voice, "from Libby."

Stomach acid responded to his words before my conscious mind had a chance to process them. I waited.

"There's something else I didn't tell you." His arm encircled my body, his hand pressed down against my hip. An audible swallow. Then a pause.

"During the week with my parents last Christmas, I slept with her. Just once. Really, only once. We both knew afterwards it was a mistake."

I still waited, conscious of the emotions now twisting inside.

"She's pregnant."

I let the message walk between us on its own legs. At least half a block passed in silence. Then: "What will you do?"

Abortion was illegal in the United States in 1967. The fifties lingered. Steve was a very kind man. I knew the answer before he replied.

"I've offered to marry her. She hasn't accepted, but I'm sure she will."

I looked up. His eyes were moist, returning my gaze. They seemed to hold a question, but I offered no response.

The three of us—Steve, the life his news was creating for us, and I—continued down the darkening street, the distressed noises of some night bird coming from far away. All three of us kept pace, stride for stride, one invisible to passersby but large and tangible to the other two.

I remained calm and reasonable, but have no memory of what I said.

Weeks later, Libby arrived in the Bay Area. Her parents lived in Oakland, but she stayed with Steve. When I was invited to visit their apartment, we were all polite and understanding. We accepted what was inevitable. Clearly, each of us felt deeply troubled by what was happening, but took comfort in discovering a shared sense of compassion that didn't assign blame. Shit happened, and guilt wouldn't help. Somehow, we would each adjust in our own way. Libby and I quickly discovered that we liked each other. She invited me to be in their wedding party, and, surprising myself and probably Steve, I accepted.

Their wedding was a small affair. Jumbled swirls of conflicting emotions bubbled up and down through my body like a lava lamp overheating. Libby's mom, Mrs. Miranda, sat in the first row of pews as sunlight streamed through leaded glass windows, making small rainbows in the entry where I waited. I tried to distract myself by staring at Mrs. Miranda's earlobes. A bit of a Bohemian, she must have spent years wearing large earrings, causing the holes in her lobes to stretch into long, narrow lines. I vowed not to wear heavy jewelry in my newly pierced ears. She sat patiently in a lavender paisley caftan she'd chosen for her mother-of-the-bride dress. I wondered how she and the country-club-tennis-playing Mrs. Bennett would manage when they shared a grandchild.

The rest of the wedding party had yet to congregate for the walk down the aisle. Steve appeared, way too handsome in a smoky blue suit. Before heading down the carpeted path to wait for Libby at the altar, he leaned his head down close to mine. No one else was around to overhear.

"You know I'm marrying the wrong woman." It was a statement, not a question. Without looking at me, he walked away.

Tears circled so far below my diaphragm I could not begin to process them. Grief meshed with a strange bit of relief. I would never have to decide whether or not to tie my life with Steve's. But the unshed tears told me I would always love this man.

FIVE

The hollow barks of sea lions echoed across Bridgeway, the road dampened by morning mist. I watched the Golden Gate Bridge shred a fog bank retreating toward the ocean, sunlight sharpening the animals' voices. Bay water lapped gently, imperceptibly eroding bits of the rocky seawall. I leaned back against the darkened siding of the former Sausalito city hall. Someone had divided the building into separate living quarters, and the old apartment I'd inherited from Martin was one of them. The apartment wall's aged cedar felt rough and splintery, warm against the bare skin my hip-hugger slacks exposed. Pleased that I hadn't battled my curly hair into submission that morning, I enjoyed the weight of it resting on my back. My small breasts were also newly liberated, freed from any restraining bra. I smiled, imagining the sunshine silhouetting their perky outline through the thin muslin of my peasant shirt. My thong sandal-straps were laced halfway up my calves, and native beads dangled from my neck. Madison Avenue wasn't telling me how to dress anymore. We were inventing our own styles just as we were now inventing ourselves as flower children, although we wouldn't know ourselves by that term until later. At the moment, we were simply feeling a deep, empowering sense of liberation.

I hummed a few bars of Simon and Garfunkel's *Feelin' Groovy*—a new song I felt certain they had written just for me—as I waited for Marvin and his friends to pick me up. The song entreated us all to slow down and stop moving too fast. With a little help from Marvin's dried green weed, I was learning to do that. Marvin and I had remained close friends; he'd even helped me work through some of my feelings about Steve. Steve's reappearance and subsequent loss from my life now lived in a place of acceptance, located somewhere beneath my sternum. I sometimes visited their home to witness Libby's swelling belly. In my newly forming life, their situation had settled into a semi-comfortable reality. Meanwhile, I found that living in Sausalito pleased me greatly. I no longer felt pressure to be married. The increasing constraints on Steve and Libby's lives contrasted with the freedom of my own. Given a choice between the two situations, I would choose my current path. That understanding felt liberating.

Tires sloshed through the puddle of last night's rain as a blue VW bug pulled up to the curb. Five people smiled at me from its open windows.

"How many clowns fit in a car?" I laughed, referring to a gig common in circuses.

"Crawl in," was the reply.

Laughter filled the already tight quarters as I pretzeled my legs among the others to hunker onto Marvin's lap. Today, we were on our way to a smallish concert in Golden Gate Park.

"Who are we going to see?" I felt embarrassed, because I wasn't as well-versed as the others on the emerging California music scene.

"Janis! You know, Janis Joplin?" The raised note of sarcasm in her voice was friendly. "Big Brother and the Holding Company?"

Crossing the Golden Gate Bridge, I looked west to see the bank of fog already hanging far offshore. San Francisco sparkled ahead like a multifaceted diamond. When we coasted up to the toll booth, the attendant waved away our proffered coins.

"Car ahead paid your toll," he said, smiling at us. In the newly forming Bay Area culture of the sixties, it was increasingly common to pay for the car behind you.

We arrived at our destination early enough to find easy parking. I untwisted my body and wiggled gracelessly through the car door. After popping open the hood, we gathered up our goodies from the little vehicle's misplaced front-end trunk. Hoisting picnic baskets, blankets, and pillows, we began strolling through the dappled light of Golden Gate Park. As we passed around a single joint, my marijuana-enhanced senses took in the beauty of the Park's Shakespeare Garden in its symmetrical, full summer bloom. I skipped a bit, swinging Marvin's hand. Our path opened into a wide area. Ancient Monterey Pines bracketed a stage just big enough to hold the sound equipment for the afternoon concert. We found a good spot to lay out our old, gray army blanket. When I plopped down on it, the rough wool gave off a pleasant, musty odor, having absorbed moisture from the grass.

That summer, even picnics were being reborn. Gone were the cold fried chicken and potato salads of our childhoods, replaced with fresh, sweet strawberries dipped in clotted cream, chocolate croissants, and a bottle of Paul Mason's slightly effervescent Emerald Dry wine poured into the cut-crystal glasses that Marvin and I had found at a Marin County yard sale. We'd laughed at the silliness of our purchase, but they were cheap and classically beautiful. Now lying on the blanket, we fed delicacies into each other's mouths while we waited for the band.

The crowd's chattering dissipated as five people made their way to the top of the plywood block structure holding microphones and a large amplifying system. By default, I reasoned that the only female on the stage had to be Janis Joplin.

"Hey, that's her," one of my friends said, confirming my thoughts. "We saw her with the Hare Krishnas in the Avalon Ballroom a few months ago. She rocked the place!"

Seeing her diminutive figure climbing onto the stage, I wondered whether I had understood correctly. That little body didn't seem likely to be able to rock a restroom, let alone a ballroom.

All the men in the band had hair below their shoulders, looking like something out of *Tom Jones* or some other movie set in eighteenth-century England. I thought their hair looked sexy, but wondered if the feeling was influenced by the lustiness of Albert Finney from the famous food scene in *Tom Jones*. I admittedly thought Indian men in John Wayne movies were sexy, riding pinto ponies with their dark hair blowing in the wind. Maybe long hair was a good look for men. Certainly better than the 1950s' crew cuts I'd always hated.

The sleeves of Janis' jacket rattled with hanging, beaded-leather fringes as she made her way to the mic. Our spot was close enough that I could hear her short-heeled sandals clicking on the hollow floor. Swinging her head around to check if the band members were ready, Janis' small chest propelled a dozen strands of beads into a flying tangle. The crowd quieted. She grabbed the microphone stand and tipped it toward her mouth. Her first words of welcome came out in a surprisingly gravelly voice as she introduced the band members of Big Brother and the Holding Company.

Janis snapped her fingers, gesturing to her group. Discordant guitar notes wound through the branches above us. Inhaling a long breath, Janis held the mic to her lips and whispered that she had been sitting by a window, watching the rain. The notes in her voice held a sweet, controlled vibrato. A few lines later, however, Janis closed her eyes and leaned her head back. "Whoa, whoa, whoa, whoa," shattered the air. She wanted her lover to tell her why. The pain in her voice and body echoed through every place inside me I'd ever felt hurt.

"No, no, no, no, no!" Dipping, shaking, whispering, then wailing, she took me through all the pain and anger in her song. I, too, had experienced things that just weren't fair.

"Why, whhhhyy, whhhhhy, whhhhy . . ." her voice leapt around the scales. It hurt her like a ball and chain. Janice dragged out the "a" in "ball," imbuing it with the agony of her pain.

The emotions she pulled us through felt palpable. I knew I had never seen a performer like this woman. The crowd erupted in reply. By the end of her set, I felt as if she had made love to us all, giving out raw, genuine emotion in an act of trust as intimate as any sexual encounter.

After the concert, we made our way back to the car surrounded by the warmth of a shared experience. Couples held hands, some danced across the grass, two girls draped garlands across the shoulders of various passersby. I squeezed Marvin's hand and he smiled back. Life seemed to be floating-free, fresh and unbound from the constraints of girdles and bras and life-scripts fed to young women. No one had given us permission to claim our own lives, but I felt as if we were doing exactly that: liberating our newly adult bodies and psyches from the expectations of a more rigid older generation.

The day after seeing Janis, I was making my first foray into the land of that older generation. The town of Orinda, where I'd spent half my childhood and where my parents once again lived. To journey from Sausalito to Orinda, a person must cross two bridges and two cities, then climb up and over the Berkeley Hills, grateful if there's no fog to hamper the journey. But sometimes the fog hangs so densely that the traveler doubts she will ever find her way. Alternatively, one can take Highway 24 straight through those hills via the Caldecott Tunnel, a mile-long portal connecting different ecologies, different climates, and different cultures.

The Orinda family home perches on an acre of land, a 1950s, ranch-style, adobe house with picture windows looking west toward the Berkeley Hills. On the east side of those hills, the suburban settlement created a safe space for white people with liberal values to raise their children. My sister Jean and I benefited from growing up there, free to roam the hills, explore the creeks, attend the excellent, forward-thinking Glorietta Elementary School, while living safely behind the geographical barrier that kept out any "questionable" people. It was a bastion of white privilege. Across the hills, a tumultuous mix of cultures, colors, languages, and beliefs clashed and coalesced, met and learned, agreed and loved, disagreed and fought. No barriers protected Berkeley and Oakland from confusion and uncertainty.

Orinda thrived through the fifties in its own semi-translucent bubble. Although my dad had always been a Democrat and felt offended that United States' voters seemed to consider Adlai Stevenson too much of an "egghead" to be elected president, my Republican mother held more sway over our childhood opinions. My girl-scout troop had happily put "I Like Ike" stickers onto all the bumpers of the cars in the Lucky's Supermarket parking lot one sunny afternoon during the 1952 presidential campaign. No one complained. Dwight David Eisenhower had brought us victoriously through World War Two; he smiled out from his campaign posters as our country's father figure. Apple pie, motherhood, and the Great American Dream ruled our suburban Orinda town. *Leave It to Beaver, Lassie, The Adventures of Ozzie and Harriet,* and *Father Knows Best* showed us what a perfect American family looked like; none of the shows included people of color. Fathers carpooled to work each day to support their families, while mothers wore aprons over their dresses as they cooked, cleaned, and oversaw the children, certain to greet their husbands each evening with perfect makeup and neatly coiffed hair. Outwardly, every family in Orinda lived up to these standards.

Mother dressed Jean and me in little suit dresses with white gloves whenever we rode the Key System trains into "the City." Upon arriving at the Trans Bay Terminal in San Francisco, Mom would stop at the first flower stand we came to and purchase a gardenia for each of us that she'd carefully pin onto our lapels. Birthday parties always had ten guests, party favors, a homemade cake, ice cream, and colorfully wrapped presents with curly-ribbon bows. Everyone kept their gardens neat, and many had small vegetable patches where they grew fresh food for their families. Children were encouraged to play outside after school until dinner, often out of sight of their parents. "Be home before dark" was the usual command.

Alcoholism, adultery, and abuse lived in the unspoken underbelly of Orinda. No one acknowledged these things; they all pretended that they happened only on the other side of the hills. Divorce was unheard of in our polite little town.

Heading into that bubble of cultural groupthink, I travelled with four large strikes against me: I had failed to get married after college; I had obviously been living with a man; I currently had no job; and I had been kicked out of a United States government program meant to broaden the educations of young people. *Ah, well. Chin up, my dear.*

An overwhelming scent of citrus emanated from the Meyer lemon bush by my parents' front door. Running my fingers around one of the sunshine-yellow fruits, I rubbed its oil behind my ears, smiling at the freshness. I stabbed the doorbell, then pushed the lever down on the bronze door handle and let myself in before anyone could respond.

"Breaking and entering!" I called out. Failing to hear an answer, I walked into the living room and looked through the floor-to-ceiling windows onto the back patio. There sat my parents with Dorothy and Paul Williams, close Orinda friends. Dorothy craned her long neck around to see the source of the cry.

"Carol!" Dorothy pushed herself up out of the padded, green lawn chair. She hugged me and then held me out at arm's length. "Let me look at you!"

I hadn't seen the Williams since I'd been a freshman in high school. Whatever my parents had or had not told the Williams, it seemed that I was not going to be treated as a reject.

"What can I get you?" my dad asked.

A large ball of my parents' favorite Dutch cheese sat on a table surrounded by crackers and highball glasses.

"Can I ask for a daiquiri?"

"Yes, and you can even have one." My dad left for the kitchen to squeeze fresh lemons.

I wondered out loud about Dorothy and Paul's children, then they asked how I'd liked school in Colorado. We all managed to politely chat our way through cocktails and a meatloaf dinner before I excused myself for my drive back across the bay. The culture of Orinda, always proper, dictated that everyone would politely refrain from asking anything about the Peace Corps training or why I was back in California. I realized that I hadn't participated in such a totally meaningless conversation in years. I would love to have told them about how part of our government was manipulating the Peace Corps in an attempt to control the entire Pacific. I would like to have talked about what was happening with Freedom Riders in the south. I would like to have talked about anything other than restaurant menus and neighbors' home additions. I would even have liked to tell them about Janis Joplin and a new kind of music, but I knew all of those topics were off-limits. I could imagine the throat clearings in the silences that might have followed the introduction of any of those subjects.

After goodbyes and well-wishes, I inhaled several deep breaths before climbing into my car. It felt as if part of my chest had been collapsed for hours, large sections of my lungs unused. I felt a suction release as my chest expanded with evening air. I loved my parents; they were good to me. But their world seemed foreign now. Shaking my shoulders and stretching my neck, I headed west with a sense of escape.

SIX

My Peace Corps' severance pay had dwindled to an ashy layer in the bottom of my bank account. Job-hunting became a daily task; one can't live on groovy vibes alone. I'd applied for a job at the University of California's Hearst Museum of Anthropology, but my bachelor's degree had qualified me only for a part-time position there. The pay would have been minimal, and accepting the job would have meant moving from Sausalito to the East Bay. I reluctantly refused their offer in favor of a more-mundane-but-financially-secure position as payroll secretary at the California Academy of Sciences in San Francisco.

I tugged at the hem of my navy-blue minidress, hoping it was appropriate attire for my first day of work. I felt a twinge of discomfort, not just because of the unaccustomed dress, but also because this was not the job I'd imagined for my future. Although the Peace Corps' rejection had squelched my vision of life in Micronesia, I still hoped to work at something culturally intriguing. But the job at the Academy would keep me clothed and fed and living in my newly adopted town of Sausalito. Perhaps I could get used to wearing a dress instead of the jeans I'd worn the two previous summers while working as an archeologist in Mesa Verde National Park.

I climbed into Sir Lancelot and headed into the city, where fog soon shrouded me in a blanket, its comforting silence quieting my nerves. Finding my way south and west, I reached the imposing edifice of the museum, hunkering in classical splendor. The large, white façade would have been at home in any number of European cities. Nervous and excited, I paused for some deep breaths, unsure of what to expect. My smart, new black flats clicked up the expansive marble steps; the double doors loomed large and intimidating. Entering the light-filled foyer, I turned to follow an institutionally yellow hallway leading to the administration area.

With effort, I pulled open a varnished door. The office I entered seemed surprisingly small with an antiquated switchboard near the door. A real switchboard: black and shiny with metal holes where colored cables could be pulled out or poked in, depending on who was being connected with whom. Even in 1966, it looked like a relic from a Doris Day movie. "Good morning, Mr. Pitts. With whom do you wish to speak?" I could hear small sucking thuds as each connection slid into place, linking academy personnel with the outside world. While researching this position, I had read that the academy had one hundred-thirty-five employees; lots of cables were being moved around.

Straight-backed and gray-headed, Mr. Brislawn, head of accounting, greeted me with a small nod, causing his neat little bow tie to bob beneath his Adam's apple. "Welcome, Miss McMillan. I'm happy you accepted our job."

I reached out to shake his hand. "Yes, I'm excited to work for the academy."

"This will be your desk." Thick, brown wood aged in place: the desk took up a great deal of space. Even the chair weighed heavily as I pushed it back and took my seat.

"This is Mrs. Hauley; she'll be your direct supervisor."

Tight-lipped and oozing a propriety equal to Mr. Brislawn's, Mrs. Hauley peered at me from her seat at the switchboard. She would be the only other person sharing this office. I felt no warm, fuzzy emanations directed my way.

Taking my seat, I was grateful for the wooden desk front that covered my knees, perhaps too exposed by my minidress. Dark doors opened off each side of the room, leading to the offices of the director and other senior staff. My duties would include typing envelopes on a clackety black typewriter, relieving Mrs. Hauley from the switchboard during her breaks, counting the till for the museum each afternoon, and delivering semi-monthly checks to the employees. Although the office staff could have been "poster elders" for an antiquated efficiency organization, they seemed accepting enough and not immediately patronizing. Their fondest hope seemed to be the creation of an excellent payroll secretary in a Henry Higgins-type experiment. I was questionable raw material, but I had potential.

Error number one occurred almost immediately—typing envelopes incorrectly. Mrs. Hauley pointed out that all lines on the address of an envelope must be left-justified against an imaginary line; my creative effort of angling them down the paper was not "how it was done."

Error number two—bare legs and bare feet inside my new black flats! For this one, Mrs. Hauley spoke softly behind her cupped hand, leaning in and shielding her polite rebuke from nonexistent eavesdroppers. "In this office, we girls wear nylons." I'd ruined the only pair of pantyhose I owned when dancing with Steve in the Avalon Ballroom. I agreed to purchase some.

Error number three—my method of coin counting! Dumping pennies into a copper pile on my desk, I gathered them up in stacks of five as I counted. For this inefficiency, Mr. Brislawn himself leaned over to inform me that in this office "we generally slide them off the desk as we count." Really? The correct form of penny-moving was required in order to pass my probation? I tried not to visibly clench my teeth.

For thirteen days, I sought to mold my behaviors into their required regimens. This position fit me more like a bulky winter mitten than a sleek leather glove. But on the fourteenth day, a kinder, gentler Mr. Brislawn stood before me with a thick stack of envelopes, one-hundred-thirty-five, to be exact.

"We like our employees to feel appreciated. Hand-delivery of their paychecks gives a personal touch that helps things run smoothly. Take all afternoon. Chat with people and ask them how their work is going. Help them feel that the museum cares. We know you'll do well at this. You'll find your way to all the offices and departments; just ask. Enjoy yourself." All this spoken with a broad smile that softened and crinkled his pale cheeks.

Delighted and astounded in equal measure, I accepted the stack and set off to explore. The museum was physically as well as administratively attached to the Steinhart Aquarium. The buildings were connected by rabbit warrens of stairs and twisted hallways. Months would pass before I constructed a trustworthy mental map. Meanwhile, I wandered and inquired, enjoying this task immensely.

Entering the aquarium for the first time, I walked past a large, sunken enclosure inhabited by crocodiles. A gum-booted man was inside, spraying them with a hose. My mouth must have gaped.

"The water's cold; it makes 'em slow," he responded to my unasked question, "so I can clean their cage and leave them food." I don't remember how I gave him his check, but I was pleased. I had just learned something interesting about cold-blooded reptiles. Nothing earth-shattering, but definitely far from boring.

I clicked my way through echoing halls, passing out aquarium staff checks, peering into water tanks from above, and increasingly enjoying myself. Entering a passageway between fish tanks, I locked eyes with a grouper. As he opened and closed his gaping mouth, I apologized to him for having no check. I winked at him before walking on. Alas, the large fish did not wink back. (Perhaps he physically couldn't. Did fish have eyelids?) I grinned and continued on through the building, accompanied by the burbling sound of air being piped into seawater tanks. The job held promise after all.

Through some mysterious tunnel, I found my way back into the museum, following an equally intriguing maze. Rube Goldberg, perhaps, had participated in the construction of these buildings. In order to reach one tiny office in zoology, I had to walk through a large "beetle closet," a place where tiny black beetles cleaned away any remaining tissue on animal bones. Before I entered the enclosure, the humans assured me that my still-living flesh would hold no attraction for the critters. I felt certain the men enjoyed my discomfort as I passed through. I tried not to shiver at the unique, soft clicking from the combined munching of a bazillion beetles. The office I entered was smaller than the bone closet. *Odd priorities in this place.*

One of my favorite deliveries required climbing two sets of narrow stairs that twisted up to a long hall leading nowhere except to one office filled with books, papers, a kind and eccentric scientist, and a golden-haired dog asleep by his chair. I remember neither his name nor department, but we came to share some friendly, relaxed conversations while I enjoyed the quiet warmth of that little room.

An impressive lab and office housed the entomology department where Dr. Edward Ross and several assistants studied countless creepy-crawly critters. The beetle closet I'd passed through earlier had been in the zoology department. I don't know if its inhabitants had been presents from entomology. How much did the separate departments communicate with each other? The physical peculiarities of the building seemed to keep them fairly isolated.

Before I opened the entomology department's door for the first time, Ed Ross's charisma nearly oozed beneath it. A silver-haired, handsome man, Ross had a reputation for charming the middle-aged matrons who attended his many slide shows and lectures. His sharp, curious mind, however, was what would keep me returning, enjoying that department's broad and ever-present range of conversations.

In my estimation, my job had shifted the minute I delivered my first paycheck. Mr. Brislawn had encouraged me to take time chatting with the employees. The extrovert in me delighted in the chance to acquaint myself with one-hundred-and-thirty-five fascinating people. Receiving checks put smiles on their faces, and I soon became one of the museum staff's favorite employees.

As summer progressed toward fall, I settled into my position. The corrections from my superiors dwindled, and I spent each week comfortably anticipating payday deliveries. My visits to the entomology department began to increase in frequency and duration. While I wished the museum included an anthropology department where I might have gotten to know some like-minded folks, the entomology department would suffice. Although I had a life-long aversion to all things small and wiggly, I discovered I had much in common with the slightly odd folks who found them fascinating. Ed Ross traveled the world collecting embioptera (a termite-like insect) and he showed a lively interest in the cultures he encountered on each continent. Contact with such diverse people left him serendipitously knowledgeable in the field of anthropology. I came to enjoy discussions in his department and soon began eating my lunches with the "bug people," listening to exotic tales of faraway peoples and places. Ross was an excellent photographer whose expeditions were partially funded by the organization. His *National Geographic* cover photos adorned the department walls. In a few months he would be heading to Africa, camping across thousands of miles of desert and bush country from Cape Town to Nairobi. Only one assistant, one cook, and his own daughter (a woman slightly younger than I), were going to accompany him. It sounded massively daring. What an adventure!

On a bright August day, I chafed at the bit, wanting to get out of work and into a splendid San Francisco afternoon. I entered the creepy-crawly domain to deliver their checks. Dr. Ross looked up from his desk. "Would you like a chance to actually be an anthropologist?"

Confused and slightly offended, I nodded, looking at him quizzically.

"The young man who was going to be our cook just broke his leg. If you want to come and cook for us in Africa, you'll have a chance to collect real ethnographic data. We'll be spending a month in Namibia, and you'll be able to spend that time gathering data on the Topnaar in the Namib Desert. There's no salary attached to the position, and you'll have to pay your own way over, but I'll take care of all expenses for the months we'll be traveling."

I stood, quite literally, speechless. Africa! In 1966, only explorers, missionaries, and scientists traveled to Africa. The continent seemed mythical. Realizing that I would need to find funds for the flight, possibly a deal-killer right there, I provisionally agreed. The fifteen hundred dollars required for my plane fare seemed daunting to a newly minted college graduate earning under five hundred dollars a month. But what an opportunity!

The following weekend, I took another trip across the bay to join my parents for dinner at the home of my family's nearest and dearest friends, the Mikas. Lil and Tom Mika, Dorothy and Paul Williams, and my parents were longtime friends. My sister and I had grown up in the tight-knit group these three families formed. My dad had worked with Tom when Shell Development in Emeryville first employed them as research chemists. Tom's wife, Lil, had been like a second mom to me, baking poppy seed cakes, toasting peanut butter, honey, and banana sandwiches in her oven, and quietly passing on her values to their daughter, Kitty, and me. Lil's model of an adult female lifestyle differed significantly from the one supplied by other trim, girdled Orinda mothers. Lil was decidedly plump. She wore her long, dark hair in two braids. By letting us blow scooped-up piles of soap bubbles at each other while washing dishes, Lil showed Kitty and me that enjoyment could be found in unexpected places, even doing daily tasks.

My sister and I paralleled the ages of the oldest two Mika children, so our families always enjoyed being together. I spent half my childhood roaming the hills above their backyard, playing deer and horses in the tall grass. Kitty was my best friend, although I was frustrated by her superior athletic prowess; I consistently lost to her in the tetherball court Tom had built in their backyard. My sister, Jean, and their oldest son Tommy were never particularly close, although they dated briefly many years later, and Jean confessed that Tommy had been a good kisser. (No further explanation or details were offered.) Pete, the "baby," was a sweet kid destined to hang out with his mom, since we older ones often ditched him from our adventures. Kitty was living in Colorado now, where she had just entered a PhD program in psychology at the same university from which I'd recently graduated. Because I'd left just before she'd come, our paths hadn't overlapped. I regretted how little contact we'd had in recent years.

On Friday evening, I drove through the Caldecott Tunnel and rolled down the off-ramp into Orinda at the "crossroads," taking the Moraga Highway out to Glorietta Boulevard. The Mikas' ranch-style home nestled in clusters of junipers and camellias. Nostalgia filled me like melted chocolate as I saw the dark-wood house on Meadow Park Court, a cul-de-sac ending in the grassy hills Kitty and I had so loved to explore.

Lil greeted me at the door with her large-bosomed hug, her now-gray hair cut short, no longer in the rather unconventional braids she wore during my childhood. Tom walked in from the dining room with his easy stride. Very fit in his fifties, he was considered the athlete among my parents' group of friends.

"Welcome," he said in his cheerful, throaty voice. "How's glamour girl number two?"

I had never been pleased with his names for my sister and me, both because she was number one to my two, but also, I had come to wonder how it made Kitty feel. Shouldn't his own daughter be his "glamour girl?" My mom had trained us about makeup and movie stars, while Lil had cared more about dogs, cats, art, and poetry. Even in my youth, I'd preferred Lil's interests, but I still resented being the number-two glamour girl.

"It's past rush-hour; I had an easy trip over," I replied, shrugging my mild annoyance off with my coat. "Still feels like home here." I smiled, moving to the couch to hug each of my parents, who were already settled in with drinks in their hands. We'd never been a physically demonstrative family. Recently, I had initiated a hugging campaign that seemed to be going well.

"If you want to go wash up, Tom will get you a glass of Mateus." Lil's call to "wash hands" had always served as the dinner bell in their home. My walk to the bathroom led past the floor-to-ceiling display of black-and-white photos commemorating the family's childhoods. A warm spot tickled my chest as I recognized myself in several photos.

When I reentered the living room, everyone had already moved to the Danish modern dining table. I took a chair facing the kitchen, my back to the large picture windows opening onto their darkening backyard.

Standing across from me, Tom poured wine, reaching out to hand the first glass to my mother.

"We saw Paul Pollaczek yesterday. His new wife seems like a very nice woman. She works as a tax accountant. I hadn't been in the house since Ann passed away." In her usual attempt to smooth out possible bumps in our social circles, my mom sounded diplomatic concerning the new marriage of an old friend. I squirmed, fearing that tonight's dinner conversation might be as stultifying as that of my last visit.

Handing me the next glass of rosé, Tom ignored my mother's remarks. "Why are you still living in Sausalito? You're working in the City, aren't you?" In Bay Area vernacular, "the City" meant San Francisco.

"I love the building I'm in. They carved the old Sausalito courthouse into four apartments. My back porch is against the hill and really private. And it's cool living across the street from Ondine. Do you know that my building is the cover picture on their matchbooks?"

The restaurant where Steve and I had eaten that first night he came was acclaimed for its cuisine and stellar view across the Golden Gate. The owners must have imagined the quaint old courthouse its entry faced would be sufficiently attractive for matchbook covers. I felt a momentary pang, thinking of Steve. No one here knew the true story of why we'd "broken up" again. My parents loved Steve when we'd dated in high school and had been pleased when he'd crossed the country to reappear in my life.

"How about your job? Are you surviving as a payroll secretary?" Lil wondered, breaking into my thoughts, undoubtedly concerned that my degree in anthropology hadn't opened any career doors for me. "Wouldn't you like to find something more suited to your sense of adventure?"

"Well, actually, I have some really great news! For months I've been eating lunch in the entomology department. Ed Ross, you know, the curator? He travels and photographs for *National Geographic*? Well, he's been getting ready to go to Africa. At least half a year camping all over the southern half of the continent! He's designed this special truck whose top unfolds like a Conestoga wagon and everyone sleeps on top of the truck, up away from snakes and things. His daughter is coming and one research assistant to help collect bugs. One other guy was coming as cook, but last week he broke his leg, and now Ross needs a new cook. Yesterday, he offered that I could come along as cook and do anthropology work too! We'd be spending at least a month in the Namib desert and I could spend every day in a Topnaar village. All I have to do is come up with the plane fare. He'll pay all expenses of the expedition while everyone's over there." I finally paused for breath, a little embarrassed that I'd let myself sound carried away.

My dad's eyebrows raised at my speech, but I couldn't read their meaning. Interest, surprise, approval, concern? My mom paused for a moment without comment, then continued cutting into a pork chop with her sauce-covered fork.

"That sounds like quite an opportunity," Lil encouraged. "I would love to have done something like that when I was young."

"But instead, you found me." Tom grinned. "Lucky woman!"

People chuckled at his joke and the conversation moved on to other topics.

Later, as the last of Lil's famous apple pie had disappeared, I collected plates and carried them into the kitchen. Tom began pouring after-dinner liqueurs at the table. Lil followed me with another stack of dishes.

"You know, it really is a rare opportunity." She spoke with quiet certainty. "It's the kind of thing you're only apt to do when you're young. Think about it. If there's a way to get the funds, I think you'll always be glad you went."

As she began rinsing plates, I fit them into the rack of her brand-new dishwasher, not yet a common appliance in Orinda kitchens. I thought of how local girls went to college, got married, perhaps worked for a while, then had two or three children, two cats and a dog, and probably counted themselves lucky if their husbands bought them a dishwasher for Christmas. Lil knew me well; I imagined she felt concerned that such a life would cause me to rattle my chains till the leg irons gouged scars into my ankles.

I spent that night and the next at my parents' home. We didn't discuss Africa further. I assumed they had not taken seriously the possibility of my going on the trip. Since they'd had to deal with my squeamishness about bugs throughout my childhood, perhaps they considered an entomology expedition across Africa an improbable fit for their youngest daughter. But on Sunday, just before I headed back across the bay, my dad said in a businesslike voice that if I decided to go, he would loan me the money for airfare. I accepted with gratitude in what I hoped was an equally businesslike voice, promising to repay the loan as soon as I returned.

On the drive back to Sausalito, I could scarcely contain my excitement: my dream of Africa would be a reality! I was set to become a reluctant entomologist, a questionably qualified camp cook, and a budding, bright-eyed, and bushy-tailed anthropologist! Africa, the dark continent of green mambas, stalking leopards, ancient cultures, and an infinite number of large and creepy insects, awaited.

SEVEN

Oversized mason jars lined the laboratory shelves in the California Academy of Sciences' entomology department. Lab tables housed terrariums where termite-like creatures burrowed tunnels against their glass-walled prisons. I climbed onto a stool to await my instructions for interacting with these critters.

Once I committed to the Africa trip, Ed Ross requested that I transfer from the payroll office into the entomology department. With less than a month to go before our departure, he wanted to make me into a passable entomological assistant, even though my primary responsibility would be finding ways to feed the four of us in some of the most isolated areas of Southern Africa. The trip's main draw was Ross's promise of a month in the Namib Desert where I could use my newly acquired anthropological skills to learn about the Topnaar Khoekhoe, who lived along the Kuiseb River. But Ross also wanted me to know something about embioptera, the subject of his life's work and his worldwide collecting expeditions.

Ross stood beside my stool in his laboratory. Gesturing toward the nearest terrarium, he pointed out that not all of the insects looked the same. Ross reached under the counter, pulled out a bottle of some type of preservative, and poured it into a clear, glass jar. "I want you to collect the antepenultimate phase," he said, picking up a long pair of forceps. Reaching his forceps into the loamy duff at the base of the terrarium, he deftly extracted a long black insect with fat forelegs. "This is the ultimate phase," he said. "These knobs at the end of his legs are his spinnerets. They emit silk like a spider and he uses them to line his tunnels." Returning the first bug, he lifted a second one, slightly different from the first, referring to it as the penultimate stage. "And this," he said, reaching in a third time and raising a smaller version, "is the third-to-last stage, the antepenultimate. Collect these and drop them into the preservative. Label the bottles with the number of the tank you've taken them from."

I had never been much of an insect-lover, but I also hadn't much heart for murder, however small and innocuous the victim. My father had tried to convince me that the writhing of an earthworm when impaled upon a fishhook was simply involuntary muscle contractions, but to no avail. I never baited a hook until he ditched the worms and offered me fat, inert, orange salmon eggs. It seemed my empathy didn't stretch to include salmon fetuses.

I took the proffered forceps from Ross's hand and reached for what I thought to be an appropriate embiid.

"That's the one," he said approvingly as I held it over the poison jar. Thankfully, it showed minimal wiggling. "Just call if you get confused." He disappeared into the next room as I relaxed my fingers and watched the small creature sink to the watery bottom, never bothering to attempt to swim or escape.

For the following days, with questionable enthusiasm, I pickled embioptera nymphs. Would the god of embioptera be waiting for me somewhere in the Bardo after I died? Some gigantic cylindrical insect with kidney-shaped eyes waiting to crunch me in his mandibles? What piece of my soul might I be selling in order to gain sufficient credentials to be taken along on this Africa trip?

Occasionally, much to my relief, Ross would decide that we needed to carry out some shopping or other pre-trip business. With the top down on his silver Mercedes, he would whisk me away to visit consulates for visas, procure Michelin maps of southern Africa, or shop for trip essentials that would soon be shipped to Cape Town, where his customized truck awaited our arrival.

As we sailed over the crest of a San Francisco hill one afternoon, he smiled at me, his wind-whipped silver hair matching his silver car. White sails dotted the bay's azure waters, our view framed by the colorful

Victorian houses standing boastfully along the street. "You know," he grinned, "sometimes I think about just starting over. Leaving my wife and buying a small villa in France or Italy." The gray eyes looking over at me made a matched set with the car and the hair.

I wondered if this comment was simple information or if it held a more pointed message. I chose to go with the former thought, though I admit to being flattered by the improbable prospect it might be the latter. I wondered if he expected any response. I gave none.

"It would be possible, you know. It would be a dream come true, wouldn't it?"

A penetrating glance across the gearshift into my eyes . . . I grunted a semi-assent. This was beginning to feel weird. Ross had groupies of elderly women who came to his lectures at the academy. He wrote articles for *National Geographic*, who supplied all the film for his expeditions. He curated the entomology department at the California Academy of Sciences, for God's sake! Was this guy flirting with me? Was he suggesting he leave his wife and we run away to Europe together?

I shifted in my seat. The leather upholstery suddenly felt sticky. Hell, he had a daughter almost my age who would be coming with us on the trip. I looked away, hoping I was misreading cues. My insides churned between feeling flattered and creeped-out.

Conversation stalled until Ross stopped to pick up some Michelin maps of Africa. It came as a surprise that San Francisco would carry such things: detailed road maps of each of the seven African countries we'd be crossing. My thoughts concerning our conversation retreated, replaced by excitement. If Michelin made maps of Botswana and Kenya, then those must be actual places on which we could drive and walk. Holding the maps in my hands began to shift my perception of the continent of Africa from a fantasy of literature into something made of rocks, grass, prickly weeds, and street signs. I let my finger trace the outline of each country's name as we drove back to the academy, the stack of maps nestled safely in my lap.

"You're going to have to cut your hair, you know. You might have any number of things getting trapped in all that hair during many months of camping with a limited water supply." We were leaving the department for the day, Ross lagging behind to turn off the rows of fluorescent lights. "You don't even want to know the possibilities of what you might carry around with you."

I glanced back over my shoulder, hoping to see an indication his words were meant as a joke. But his face remained serious as our footsteps echoed down the marble-floored corridor.

"And you'll want to buy a safari jacket, good boots, and khaki pants. Light colors tend not to attract insects, and tall boots are necessary, especially in the desert. In Namibia, there's a viper that buries itself in the sand so only its nose and eyes are exposed. It's small, and can only strike as high as your ankle, but the venom is deadly. When we're walking in the sand you will definitely want sturdy leather covering your ankles."

Was he deliberately trying to discourage me? Had I been a disappointment as a research assistant? Had I been pickling the wrong stage of embiids, and now he no longer wanted me on the trip? I didn't want to cut my hair. It curled nearly to my waist. I loved the feel of it in summer when I could turn my head and enjoy it swishing across my back. It would take me forever to grow it long again.

"We'll each be able to send one or two suitcases ahead. Weight doesn't matter, since the ships charge by volume. Choose necessities that you might not find after we're there."

So he wasn't trying to scare me into not going. I realized he was right about my hair, of course. Lengthy shampoos would not be conducive to many months crossing deserts with water at a premium.

"I'll see you out at the house tomorrow? Do you know how to get there? And your folks too, right?"

He and his wife had invited us to dinner at their home the following evening. Everyone would be meeting. My parents would meet the Ross's, and I would meet their daughter, Marty, the other female member of our expedition. "Marty" (Martha) was a few years younger and according to

Ross, had a strained relationship with her father. He told me he hoped my love of science and natural sense of curiosity would interest Marty in what had always motivated him. Marty had become what Herb Caen, the beloved columnist for the *San Francisco Chronicle*, had recently begun calling "a hippie." Ross had little patience for her seeming lack of direction in life. I'd gotten the feeling that he didn't have much interest in understanding her, but hoped that she might begin to appreciate him. I didn't look forward to being the designated go-between or hold out much hope for success. Ross admitted that one of his greatest regrets was leaving with his wife on an eighteen-month expedition without telling Marty and her brother goodbye. They had left them at their grandparents' house, slipping out while their children were playing on the living room rug. I think he said they had been three and five. His wife never traveled with him again. I couldn't imagine how those little children must have felt, and what anger and resentment they probably still held as grown-ups.

Mrs. Ross welcomed us into a Marin County house nestled against a forested hill. She introduced us to Marty, huddled into an oversized living room chair. Marty's light-brown hair formed a blunt line encircling her head just below her ears. Her hooded eyes glanced up only for an instant as she grunted a response. Ross came out of the kitchen to offer drinks in a hail-fellow-well-met kind of voice. My parents, adept at social skills after years of entertaining my dad's business associates, carried on a pleasant conversation with Mrs. Ross. Her husband returned with our drinks, then gestured toward a large plate-glass window framing a hillside view. "Can you see my path? Every day I walk that trail. It loops through the backyard. Here, why don't we take a tour? Bring your drinks along."

I rose immediately. My father looked at my mother, who demurred but gestured for us to go on. One glance at Marty told me she didn't share my enthusiasm. She heaved a sigh. Ross must have led her around his trail many times, trying to elicit interest in its six- or eight-legged inhabitants.

Three of us headed across a small lawn and up some natural stone steps.

"Look, just here. See that? Something's been feasting on that rose petal. Could have been any of several beetles." Ross rattled off the Latin names of his suspects.

"Look around for what's happening." He crouched down. "Here's a young spider spinning a new web. Mostly, they spin them at night. She's starting early this evening!" Ross beamed, obviously enjoying his captive audience.

We climbed the hill, proceeding in a game of follow-the-leader, stepping over tree roots and ducking below pine branches. Every few feet elicited a new explanation of tiny goings-on along the path.

"Just yesterday, a praying mantis cocked her head at me. The whole world out here changes daily!" He looked at me. His speech held a lesson: pay attention and you'll find so much. Traveling with Ross, I wouldn't just see lions and giraffes but all the smaller flora and fauna that I might otherwise miss and therefore fail to understand.

Excitement bubbled through me by the time we returned from our backyard safari. Marty glanced up as we entered. Judging from her semi-slouched posture and half-lidded eyes, I guessed nothing of her father's world excited her.

When we filed into the dining room, I held back to walk beside her. "So, you're going to come with us to Africa?" I ventured.

"I haven't really decided," she replied in a flat tone. "I probably will . . . but I don't know for certain."

"It feels to me like the chance of a lifetime. I can hardly believe that I'll be going! Africa doesn't even seem real. I think part of me doesn't believe that Africa actually exists." I laughed. "Have you ever been on one of your dad's expeditions?"

"No, he's never really asked me before. It could be strange to travel with him."

An uneasy silence followed. It didn't seem appropriate to probe her for an explanation of her comment.

"Are you going to school?" I finally said.

"Naw, I'm just hanging out."

Having depleted my reservoir of conversation-starters, I tucked myself into a carved walnut chair at the beautifully set dining room table. Marty plopped into the vacant seat beside me, opposite her father. The others chatted politely. Ross, comfortably holding court, began recounting his adventures.

Marty didn't appear to be interested in who I was or why I would be going with them to Africa. Anxiety seeped into my chest at the thought that she might not come. If she didn't, I'd be the only woman traveling for months with Ross and his assistant. Alan, whom I hadn't met yet, was still in school down on the peninsula. Since he was an entomology major, he had to be viewing this expedition like a gift from the insect gods. Ross must be a bit of a legend to him, I surmised. Ross hadn't said much about Alan. I had the feeling they didn't know each other well.

Realizing how much I'd been hoping Marty would come, I tried again to draw her out.

"I went to see Janis Joplin with Big Brother and the Holding Company in Golden Gate Park. Have you heard her?"

"Yeah, she's groovy."

"I've never seen anyone give so much energy to an audience. We weren't just listening; it was like we were all dancing along with her. I really dig what she does."

"I know." Marty sat up and turned toward me. "Country Joe and the Fish are cool too. Do you know their song? The one about Vietnam? They tell it like it is."

"Did you go to the peace rally? There were so many people there who don't think we should be fighting in Vietnam. Why kill people halfway around the world?"

"Yeah, but it's not going to last." Marty looked down.

"What do you mean? What isn't going to last? The war or the protests?"

"Oh, the war will go on, all right, but I bet the protests won't."

"Why?"

Marty looked at me sadly. It was almost like she pitied me, like she thought I just wasn't getting it. Then she looked away, studying a pea she was chasing around her plate with a fork.

I waited, but nothing further came from her frowning mouth. I turned back to my food and finished the meal in silence. My dad and Ross were involved in a mutually enjoyable, intellectual conversation. My mom rose to help clear the dishes. Mrs. Ross took my plate. Since Marty showed no sign of offering to help, I stayed seated too, hoping for more conversation.

My mom and Mrs. Ross remained in the kitchen. I fidgeted, unable to pay attention to the men. Marty stayed silent beside me. I tried to imagine what thought had wormed its way in and destroyed our conversation. When the women returned, Mrs. Ross's eyes had reddened. My mom's lips had curled inside her mouth, a sure sign she was annoyed. Unexpected trains of thought were snaking through this house, none of which I could decipher.

After dessert and coffee, we said our goodbyes and left, reminding the Rosses they needed to drive back across the bay that night. As we headed toward my apartment, my mom, usually a chatterbox, stayed silent.

"Well, Ross is quite a person," my dad stated. "He certainly loves his bugs!" He smiled, drumming his fingers lightly on the steering wheel.

"Marty was almost impossible to draw into conversation. She's really angry at him. But I hope she comes with us; I'd hate to be the only woman."

My mom cleared her throat. "Yes." It came out loud and a bit angry.

I looked at her, uncertain of how to process her outburst. Maybe she'd felt ignored by the men? I was missing something, or several somethings important to her, but I had no clue. Disquiet twitched like a confused butterfly trapped inside my chest.

"I liked your dad a lot. Intelligent man!" Ross beamed across the top of a jar into which I'd condemned mildly resistant penultimate embioptera. "I think you take after him."

I looked like my dad, but I didn't think Ross was talking about facial resemblances. I knew he meant his comment as a compliment, so I smiled while he continued on.

"I'm glad you had a conversation with Marty. She's having problems. I wonder if she's in some kind of trouble. She's nervous, even jumpy. Did she tell you anything? She isn't pregnant, is she? I just wish she'd go back to school and find a real career. I don't mind if she doesn't choose my field, but just to see some spark of intellectual curiosity . . . I've been looking for it for so long. I know I haven't been the greatest father to her. I'm sure she holds me responsible for a lot of her troubles, but she won't even try to see the joy in science!"

Ross seemed to address the last part of his monologue more to himself than me. I didn't relish the idea of spending many months in Africa spying into the workings of his daughter's psyche. I suppressed an impulse to share her excitement about Janis Joplin's music and the peace rally, but I imagined he wouldn't understand Marty's ability to find joy in the things he'd find inexplicable.

I needed to give him my response. "I hope she decides to come. I'd like to get to know her. I think she knows a lot about the social movement that's happening right now."

"I wouldn't call it a 'movement'," Ross scoffed. "Just a bunch of kids rebelling against their parents' values. No comprehension of the work it took to raise them, to give them a good home. They take things for granted. Having food on the table, education, cars in garages. They think they can just listen to music and smoke marijuana and never have to work. Maybe they think food just magically appears on tables and there will always be a roof over their heads. I know I've done some things wrong as a parent, but my values are good ones. I just haven't managed to pass them to my children." Anger, confusion, and sorrow braided through Ross's rant. I imagined that Marty suffered similar feelings. Ironically, what they shared most might be feeling judged by the other.

Passport photo.

By the next Saturday, I'd purchased most of the things Ross had directed me to. I'd watched my hair fall to the floor of a fancy San Francisco salon. The price had been extravagant, but if I were going to lose the hair I'd been growing for years, I wanted someone to do a good job with what was left. My passport photo, although a new look for me, was acceptably flattering.

I'd packed two small cases to be shipped and left them with Ross. As I headed to my folks' house for the weekend, it seemed like a nest of benign hornets had taken up residence in my body. Every part of me buzzed. I found it hard to sit still or stay focused. By then, I figured I'd probably pickled countless, ultimate-stage embiids in the same jar as the penultimates.

I watched whitecaps rise and melt back into the dark-blue waters of San Francisco Bay as I sped across the bridge to Oakland. In less than two weeks, if I didn't break a bone or contract pneumonia or simply drop dead, I'd be in Cape Town, South Africa, a bustling city that looked shiny and beautiful in all the photos I'd found.

My mind was aflutter. For the rest of my life, the African landscape would be cemented into my brain because I would have set foot on its soil. I would have drunk its water and eaten its food. African molecules would become part of my body. After so many months there, would I be made up of more African molecules than American? What a thought! I would slowly become African. Would African molecules bring about more African thoughts? Could my physical makeup change my mental makeup? By the time I reached my parents' house, my brain hurt.

Entering their home, I was greeted by the sight of photographic paraphernalia laid out across my parents' dining room table. I saw a fifty-millimeter lens for regular shots, my new three-hundred-millimeter telephoto lens for animal shots, and extension tubes for macro-photography close-ups. Ross would be tutoring me in insect photography. He said that I might be able to sell an article to *National Geographic* on the Topnaar Khoekhoe, the tribe I'd be spending my days with in the Namib Desert. It felt unreal to imagine that all this equipment would soon be used to photograph giraffes, elephants, and desert-dwelling humans!

I gave my dad a broad grin of gratitude for his help. He had been an avid photographer all his life, and one of my fondest memories was sitting on a stool in the tiny darkroom he'd built, using tongs to fish out photographs from a flat, ceramic pan filled with developer, then sliding them into the fixer pan. Although they were undoubtedly toxic to my young body, I'd loved the smell of those chemicals and the glow of the red light designed to protect the black-and-white prints from exposure. I'd gotten my first camera at ten, a Brownie Star Flash. Blue bulbs sizzled and smoked inside the cupped reflective flash casing whenever I took a picture. The smoke they emitted was also undoubtedly toxic, but I loved that smell too as I popped a used bulb out and inserted another, ready for my next shot. Dad had helped me develop my prints along with his own. I remembered our visit to West Point and the ridiculous number I'd taken of handsome cadets. Dad never commented on the subject matter or suggested I was wasting expensive film. I loved photography and was about to be tutored by a professional! My father was happy for me and enthusiastically helped me get the right equipment for the trip.

For photographing insect close-ups, Ross gave me a large, blue-plastic rectangle to hold behind insects as a way to mimic the sky. I slid it into a pocket of a faux-leather shoulder bag I'd be using for my equipment.

"And your flash," Dad added, handing me a black cube, "and light meter and shutter-release cable." His voice sounded husky. "Put on your safari jacket and let's go outside and take some pictures."

The afternoon sun had turned the hillside golden behind me as I stood with a stick over my shoulder, holding a teddy bear upside down by one leg and grinning triumphantly. This big-game hunting mockery was my dad's idea, but I enjoyed its silliness. I wondered what each of my parents thought about this African adventure. How much danger did they imagine they'd be sending their daughter into? Ross had impressed my dad. He'd done so many trips already that Dad probably felt he could trust him.

Changing out of my Africa togs after the humorous photo shoot, I went into the kitchen to help Mom with dinner. She bustled around the stove, distant and distracted. "You can set the table. How 'bout a little wine? There's an open bottle of Emerald Dry in the fridge."

"Are we eating on the patio or in here?"

"Patio, I think." While she sounded normal enough, her tone carried tension.

I carried placemats and utensils out the glass door to the backyard. Returning for the wine, I heard my mom clear her throat.

"Do you feel certain about going on this trip?"

"Sure. Why?"

"I just want you to be careful."

"I plan to. You know that Ross has done these trips a lot."

"Yes, I know." Mom turned and looked at me, giving me her full attention. "When his wife and I were in the kitchen at their house, she said that I had no idea what she'd been through, that he has done this over and over again. She cried a bit when she said it. I just want you to think about what you're doing."

"I guess it must be hard to be left behind all the time," I said. "I think it has been especially difficult for Marty and her brother. But the kids are grown now, so maybe she should go with him. Maybe she could come along with Marty."

Mom gave me a long look, then turned back to the vegetables she was cooking. I felt again as if I'd missed something.

Monday found me back in the lab, this time pickling the adult embiids. What in the world did he intend for them? So many little lives seemingly lived meaninglessly, just to end up on a laboratory shelf! I'd had my fill of this task and was more than ready to be on my way to Africa. I even preferred the thought of being back at my desk in the payroll office than continue my role as insect executioner. I missed wending my way through the labyrinthian corridors of the academy to deliver employee checks. I realized I hadn't even said goodbye to anyone. Echoing footsteps interrupted my rebellious musings.

"I looked through your bag." Ross hefted my smallest suitcase onto the bench. Clicking the tongued latch open, he lifted the lid. "Why in the world would you bring this cotton wadding?" He poked at a bag of cotton balls in the center of the case. "We can get this after we're there! Africa has stores, you know." His tone was grim and mocking. His face twisted in annoyance, showing a side I'd never seen before.

I'd packed the cotton balls for applying my Ten-O-Six astringent lotion to keep my face from breaking out. I felt shame descend like a curtain, but a sense of indignation kept the curtain from closing over me. What did I know about anything that might or might not be available in Africa? I said nothing as he closed the case and carried it back with him.

"By the way," came the same gruff voice from the other room, "Marty's decided to come with us."

EIGHT

Women in high heels clicked past me, men in dark suits hoisted travel bags over their shoulders, and children stumbled to keep pace with nervous parents hurrying toward departure gates. San Francisco International Airport brimmed with the promises and memories of its arriving and departing passengers. Sitting quietly amid the bustle, I adjusted the hem of my new green dress, pulling it over nylon-clad knees. My sweaty hands clutched the novel I hoped would distract me from a potential twenty-five hours of torture.

Four members of the California Academy of Science's entomology expedition were about to embark on an adventure: Ross, Alan, Marty, and I. My father was taking a business trip to New York and would be joining us on this flight. Knowing my visceral fear of flying, his presence probably wasn't coincidental; he may have adjusted his schedule to help me over the first hurdle: San Francisco to New York.

Dad led me down the narrow aisle to our seats. Once settled, my father began asking about what I had packed, what lenses I had for my still-new Pentax, what routes we were planning to take once our expedition got underway. I knew he was trying his best to distract me from the imminent flight. Only half-listening, I thought instead about the trip.

After the flight landed at Newark, New Jersey—thankfully without any big disasters—we would be taking a short hop over to the New York Airport recently renamed "Kennedy" in honor of our assassinated president. From Kennedy, we would fly to the Canary Islands, to Johannesburg, then end at our final destination: Cape Town, South Africa.

From then on, we would be camping across the outback of seven countries in sub-Saharan Africa. The trip would not be easy. I'd made a conscious decision concerning my mortality before I agreed to go. Political unrest, wild animals, disease, creepy-crawly critters, or vehicle malfunction could easily result in my demise. I'd decided the adventure was worth that risk. As irrational as this was, none of those possibilities scared me as much as my potential death in a fiery plane crash.

After taxiing to our assigned spot, the plane turned, revved its jet engines, and lumbered forward, gaining speed. The massive mixture of steel, aluminum, plastic, and human bodies shook and vibrated. I took a death-grip on both armrests. Long after I was certain we had run out of runway, the plane gave a final bump and rose into the air. All became smooth. As my iron grip released from the armrests, we hit an air pocket and plummeted like someone had just pushed the "down" button in an elevator. Stomach in my mouth, I stopped breathing until we resumed our climb.

The hours we spent crossing the country peeled away my resolve. I imagined every bump, every rattle threatening imminent death. I was soon emotionally exhausted, and probably more than a little bit drunk.

My mental state did not improve when we encountered storms somewhere over the Midwest. The breathtaking expanse of cloud beneath us couldn't compensate for the turbulence they caused for the rest of the flight. When at last we neared New Jersey, the weather turned from bad to atrocious. We circled the airport, bumping, dropping, dipping, and turning. Rain flew past the window. The plane began losing altitude. I heard the landing gear grind into place. Experience had taught me to listen and be grateful for the final metallic *clunk* that assured the gear had locked into place. Wind buffeted the plane left and right as we neared the runway. We were already passing the airport's tower while our pilot still struggled to land the plane. After slamming onto the wet concrete in a bone-jarring landing, the engines roared in reverse thrust. Careening sideways, we came to a stop as the red-striped, end-of-the-runway barrier appeared right outside my window. Spontaneous applause burst from all one-hundred-and-seventy-five passengers. I felt numb as I tried to remember how to breathe.

We disembarked from the plane and my dad turned to Ed Ross. "We're going to take a cab. We'll meet you at Kennedy."

I choked back tears. There was no way my mental state could have handled continuing on that plane. If the aisle where we were standing had been a bit wider, I might have kissed my dad's feet.

The thirty-five-mile taxi ride to the New York airport must have been ridiculously expensive, but it gave me a much-needed hour to recover my nerves. When we arrived at Kennedy's "Departures" and found the appropriate gate, Dad deposited me with my carry-on bags.

"Thanks tons for that. I couldn't have gotten back on a plane right then." I hugged my dad.

"It was just as fast," he responded, kindly overlooking my need for recuperation between flights. "Curly, be sure to write whenever you can. We have the names of the towns where you'll get mail at general delivery. We'll write too." I heard the gruff affection in his pet name for me. After choosing this ironic name for his bald baby, Dad had never called me anything but "Curly." We hugged goodbye and he went off.

I put the cross-country flight behind me as much as I could. Ed, his assistant Alan, Marty, and I gathered our belongings and joined the line boarding our aircraft. The four assigned seats turned out to be scattered around the plane. Ross and his daughter had seats near the front, Alan found his about halfway back, while mine ended up being toward the very end of the plane. Settling into a window seat in the back row, I appreciated the moderate isolation. Time to regroup.

I made myself think about how amazing this trip was going to be. I imagined a giraffe. I comprehended the reality that I would be seeing a giraffe on the plains of Africa, a giraffe that would be standing tall and spotted on the plains of Africa! In 1967, no one I knew had ever been to Africa. No one I knew even knew anyone who had ever been to Africa. Africa was the continent of Joseph Conrad and Doctor Livingstone. In movies, Humphrey Bogart waded through leech-filled swamps, steering Katharine Hepburn through the murky water aboard the old wooden African Queen. Only a decade before, the Mau Mau had risen up in a perfectly timed rebellion. On cue across Kenya, family servants used curved, razor-sharp pangas to slay the white colonizers oppressing them. Julius Nyerere now headed Tanganyika, freshly renamed "Tanzania," after the country's peaceful revolution of great socialist idealism. And this little white girl from the San Francisco Bay area's suburbs now had boarded a plane that would fly (hopefully) for twenty-five hours, landing briefly in a few places, before depositing her on the soil of that continent half a world away.

I tried to envision how soil would actually look in Africa. Did dirt look like dirt wherever you went? I pictured the dry, eroded-sandstone dirt I played in while growing up in Orinda, and thought, "no." Orinda dirt was different from the soft, black soil of my grandma's farm in Illinois. Once when we'd visited her there, my dad picked up a handful of the rich, dark, loamy soil, smelled it, and commented on how Midwesterners just took for granted such a treasure. Peering into his hands, I'd expected to see little diamonds or emeralds hiding in the soil. But Dad had merely sighed, scattered the dirt, and dusted his hands. No jewels had fallen out.

Did African soil look like Orinda's sandy clay or the dark soil of the Illinois family farm? I imagined a road cut, exposing the skin and body of Earth's dark continent, something I would soon see for myself.

I stuffed my red plaid flight bag under the seat ahead, grateful to have something to rest my feet on. I grappled with my seatbelt, nervously trying to pull it tight. The glow of forthcoming adventure faded to gray nausea. Thinking about giraffes and dirt could only distract me for so long. Stepping onto any airplane put me into the presence of my own death; its method, time, and manner were all secondary to the comprehension of mortality always consuming me. My face tightened with the tension of what awaited. Despite having survived our first flight, the idea of sailing through the air and crossing the Atlantic inside a thin, metal eggshell still seemed unreasonable.

As the plane took off, my toes and fingers again attempted to hold onto solid ground, squeezing nonexistent life out of shoes and armrests. My eyes closed. Each dip and curve told my screaming psyche these were the last moments before impact. Shifts in the engine's tone signaled imminent mechanical failure. Cabin vibrations, unnoticed by the stewardesses, warned me of impending breakup due to metal fatigue.

Attempting to contain my nerves, I inhaled slow, deep breaths. However much we may want to ignore the fact, we all realize that we will die someday. We often have our first gut-gripping experience as teenagers comprehending the fact of mortality. Those lucid moments usually remain few and far between, but when I stepped onto that airplane, I knew I would die. Positively. Not a speck of room for doubt. People had often tried to soothe me with physics and safety statistics to no avail. The point was not that this particular plane would or would not land sometime in the future; that didn't matter. A safe landing would merely be a stay of execution.

When the airliner leveled off, I opened my eyes. Gazing around, I noted that the other passengers had settled in for the long flight. No one shared my private hell; they believed the plane would fly. Death had not come at take-off. I would be forced to wait twenty-five more hours.

A stewardess moved past my seat to assist another passenger. I debated asking whether she had something to render me unconscious for several dozen hours. If she did, she probably would be forbidden to administer such a powerful drug unless I seemed dangerous to myself or others. I filed that idea. The flight crew would know what to do if I suddenly lost my self-control at forty-thousand feet. The thought was slightly comforting. Emotionally, I surrendered my first bit of control.

Okay, I'm scared. Why not simply be scared? The novel idea of embracing my fear cheered me a bit. I breathed slowly and allowed myself to inventory what fear felt like. Turning my full attention inward, I experienced fear as something cool and gripping inhabiting my body. Merely a sensation, it felt no worse than being outside on a chilly afternoon with insufficient clothing. I sat with my fear. I chatted with my fear. Eventually, I became moderately comfortable in a state of fear.

After deciding I could survive twenty-five hours hanging out with fear, to my utter dismay, fear shifted into terror. My stomach dropped. My insides clenched. I breathed shallowly until I reminded myself to try taking deeper breaths. After concentrating until I could fill my lungs with air again, I remembered that fear had been okay once I'd accepted it. Maybe this could work for terror too. Regaining my newfound detachment, I decided to give the terror full rein. *Go for it, terror. You've got me for hours. What can you do?*

Terror's response to my challenge surprised me. The moment I stopped fleeing the emotion and accepted terror's presence throughout my body, its quality changed. A new sensation, more peaceful, washed over me in waves. Observing, I tried to give it a name. The word that came to mind was a total surprise. Orgasm. The most similar sensation I had in my emotional/physiological encyclopedia was orgasm! Waves of uncontrolled feeling resting in a backdrop of nothingness.

I gave up any sense of time and had no consciousness of the airplane that held me or the passengers around me. I disappeared inside myself. This experience was all about death. Death was the thought that brought terror. To embrace my terror, perhaps I must embrace my death. Dying required letting go. Losing me. I wondered what it meant to lose "me."

I began taking inventory of what I considered to be my "self." I looked down at my hands. My sister always told me that I had good hands. They tanned to an olive brown. They were soft, flexible, skilled: an artist's small, dexterous hands. My hands would not survive my death. I sat focused on the loss of my hands, feeling intensely sad, grieving the loss of this part of "me."

Continuing my inventory, I realized I'd be losing the bad stuff too. Flat feet! My bad connective tissue had always been a problem in a family that loved to hike. I often lagged behind. My feet always hurt. Whatever else death might bring, I knew I wouldn't be going there with flat feet.

Then I thought of my voice. Years of vocal training. Solos. Musical comedies. The joy of singing a piece perfectly. The high of an audience's appreciation. Gone. Every hour of work and study no longer mattering. *Poof—just like that.*

Piece by piece, I inventoried my body, my hair, my acquired knowledge, my talents, my connections with others. Honoring and releasing each, I grieved its loss. Waves of sorrow. I felt myself shrinking. Overwhelmed by sadness, I continued to diminish as I contemplated each aspect of myself that would be gone.

After an unknown amount of time, I had inventoried and mourned the loss of every aspect I identified as myself. I felt shrunken to a mere point of existence, to a place of pure aloneness, feeling separate from all I had ever known. All connections had been illusions. I'd been born alone and I would die alone. I was totally alone. There was nothing left of me, nothing but an infinitesimal point continuing as my consciousness. Boundless sorrow.

Just as with terror, a change happened when I comprehended the truth of my absolute aloneness: my entire being was suffused in inexplicable bliss. I knew I could shrink no more. As is true of matter and energy, I understood with complete certainty that consciousness could neither be created nor destroyed. I was something more than the collection of traits I had just released. The essence of "me" existed as part of the Universe; it could not cease to be part of the Universe. Something new, fresh, and sensory filled my experience, something vastly different from the usual five senses. More than a combination of sight, sound, taste, smell, and touch, this new sensation floated me out of my body, out of the airplane, and into an ethereal place of vast and total comfort. I merged with a light I couldn't see, but that encompassed all of me. A sense of safety and compassionate love embraced me. I was resting in a love bigger than anything I'd ever felt. Infinity held me and became me.

I have no idea how long the experience lasted in the temporal world. I descended back into the airplane, reuniting with the body I'd abandoned. Joy remained, and wonder at the limitless bliss I had experienced. I had existed as part of everything, and everything was an infinite oneness.

In vain, I searched through the English language, hoping to find a way to codify the journey. Words and even memory seemed insufficient. I thought about how when we feel loved by someone, the sense of our aloneness dissolves. That feeling of connection might be likened to the tying of two threads in a tapestry. At that moment, I'd felt woven into an infinite tapestry, a tapestry holding every star, ocean, dog, beetle, person, and unknown species from every unknown planet. The Universe was the Universe; there existed but a single Oneness. I could not separate from it; I could not die. My body would eventually disintegrate, but the essence of my consciousness could not. I was of the Universe. There is no quantity in infinity. One cannot name the portion of the infinite Universe that I became. I merged with infinity. I understood that I was everything. We were everything.

A calm surrounds us when we feel at peace, but "peace" was a tiny attempt at naming what I felt. Enormous peace. Total calm. Infinite joy and love, and a sense of returning, reuniting with that from which the illusion of my life had separated me. True reality is essential consciousness, not separate from matter and energy, but another aspect of it.

My eyes opened slowly, looking around at my fellow humans confined within a flying metal structure. Outside my window, night emptied the physical world of all matter, save for the flashing light periodically revealing the expanse of wing supporting our airborne capsule. My cheeks felt damp. I found a tissue to wipe the tears I hadn't been aware were falling.

"We will soon begin our descent into the Canary Islands. This plane will remain on the ground for one hour for refueling, during which time you are free to deplane. If you are continuing on with us to Johannesburg and Cape Town, please find the 'Occupied' card in the pocket in front of you and place it on your seat when you leave." The strangely accented voice droned on while the engine noises rose in pitch.

The plane began to fall. Not to crash, though the pilots were allowing gravity to have its way with us. Adjusting flaps and engine speed, our captain guided the descent toward the Atlantic Ocean. I pictured their tiny target, far ahead beneath us. An island they must find in the vast blackness. A strip of asphalt, barely wider than a two-lane road, exactly aligned with the trajectory of the craft. Air pockets and wind gusts began jostling us through all three dimensions. How did humans routinely accomplish this feat of dropping thousands of pounds of mass onto a small strip of land at the exact speed needed to preserve our corporeal beings?

Hearing the grind and thump of landing gear locking into place left me serene. My hands, curling around the plastic armrests of the Boeing 707, felt relaxed and dry. No sweaty palms scrabbling to keep the plane airborne until the last possible second. Looking out the window I watched lights twinkle into view. I remembered the feeling one night as a child in Disneyland when our magical caterpillar cart seemed to float down a leafy track at the end of the Alice-in-Wonderland ride. A fairyland spread below me and I descended into its enchantment. And, just as it had long ago in Disneyland, this new magic cart carried me gently down to land in an unknown world.

As others began deplaning, I debated leaving everything I owned on board and simply stepping into the uncharted world of the Canary Islands. Would people care for me? Would I be fed and eventually returned to the life I'd known? Or, rather, into a new, unimagined one? I smiled and decided that stepping off the plane with no possessions would unfairly test my newfound Tapestry and its concept of Oneness. I remained seated until the plane reloaded and once again rumbled down the runway, then floated up into the night sky.

A new seatmate settled in beside me, a woman about my age. Her shoulder-length brown hair curled gently onto the collar of her pale pink cardigan. She smiled and nodded a greeting. Having been preoccupied with internal explorations, I'd scarcely noticed her predecessor. Now I felt curious about someone boarding from the Canary Islands. Did she live there? Where would her future take her? Where was she headed now? It turned out she was flying to her wedding, flying into the married life that I had recently thought I wanted.

"You're American, aren't you? Are you going on safari?"

"Well, sort of. It's a scientific expedition."

"Oh, that will be nice." Nervous energy spun her away into concerns about her impending wedding, worries about the condition of her dress travelling with her, and a detailed description of the husband-to-be. Big-game-hunter handsome. Khaki safari shorts and all that. The stuff of movies. She soon would tie her life to his.

I awoke at dawn when the plane touched down in Johannesburg. My seatmate and I said our goodbyes. I watched her gather a long garment bag from the stewardess and give a final wave before disappearing down the aisle, leaving me to wonder whether or not I wished we had switched life-paths during the night.

A boy soon reoccupied her seat while his mom settled in across the aisle. Nattily dressed in knee-socks and short pants, the friendly lad proved to be as talkative as his predecessor. Maybe it was something about that particular seat. I learned he was headed back to his German School. I had discovered that various ethnic groups in South Africa were divided by the languages they spoke. White students attended either Afrikaans (Dutch), English, or German schools. Black Africans had their own schools, if they were fortunate enough to attend. The boy was doing quite well in all of his subjects except maths, and quite feared flying; he felt nervous about this trip. As we began taxiing, he nestled against me. I reached my arm around his shoulders, happy to offer soothing words to calm his fears. Glancing across at his mother, I accepted her smile and nod of gratitude. If I were marrying a big game hunter, would it then follow that I would be comforting my own child? How would that compare to my current life path? Would the Tapestry be better served by creating family connections, or didn't that matter since all was interwoven anyway? By the time the plane landed in Cape Town, I had answered none of those questions, but the boy was asleep, cuddled against me.

NINE

Our exhausted bodies straggled out of Cape Town Airport's baggage claim area and found a waiting taxi. The ride to our hotel showed us little of Africa other than darkened city streets. After checking in, Ross handed Marty and me our keys. We found the room and flopped onto our beds. Her rhythmic breathing told me she had almost immediately fallen asleep, but I sat up, needing to record something of the flight's life-altering experience before it blurred in my mind. Hoping only for something that would jog my memory the next day, I scrounged for a pen and wrote a poem.

> "Perhaps She Died"
> *She prepared herself for death.*
> *I think perhaps she died.*
> *That's her suit lying on the dresser,*
> *But she's not wearing it.*
> *Some, perhaps, might think her me,*
> *But she didn't know about the*
> *Blue quilt at her destination*
> *And I do.*
> *Knowing the quilt and the*
> *Funny trees on the wallpaper*
> *Sets me quite apart from her.*
> *I last saw her on an airplane*
> *With her arm around a little boy.*
> *She can't know what I'm*
> *Thinking now because she was*

On a plane that is no more.
But it's all right.
She was ready
To be gone,
And now I'll
Continue in her place.
No one will know.

Marty and I slept until two the next afternoon. When I woke up, I realized my world had shifted and I needed to try to relay that shift to someone else. Marty was the most likely candidate. I decided to share my poem with her. While I didn't think it was very good, it did express something true. She read it and nodded.

"Yes, I understand," she said, looking me in the eye as she returned my poem. Without speaking, she handed me a book on Buddhism, open to the page she had been reading. "When the student is ready, the teacher will appear."

Whoa! This seriously scrambled my already protesting mind. Did she really understand what I meant by my poem? Perhaps a wider and much weirder world had opened to me once I'd experienced abandoning my usual definitions of reality and self. Did Marty already know about the things I'd experienced on the plane?

We joined the men early in the evening, leaving the hotel to find dinner. We passed a construction site piled with stacks of building materials. Raw dirt lay exposed and trampled between the supply bundles. I recalled the thought I'd had before leaving the San Francisco airport, so recent and yet a lifetime ago. I'd wondered what African soil would look like; now I stepped off the Cape Town sidewalk to find out. Kicking a bit of loose dirt with the toe of my black flat, I saw that African soil looked very much the same as California soil, but the eyes that viewed this land were focusing through new lenses. My world had shifted. I doubted if even California soil would ever be the same again.

We were all too dazed to pay much attention to what we ate. After dinner, we returned to the hotel for another long sleep.

Dedicating a day to jetlag recuperation, the following morning, we decided to leisurely explore the city. To my surprise and even annoyance, Africa looked much more like the city I'd just left than the steamy jungles of literature. Geographically, San Francisco and Cape Town had a lot in common being equidistant from the equator, one to the north and one to the south. Letting that fact sink in made me contemplate the vast expanse of travel lying before us. To get to the equator from San Francisco, you'd have to drive south down the rest of California through Mexico and Central America, clear down through Colombia to the border of Peru. From where I now stood, we would be taking mostly unpaved roads and dirt tracks through seven countries, crossing two desserts, wide savannas, vast swamplands, and dense forests before reaching our destination of Kenya at the equator. Africa suddenly struck me as huge. And we'd be crossing it with gas and water tanks that were hopefully large enough to get us from one supply place to the next, but with no firearms or other weapons for finding food if we ever got stuck. Well, Ross had done these kinds of trips many times before and survived unscathed. I decided to trust that he knew what he was doing.

The comparable but geographically opposite latitudes of Cape Town and San Francisco meant their climates would also be similar—no snow and mild summers. The September temperature was in the low seventies in both places, but in one place it was early spring; in the other, early fall. Also, like San Francisco, Cape Town wrapped around the shore of a large bay, and Table Mountain provided as stunning a backdrop as the Berkeley and Oakland hills did at home. Fog had rolled in during the night. Trapped against the side of the mountain, it then settled back over the modern city. Had San Francisco teleported to Africa during our flight? Would I find barking sea lions and the Golden Gate bridge? The similarities, to be truthful, disappointed me. I wanted giraffes and lions.

As we strolled through the city, I found a place inside myself to hold the airplane experience until I could examine it fully, perhaps eventually discuss it with someone. If I ever did try to verbalize these thoughts, Marty would be the most likely listener. Musing about the airplane experience as we wandered, I was disoriented and distracted. As I stepped off a curb to cross my first street, a dark green Land Rover slammed on its brakes and swerved to avoid flattening my unwary American body. When the British brought automobiles to South Africa, they also brought left-handed driving. Cars came at pedestrians from the right. The lorry driver scowled at my carelessness and continued on. Conscious street-crossing would be required. I needed to tune back into the material world.

The first animals we encountered in Africa were not even African. The park we had wandered into contained a small zoo. Near the entrance, exotic-looking red-beaked finches fluttered around their cage. All of us scurried to be photographed with our first African fauna. Then, as we read their identification sign, we felt slightly deflated. The birds were "Java Finches" from Indonesia. In Cape Town, of course, just as at home, the exotic animals on display would be transplants from other continents. Why would anyone want to see a cage full of robins in San Francisco? No zebras here, either. Apparently, people in Cape Town didn't find zebras interesting enough for a zoo.

As afternoon slid into evening, I found the darkening heavens discombobulating. The sky was all wrong. While I'd never bothered to learn many constellations, the star patterns I'd seen all my life inhabited an area of my brain now labeled *aspects of home*. Their consistency existed as a basic assumption of Universal Truth. South of the equator, the heavenly view from Earth looked out at a different canopy of stars. The foreign dome covering us at night surprisingly upset my sense of rightness. Cape Town was revealing itself to be a jumble of things unexpectedly strange yet surprisingly familiar.

By the third day after landing in Cape Town, we felt sufficiently recovered to finish the necessary city business and begin our expedition in earnest.

During our stay in Cape Town, I had learned only one phrase in Afrikaans, the primary language of apartheid South Africa: *"Geen Stompies in Pan Assambleif."* This message was posted in all public restrooms. "No cigarette butts in toilets, please." I hoped to gain a more useful knowledge of the languages I would encounter in the future.

A cab took us to the where Ross's grass-green, three-quarter-ton Chevy truck awaited our arrival. My first impression was of a normal truck with a large aluminum box attached to it instead of the usual bed. Ross had designed this truck several years ago for his camping expeditions. After his previous trip through Australia, he had shipped it to be stored in Cape Town. I clambered through a back door to find a seat surrounded by shelves and drawers with a built-in desk in front. I could see across the shoulder-high opening to Alan's seat on the other side. Marty rode in front with her dad as Ross revved the engine and we headed out.

After an hour or so driving south from the city, we found an isolated campsite on the seventy-mile-long peninsula that ended in the Cape of Good Hope. The untouched beach of Haute Bay extended for miles alongside us. Thin grass covered white sand in a clearing surrounded by spidery starbursts of wild protea, a shoulder-high plant whose flowers could look like anything from oversized roses to silvery pinecones. At last, I saw something totally foreign to my American concept of vegetation.

Camp at Haute Bay.

As we set up camp, I came to further appreciate our vehicle's elegant design. Ross and Alan climbed small ladders to lift the shallow, inverted aluminum box covering the top of the truck. As they lifted and slid it to one side, legs unfolded from either of its sides. Ross and Alan hooked one edge to the truck and extended the legs, creating an awning. A side door of the truck lifted off, its hidden legs unfolding to create a large table that would become my kitchen area under the awning. The space behind the door held pots, pans, and containers for food storage. Gathering those up, I filled a pot with water from our hundred-gallon tank, then carried the dishes off to wash and scrub away accumulated dust before beginning our journey. Sitting cross-legged on the warm grass felt liberating. I sloshed soap bubbles between the pans. As I stood to fill another pan with rinse water, I looked up at a small hill just above camp.

"Zebra!"

Luckily, the focus of my excitement remained unmoved by my whoop. Hurrying to find cameras, we began stalking our prey. The large, dark eyes in his striped face calmly took us in. Perhaps campsite zebras, like campsite deer back home, aren't really wild. Posing majestically on the top of the rise, he satisfied our need for a picturesque photo of our first truly African animal.

Returning to our chores, I watched as Ross and Alan each grabbed a rope on opposite ends of the truck. One end of each rope was tied to something on the top of the vehicle. As the two men pulled, a Conestoga-like tent rose up, creating a relatively safe and airy sleeping space for the four of us on the top of the truck, high above wandering carnivores, reptiles, and a myriad of creepy-crawly critters desirous of our flesh. I stood happily awed.

While they were busy transforming the vehicle into our camp home, I was gratified to see Ross's silver hair flop into something more casual from its usual slicked-back neatness. Alan's plaid, polyester, short-sleeved shirt untucked itself from beneath the belt of his neat khaki trousers, declaring its freedom from confinement. I smiled to watch our expedition get real in many ways. Our first camp meal consisted of ham sandwiches on seedy, heavy South African bread, pickles, and excellent green-grape juice. (In another similarity to California, South Africa grew grapes and produced superior wines.) This first humble demonstration of my skills as camp cook impressed no one.

During our preparation, we took our first forays into the semi-wilds of the Cape Peninsula. As the personalities of our group began to show themselves, we established patterns of interaction that stayed with us throughout our journey. Dr. Ed Ross led as our undisputed captain, while Alan bounced around as his Labrador-puppyish assistant. I took the role of a contrary independent who didn't hesitate to speak up when Ross's decisions seemed unreasonable. Marty sulked behind her round-rimmed glasses, partially hidden by a shock of tawny brown hair falling across her face. Stoned on her not-very-secret stash of marijuana, Marty readily enacted the part of the mostly uninterested, post-teenage daughter coming along on the journey only to please her father. When I thought about her response to my poem, I felt certain some deeper knowledge must live inside her—deeper than the rather spoiled daughter who'd gotten away with seldom lifting a hand around camp.

    These roles played out almost immediately in an incident on our third camping day. Bumping along a one-lane dirt road, Ross suddenly slammed on the brakes. Outside my window, I could see a large, brown-patterned snake in the nearby brush.

    "Puff adder!" Ross leapt out of the truck, grabbing a long-handled butterfly net. "Alan, set up the movie camera on the tripod."

    Previously, Ross had reviewed some of Africa's deadlier creatures that we should take pains to avoid. Among the snakes, green or black mambas ranked first for their deadly venom and their propensity to come after people. Cobras moved quickly but generally weren't as deadly. Puff adders, the fourth on the list, owned that position because of their mellow nature, but their venom killed quickly. Recalling the list, I warily stepped out with my camera in hand, but did not venture far from the raised safety of the truck. Marty remained inside, scarcely glancing at the snake. Alan dutifully set up the movie camera beside the truck, while Ross ventured into the bush. Hooking the snake with the end of his net, Ross flipped it onto the road, where it instantly coiled itself into a protective knot.

"Start filming!" Ross bellowed.

Alan focused and held down the button that rolled film within the camera.

Darting its head from side to side, the snake began to uncoil in front of our truck. At this point, I leapt back into my seat, closing the door behind me.

"Keep filming!" Ross's voice apparently had control of Alan's body as the snake began making its way directly toward the base of the tripod, behind which Alan's feet were firmly planted. "Keep filming! Great stuff!" Ross nearly danced with enthusiasm.

Unable to stand this insanity any longer, I out-bellowed Ross. "Alan, get in the truck!"

Alan stood frozen as the snake nearly reached his boots.

"Now! In the truck!"

Alan finally jumped away from the snake, and Ross didn't contradict me. Would he have sacrificed his assistant in the first week of the trip?

During the four-month expedition, never once did I see Alan question Ross's orders. I backed off, leaving Alan to take care of Alan, but I think this early incident established that Ross would not be yelling orders at me. And he never did.

Camp began to take on a fairly comfortable routine. Ross prepared materials for the upcoming months of insect collection, I cleaned and organized the kitchen area, Marty hung out in the shade reading a book, and Alan helped where he could. One day, I convinced Alan to read *The Wastemakers* to me while I sewed a new zipper on the tent. The book was an exposé of "the systematic attempt of business to make us wasteful, debt-ridden, permanently discontented individuals," as the jacket explained. Since we'd be living for months with very few amenities, this book offered something we could be thinking about before we returned home to American "civilization."

A light wind blew as I stitched the heavy fabric. Alan sat cross-legged on a sleeping bag, reading out loud. He didn't comment much on the content of the book and was willing to go on reading it. Marty leaned against a tree on the far side of camp, her usual, reclusive self. As I nearly finished working on one side of the new zipper, someone began clacking the cupboard doors below us. Since the area around the kitchen was usually my domain, I peered over the awning to investigate. To my surprise, Marty had opened a loaf of bread and laid out a row of slices. *Was she making lunch?* The smell of tuna fish wafted up. Then I heard her rustling open a bag of chips, announcing that lunch was ready if we wanted it. Marty retreated back to her tree, carrying a sandwich and her book.

Alan and I exchanged glances, acknowledging a hope that this might signal an attitude change on her part. I finished stitching the last bit of the zipper, then we climbed down the ladder to have lunch. Five sandwiches lay uncovered on the table. The greasy tuna can sat empty beside a knife lying in a puddle of oil. Chips spilled from the wide-open bag. Flies buzzed around their unaccustomed feast. All my excitement about Marty finally pitching in to help drained away with the tuna oil plopping drop-by-drop onto the ground. Shooing flies, I put two sandwiches for Ross onto a plate and covered them with an upside-down bowl. Grabbing a paper towel, I sopped up most of the oil, waiting to really clean the table until after lunch when I'd have soapy water. Alan scooped chips onto his plate. I took some and sealed the bag after carrying the tuna tin and oily paper towels out to where we had a garbage bag. Lunch went down my throat with a swig of bitter-flavored annoyance.

Heading over to Marty's tree, I tried to find words that wouldn't add to the strains developing in camp. "Thanks for lunch. The sandwiches were good."

"No problem."

"I appreciate you helping with meals, but you left everything quite a mess. There's tuna oil all over the table and flies were crawling on the food."

"Well, I called you for lunch. If you'd come down when it was ready, they wouldn't have beat you to it, would they?"

"I covered your dad's sandwich."

"Bravo for you! I know you want me to do more, but the kitchen is your job, not mine. If you think I'm spoiled and lazy, you're probably right. But that's the way it is and that's the way it's going to be, so you might as well chill out and get used to it."

I had no response. I went and got water and began cleaning up. Dealing with Marty was going to be a dilemma.

Finally, all was ready. We packed up and headed north toward the deserts of Namibia. Windows down, wind blowing my newly close-cropped hair, I had my bare feet propped up on the dashboard. *This*, I thought, *is me!* No more nylons; my black flats were packed away into the truck's dead storage space.

The road wound up through the Misty Mountains and over Du Toit's Kloof. During a collecting stop, Alan found a large chameleon with independently swiveling eyes. I created a cage for him out of woven twigs. Whenever we stopped, we'd place him on a branch, hoping he could catch himself a sufficient meal. He never ventured far enough that we couldn't find him again. We called him "Du Toit" in honor of his homeland, and imagined he stuck around because he liked us.

As the road increasingly deteriorated, we entered a rocky desert that looked annoyingly similar to the southern Colorado and Arizona deserts where I'd recently spent two summers working in archeology. Even though the terrain had changed greatly, it didn't look anything like a setting for a Tarzan movie. I still wanted Africa to look more exotic and less familiar.

Since we'd been traveling through relatively populated areas, Ross hadn't filled our water tank to capacity. For the last hundred miles or more, humans had become sparse and we had run out of drinking water. Hot and thirsty, the three of us began to grumble. Ross assured us we'd soon cross the Orange River marking the boundary with Namibia and that we'd be able to resupply there. Sure enough, eventually the rocky road wound down to a bridge crossing a rather grungy-looking river. We stopped at a pump near the gas station; a large pipe led directly to it from the river.

Cape Town's water had been clean and potable, so this would be our first use of army purification tablets. Grabbing my canteen, I went over to pump water as Ross got ready to fill the truck's tank. As orangish, mucousy blobs gushed out with the water, I understood how the river had gotten its name. I overlooked the slime and filled my canteen, dropped in a tablet, shook it vigorously, and anxiously waited the prescribed minutes for the chemicals to render its living organisms harmless. The sun glared down and reflected off the gravel. I couldn't remember ever having been so thirsty. As soon as the necessary time had passed, I chugged my entire canteen. Amazing, I thought. When you're seriously thirsty, you don't care what the water looks like. African real-world lesson number one.

Before leaving the Orange River, we replenished a few supplies. Ross returned to the truck with icy bottles of Coke. Despite having quenched most of my thirst with the grisly river water, I gratefully accepted and started drinking. Ross leaned up against the truck, watching me drink.

"You know you're making an air seal, don't you?"

I looked up in confusion.

"When you put your lips all around the top of the bottle," Ross continued, "you make a seal and air can't get in. That's why there's that little popping sound when you stop. You need to leave an air vent."

I screwed up my forehead in disbelief. Really? Did I need to drink the way Ross wanted me to? He had an opinion on the correct way to do everything, and he obviously expected me to do things his way once I'd seen the light. Technically, Ross obviously was right, but who would try to make somebody change the way they drank from a bottle? He kept watching expectantly, so I merely attempted to follow his dictate, pouring Coke into my mouth slowly, incredulous at the man's audacity.

We pulled away, our gas and water tanks filled, and me still shaking my head at Ross's behavior. Was there no end to this man's control issues?

Ross soon turned the truck onto a barely discernable track. We bumped across its flatness for several miles until, with no warning, the land dropped away into a massive canyonland. We pulled to a stop near the rim.

"It's the Fish River Canyon. The second biggest canyon on Earth after the Grand Canyon," Ross explained as my jaw dropped. "Those are kokerboom trees."

Sprinkled like sparse hairs on a balding man's head, the plants made me think of giraffes wearing spiky helmets. Long, thin trunks exploded at their tips into clumps of short green blades. I grabbed my camera as we poured out to explore. Alan convinced me to photograph him standing on one leg, reaching out over the canyon rim, his butterfly net poised in pursuit of an imaginary insect. As the sun descended toward the horizon, I pleased myself with a photo of the orange globe sinking behind a kokerboom tree, all reflected in the dark lens of Alan's sunglasses.

We set up camp for the night near the canyon's rim as the light faded, marveling at the changing colors working their way down its cliffs. I redeemed myself as cook that night with a tasty curry dinner. Ross broke out a bottle of gin that we mixed with warm soda. Sitting around the fire, we continued drinking.

The campfire's light separated us from the blackness of the surrounding desert. Suddenly a flat, black form scurried past my foot, darting across the circle near Ross. About a half-foot long, the critter triggered no recognition in my catalog of earthly inhabitants.

"Solpugid," yelled Ross, leaping up. He raced to the truck, returning with his collecting forceps: long metal tongs meant to keep his fingers safe from bites or stings of odd African critters. "Watch your feet! It could saw through your toes in seconds!" At his warning, wearing only sandals, I pulled my feet into my chair as the critter raced by again. Too big for an insect and too flat for a mammal, I still had no category for it except *dangerous thing to be avoided at all costs.*

Marty coiled as far into her chair as I did, and Alan, who was supposed to be the deputy critter-catcher, also lifted his feet, hugging his knees into his chest as Ross chased the long, eight-legged thing in and out of the firelight's circle, waving his tongs. Considering his degree of inebriation, his eventual capture surprised me. To my horror and fascination, he held the critter aloft for us, its nearly inch-long saw blades extending from its jaw.

Slightly slurring his words, Ross told us the critter was related to spiders, but to me it looked like some monstrous, mutated, flat cricket from the depths of a nightmare I'd not yet had. I didn't breathe freely again until after he'd secured it in a box holding a cotton wad infused with chloroform.

Obviously pleased with his success, Ross turned to me, wide eyes slightly maniacal in the fire's glow. "What should I capture next?" He chortled.

I laughed at first, but his gaze focused pointedly on me. I sensed very questionable intent as he walked toward me. I stood up and moved away from his outstretched arms.

"I don't know what you're doing, but it's not okay." I circled the fire, moving backward, away from him.

"But I can offer you a life you've never dreamed of. I'll buy you a Mercedes sports car. We'll drive throughout Europe. I'll get a divorce. We'll start a new life."

His daughter sat before us, taking in the entire scene but not speaking. I glanced at Alan, seeking some assistance, but Alan looked away, apparently unwilling to risk his alliance. No reinforcements were going to help me handle Ross's drunken behavior.

"Are you out of your mind? Stop it!" I raised my voice, continuing my circular retreat.

After three complete circuits around the flames, Ross finally stopped his pursuit. I stormed away, walking into the night to cool off. *How naïve had I been?* I'd let myself believe he enjoyed our conversations, that he wanted to offer me a chance to begin as an anthropologist. In the insulated suburban community where I'd been sheltered from some of the ugliness of the world, I'd been led to believe that a fifty-plus-year-old man would never lust after someone the same age as his daughter. The rules of 1950s television broadcasts limited their content to *Leave-It-to-Beaver*-type sitcoms. Nothing like this existed in my worldview.

I wandered until I reached the edge of the canyon, where I was forced to pay attention to my surroundings. The sky brimmed with stars, clustered so densely in places they formed clouds of shimmering light. So bright were the moon and stars, I was able to detect colors in the rocky formations below me. Pillars, temples, and obelisks had been carved by wind and water from the layered stone. My anger at Ross dissipated, eroded by awe and wonder. Did I need to abandon all that might lie ahead in order to escape Ross's urges and duplicity? Anger roiled up again. *Yes*, my pride and self-image answered. I could not submit to months of wondering whether or not I'd be safe from his sleazy advances.

Something tickled across my toe, startling me into a jumpy little dance. The captured solpugid probably had friends, and I still wore only sandals. Returning to climb into the tent, I made my way past the already softly snoring bodies of my campmates to wiggle into my sleeping bag. With my brain swirling in a soup of sadness, anger, awe, and indecision, I eventually fell asleep to the cricket-like sounds of unknown desert-dwellers.

The following morning, I broke the stony breakfast silence. "I'll be leaving the expedition when we reach Windhoek. I think I came along under some false assumptions as to why I was invited on this trip."

Ross set his coffee down onto the sand immediately and rose to take a step toward me. "No, no. Please." He dropped his head and turned away. "I don't remember everything about last night, but I know I behaved badly and I regret that very much. Why you were invited to come was because I knew how much you'd enjoy Africa. I wanted your enthusiasm to be contagious. I hoped that Marty might catch a bit of it."

"But instead, you humiliated her along with me. How do you think she felt watching her father chase me around the fire!"

Turning to Marty, he let his shoulders slump. "I know. I owe you both an apology. I had too much to drink. I won't let it happen again." Ross might have been acting, but he sounded sincere.

Three of us turned our gazes on Marty. She reddened slightly but didn't comment.

"How can I know that will be true for all the months ahead?" I held enough anger in my voice for both of us.

"It was a mistake. I got carried away." He turned back toward me, meeting my stony gaze for the first time. "Don't go."

Alan and Marty remained silent, supporting neither side. Their loyalties lay necessarily with Ross, but they could not ignore the ridiculous scene they'd witnessed the night before. I turned and cleaned the breakfast dishes before determining my reply. If I left, I would be losing the adventure of a lifetime, the chance to be a genuine anthropologist in a Topnaar village. But if I stayed, what else might this man do? Realistically, I knew he had a reputation to uphold in California and that Alan and Marty's presence would undoubtedly prevent any extreme acts. I demanded one additional assurance on his part.

"No more suggestions like that, ever! Okay?"

Ross nodded, "Okay." He looked totally gray: gray hair, gray safari jacket, and gray pants matched by morning-after gray skin tones. He sounded and looked pitiful—and relatively harmless.

I agreed to continue with the group. But a chill had established itself between us that would never totally dissipate. My newfound Tapestry worldview helped me deal with Ross's ego increasingly displaying itself as our trip progressed. He could be a bombastic bully, but even when his energy focused on me, my main response was a feeling of pity that this man had to live inside his brilliant-but-insecure identity.

The road we took from South Africa north to Windhoek, Namibia, lay inland about a hundred miles from the Atlantic Ocean. Soon after we left the Fish River Canyon, Ross turned west, heading out toward the coast on a route through miles of dunes. Ross explained how the Atlantic met the southern part of Africa slowly, foaming its way landward over shallow shoals with countless diamonds imbedded in their matrix. Continuously eroding out, the stones washed ashore, mixing into the sand of the dunes. Many ships had run aground on this rocky area known as the Skeleton Coast. If a sailor managed to reach shore, he might be surprised to find diamonds sparkling across the beaches. Filling his pockets, he would be doomed to die of thirst trying to cross the desert, unable to cash in his treasure. Due to the abundance of diamonds here, the area was fenced and patrolled. Ross's status as an entomologist had gotten us special permission to collect insects in the restricted area. Driving through the gates at night felt as if we were entering a vast prison yard, complete with spotlights and guard posts.

In the morning, I made us a breakfast of cold cereal, since there was no wood or anything else combustible for a cook fire. After Ross and Alan headed out and I'd finished the dishes, Marty and I set off to explore, sliding a half-step backward for every forward step we took up the steep-sided dunes. From the top, we looked around. The dunes seemed to extend in all directions. I made a mental note to be certain we didn't wander far, realizing how easily we could lose our way if a breeze should arise and obliterate our footsteps. I thought of the men, and maybe some women, who had died here. Dying of thirst is said to be a horrible way to go. I didn't relish feeling thirstier than I had when we'd reached the Orange River. I thought of the airplane experience and wondered if everyone got the image of themselves as an indivisible part of the universe right before they died. I hoped so.

Marty and I slid up and down a few dunes, trying to stay headed in one direction. In a shallow vale, I found a wind-exposed cache of translucent stones that had seemingly been worked into simple, flaked tools. Laughing with excitement, I called Marty over to see my "diamond arrowheads." I pocketed the five stones and we headed back, following the trail we had made in the sand.

"Do you really think they're diamonds?" Marty looked at me quizzically, with more interest in her voice than I'd heard before.

"Oh, they probably aren't. Probably they're quartz or something." I laughed. "But if they were, they'd scratch glass."

When we reached camp, Marty gestured toward the truck. I nodded, understanding what she meant. I casually drew the edge of one flake over a small corner of the truck's windshield. Expecting nothing, we both sucked in our breath as the stone etched a line across the glass.

We never told Ross or Alan. I fervently hoped neither would notice the small scratch on the windshield. I smuggled my gems out of the area and would keep them safe thereafter, enjoying the fact that I might have acquired a secret fortune. Uncertainty about their value seemed more fun than risking disillusionment by having them tested.

After several days of desert travel, we reached the small capital city of Windhoek, where we resupplied in a "real" grocery store. I bought rice, pasta, cabbage, onions, hard cheese, vinegar, dense and seedy bread, and various canned meats and sauces; I couldn't buy anything that needed refrigeration. We refilled the gas and water tanks, then drove down off the central Namibian plateau into a natural blast furnace called the Namib Desert, more formidable than the last desert we had crossed. One hundred twenty-five degrees Fahrenheit registered on our truck's thermometer. Sparse yellow grass shimmered in heat waves through the headache throbbing behind my eyes. A large antelope, a gemsbok, fled before the truck. As he raced across the plain, long horns curved toward its back, and striking white-and-black lines ran from his face to the tail streaming behind him. I wondered where he might be headed into that vast nothingness.

Ross had told us about the life forms that evolution had adapted to this ancient desert. Crickets had developed snowshoe feet, excellent for hopping on dunes; sightless moles could swim through the sand, their coats the color of spun gold; and there were spiders that could bend their legs in half and roll like wheels down a dune's face when escaping danger. Here I was to be given my anthropological wings. A deciding factor for my presence on the bug-collecting expedition had been the promise of doing fieldwork in a Topnaar village. In their own language, they are called the "=Aoni group of the Nama people"; the "=" represented one of the five "clicks" used when they spoke. In anticipatory delight, I had divided and tabbed the blank pages of my notebook into appropriate categories: childrearing, subsistence, religion—all the textbook headings from Anthropology 101. Spare bottles of waterproof ink were tucked into the truck's nooks and crannies. At last, I was "in the field." A real anthropologist.

The cooling air of evening coincided with our arrival at Gobabeb, a two-room research station staffed by a young couple from Pretoria. We set up camp, quite literally, in the Kuiseb riverbed. With rainfall averaging less than two inches per year, the one "river" coming off the central plateau flowed beneath the sand. For a thousand miles to the south, unbroken salmon-colored dunes reached heights of nearly a thousand feet. North of the Kuiseb, a white gravel plain stretched nearly as far. Running from east to west, the riverbed offered the only shade trees for perhaps thousands of square miles. Human life had existed here virtually unchanged for millennia, dependent on the silent passage of the Kuiseb's hidden waters four feet below the sand.

Kuiseb River Camp, Namibia.

This Martian landscape was home to a dozen small Nama villages dotted along the riverbed. After passing two or three groups of dome-shaped brush structures on the road to our campsite, I could scarcely believe the next day's prospect for genuine "anthropologizing." We'd agreed I could make sack lunches each day for our group. They would leave me in the mornings at one of the villages, go off to collect insects in the riverbed, and then pick me up again each evening. A month of immersion in one of the least-changed cultures on Earth awaited my budding ethnographic spirit.

The following morning, just as the sun turned the dunes from gray to pink, we bounced eight miles down the desert track to the nearest village. An array of half-tanned goat hides spread across the sand in a white, brown, and black patchwork quilt. A small group of women and children sat on the ground in front of bentwood huts. As I climbed out of the truck, a young woman dressed in a soiled blouse and skirt picked up her baby and left the group, walking toward me with a pleasant look on her face. I was ecstatic. Turning to lean inside the truck, I bade goodbye to the others.

As the truck left a dust trail down the riverbed, the young woman and I exchanged smiles and nods.

"Do you speak English?" I asked.

Her face took on a puzzled look. "No English," she replied.

Gesturing toward the small group working on the goat skins, I smiled more broadly and continued, "Does anyone in the village speak English?"

Now her puzzled expression shifted to something more like an annoyed scowl. "No! No English!" With back turned and hips swaying, she strode away to rejoin the group. She gave no backward glance, no gesture for me to follow.

The ambient temperature rose steadily. I stood alone in the sand, eight miles from the nearest familiar face. Wow! Did this ever happen to Margaret Mead? What in the world had I been thinking? Some lily-white foreigner bopping into their village, assuming I'd be welcomed with open arms? What did I have to offer them? Oh yes, and tell me again, exactly why did I want to be an anthropologist? Approaching that woven hut village for the first time, I felt more like a kindergartner knocking on her classroom door than the anthropological adventurer I wished to be. Shy and nervous, I knew from my ethnographic training that days could pass before anyone began to accept or understand my presence.

Collecting insects in the Namib dunes.

I sat down on the far side of the drying goat hides, keeping my eyes cast downward in what I fervently hoped might be seen as respect. No adult looked at me. Occasionally, a child would peer at me until our eyes met, then would giggle and dash behind the safety of his or her mom. Ah, a mother! I wanted mine! I tried wishing myself into the size of a peanut, but felt more like an elephant sculpted of foolishness. This was a nightmare; couldn't I just teleport home?

Over two-and-a-half hours passed in this bizarre standoff. Suddenly, the young mother rose again and gestured for me to come into the nearest hut. Immensely grateful to be out of the sun and doing anything at all, I followed the women's group into a small wattle dome. She picked up a red stool, brushed it off, and gestured for me to sit. As I did so, the others formed a semicircle on the sand floor beside me. Going around the group, the young mother pointed to each member and said a name. She was "Ruth," her baby was "Alexander," and a young boy was "Moses." The names sounded strange amid the clicks and stops of their language. I introduced myself, and "Carol" was repeated with varying, interesting accents.

Then, silence. Every eye looked toward me. Something was expected; I had no idea what. Smiling like an idiot, I simply nodded and sat there. More silence. Finally, Ruth retrieved an ancient, leather-bound book, beautifully handwritten. She held this open before the group, and everyone began singing. The sound was incomparable! Fluid tones in a language I had never heard before that morning: deep, popping sounds intermingled with wide vowels and clicks.

Seemingly satisfied with my obvious pleasure, after several more songs, Ruth led us back outside and the daily tasks resumed. This time I was allowed to sit with them, continuing to silently nod and smile in what I hoped were appropriate places. Most of the earlier tension seemed to have dissolved into the sand.

The morning had seemed interminable, but the afternoon slid past too quickly. Waving my arms around like a floundering swimmer, I attempted to ask permission to return the next day, hoping my gestures and English phrases communicated the question. Nodding their scarf-clad heads, the group seemed to like the idea. Perhaps I had become a harmless novelty. When the truck reappeared, the group saw me off with friendly gestures.

In the evening, as we assembled for coffee, our Gobabeb hosts seemed eager to hear the details of my adventure. My confusion about the young mother insisting on introducing me to everyone elicited laughter.

"A missionary, of course!" they chuckled. "Any white person who's entered their village before has been trying to save their souls. They were waiting for a sermon."

Click. A reasonable picture replaced my interpretation of the day's seemingly odd behaviors. The names that "Ruth" had used to introduce the group were never spoken as forms of address. They had been used for my benefit—bestowed upon them in some previous flood of Biblical fervor—but they were not the names they used for each other. With no clue what to do with my unexpected behavior, they had simply shrugged their mental shoulders and allowed me to hang out with them.

During the following weeks, for the five or so hours I spent in the village each day, the five women did little work. At dawn, their dogs herded goats from the woven-stick kraals down into the riverbed to feed on pods of acacia trees and other vegetation. Sometimes, they drew water from wells dug into the riverbed. Goat hides were stretched and tanned. Small vegetable gardens were occasionally weeded. One day, two women pounded dried wild figs into a powder to be stored for later use. They never invited me to share in performing the few daily tasks I observed.

I didn't bring my camera or recording devices into the village, not wanting to disturb things any more than my foreign presence did. However, one of the greatest bonding incidents occurred during the final week when I decided to break my own rule and bring a small, reel-to-reel tape recorder into the village. The group of women gathered around, interested to see what the mysterious object did. When I spoke into it, rewound, and replayed my voice, screams of laughter followed. Everyone wanted to hear their voices repeated by this small machine. Finally, Ruth grabbed my hand, more animated than I'd ever seen her. Pulling me along, she started up the riverbed at a half-jog. Excited chatter surrounded me in a language I still couldn't understand.

Playing back the tape recordings.

A mile or two up the river we entered another village. At last, my question concerning the absence of males was answered, at least somewhat. Here were huts used by six or seven men of various ages. Ruth sat me down and indicated I was to record her as she started speaking. After a short but obviously eloquent narration, she gestured for me to play it back. Total awe on the faces of the men met equal glee from the women. Apparently, the battle between sexes was not merely a Western phenomenon. Ha! Had they ever showed these men something!

I was pleased to have supplied that small pleasure to women who had given me a month's hospitality. I never found out why the men and women lived separately. Was it only during the day? Was it temporary or a permanent pattern? Our expedition group left too soon to answer that question and many others. I discovered little about marriage patterns, political structure, or any other anthropological concept. Are they matrilineal? Do they practice "exogamy" (marrying outside the community)? My tabbed notebooks remained relatively empty. I couldn't answer those questions, but I answered a far more important, personal question: a human Tapestry does, indeed, encompass us all.

Perhaps being unable to communicate verbally helped us see past our differences; we could never discuss topics of potential dissension. I tried my best to be inoffensive, respecting all the cultural customs I could perceive. I suppose I was young enough to appear harmless, and my errors, such as not covering my hair (only later in the trip did I realize this was customary for adult women), were seemingly forgiven. So, we laughed and hung around together. It felt good. We "connected."

Because of a month spent with a small group of people in a sandy riverbed, my worldview continued to weave itself into a sense of Oneness. The Tapestry connecting us all clearly included both Namib desert hut-dwellers and suburban California white girls. I became friends with women who did not share a single common word with me. Humans may have vast cultural differences, but laughing and working with this group of women gave me empirical proof of the "interconnecting Tapestry." The goat-herding women's kindness and acceptance cemented my conversion from nationalistic patriot to global inhabitant: far more valuable than any data I might have collected on matrilocality.

TEN

Our weeks in Namibia included many side trips and forays into unanticipated jewels of experience. On a supply run to the tiny port town of Swakopmund, Ross decided to explore the coast north of town. Camped in low, windy dunes, I noticed that the leeward side of each crest was outlined in a reddish wave. Lying on my stomach to peer at the sand, I saw that the grains were miniature garnets. I skimmed them into a collecting tube, gathering a treasure to take home.

Ross wanted to show us Welwitschia, a plant endemic to the Namib desert, so we took another side trip to visit a rocky gorge at the edge of the salmon-colored dunes. He had told us Welwitschia were "trees." When we rattled down through a dry wash, I scanned for something tall, maybe similar to a saguaro in our southwest deserts. Instead, Ross stopped the truck amid three-foot-high clumps of tangled green fronds. The long, leathery "leaves" grew from the edge of a circle on the top of round stumps. Ross showed us small black-and-yellow bugs living in the bark-covered shallow bowl forming the top of the "trunk." They looked like what we called "stink bugs" at home. Ross called them Welwitschia bugs. They evolved along with those trees, living nowhere else. He pointed to one of the nearby plants whose tangled fronds covered an area about six- or seven-feet square, saying it was probably thousands of years old.

We might as well have been on Mars. The antiquity of this desert had allowed it to evolve an entire ecosystem like no other on Earth. I could come up with no explanation of the warm sense of belonging and of "home" I felt here in what should have seemed a hostile environment. I loved the Namib. Welwitschia, however, just felt weird and foreign. I couldn't conjure up much oneness with Welwitschia. I'd work on it.

After returning to the Kuiseb, late one afternoon we headed out to Windhoek for supplies. Ross drove the truck to an outcropping of house-sized red rocks, made even rosier by the setting sun. He told us this was "the Marshall's desert ranch," where we would camp for the night. I didn't know how Ross had communicated with Mr. Marshall, but soon a jeep bounced into camp, throwing up pink, evening dust. A stocky, white-haired man climbed out, brushing fine sand off the shoulders of his khaki safari jacket.

In Camp with Alan, Carol, Marty, and Laurence Marshall

Laurence Marshall had postponed a trip to Cambridge in order to see Ross. He told us he was delighted to have company in "the middle of nowhere." After a relaxed conversation, Laurence left us to set up our camp, promising to return later. I made mutton curry for dinner, accompanied by Major Grey's Chutney, available even in the tiniest groceries across southern Africa. In the last of the desert light, we ate silently, enjoying the chorus of small inhabitants that ventured out after a searing sun set for the night. Ross said these insect voices signaled the desire for some hanky-panky with like-minded individuals of the opposite sex. I glanced over, but he was looking into the campfire and seemed not to have been suggesting anything untoward.

As I was finishing the dinner dishes, Mr. Marshall and an assistant returned to our camp in a van fitted with a fully stocked bar. After adding two chairs, they joined us around our campfire. Cocktails and quiet conversation filled the night. Watching Ross consume quantities of Laurence Marshall's fine liquor, I began to feel uneasy, but Mr. Marshall and I started chatting, and I abandoned Ross to his own concerns.

Laurence laughingly told me that he was a multimillionaire who started a flashlight manufacturing company. At first, he made "light" of his success, but suddenly he leaned forward in his camp chair, furrowing his brow with sincerity.

"The success of Raytheon wasn't due simply to the quality of our product." He sat up straighter. "Mind you, we made fine flashlights. But what was most important was how I structured the company."

I wondered aloud how the structure of a company could make its product successful.

"Trust. It's all about respect and trust." He leaned toward me again, passionate about this concept he wanted me to understand. "I don't know a lot about light bulbs. I'm no expert in marketing. But I hired people in each area who were specialists and then I trusted them."

"So you were more like a facilitator than a director?"

"Yes, exactly." Laurence got up to refresh our drinks as he continued. "We made decisions as a group. By respecting the knowledge of each individual, we got buy-in. Everyone knew they were an important unit in the company and had pride in what they did."

"So they worked harder?"

"They did. We functioned as a group. Now Raytheon makes rocket ships instead of flashlights; we've come a long way."

Laurence sat back in his aluminum camp chair. His satisfied smile radiated the belief that I understood. Perhaps, I did. Laurence Marshall had built a company based on the interconnection of the people working there.

I smiled back. "It's funny, but that sounds like something I've been thinking about a lot. Coming to Africa made me see things in a different way. I think the most important thing is that we really are all interconnected." I paused to sip my drink. "Operating your business from that place of connection had to have just felt right for everybody."

"Exactly."

Laurence was talking about something more than just being kind to your employees. I wondered about the concepts we seemed to be sharing. Could I have had a similar conversation with other men of my father's generation? As dear to me as my dad and his friends were, I couldn't imagine that they would run things the same way. Laurence and I sat in silence. I watched Ross wobble a bit as he added a broken branch to the fire.

After a few moments, Laurence guided the conversation in a new direction. "You're an anthropologist?" I nodded and he continued. "My wife, Lorna, studied anthropology. For the first half of our marriage, I got to do what I wanted, so for the second half of our marriage it seemed only fair that we would do what she wanted. We spread a map on the living room floor, and the family looked for the largest stretch of uninhabited land we could find. Uninhabited by whites, that is. We wanted to find someplace where she could do anthropological research. Our son, John, pointed to Namibia, so here we are!"

By now the others were also listening to his story. I was surprised and excited that his wife was an anthropologist, but disappointed that she hadn't come here with him. Lorna and son John, Laurence said, spent great amounts of time with the !*Kung* bushmen in the nearby Kalahari Desert.

"So you've gotten to know the !*Kung*?" I asked, pleased with the fact that I could make the popping sound preceding the rest of the word "kung." Ever since Anthro 101, I'd heard about the egalitarian example of the !*Kung* society. "Oh my gosh, they must be fascinating!"

Laurence laughed and said he didn't really know the !*Kung* himself. When they were in the Kalahari, he had acted only as a supply train for his wife and son. "John made a film about a giraffe hunt. I think it was quite well-received."

"Not *The Hunters*?" I exclaimed.

"Yes, that's its title. Have you seen it?"

"Of course! Anyone studying anthropology has seen it. It's wonderful. You must be so proud." My mouth was hanging open in astonishment. The movie followed a group of *!Kung* men on a giraffe hunt lasting several days. It was a staple of introductory anthropology classes. I couldn't believe I was sitting with the man whose son had made the film.

"Well, yes, I rather am. And of my wife too. Lorna has published several articles on the bushmen's concept of "*!nau.*"

"*!nau*?" I'd never heard the word.

Laurence paused, recognizing that he had everyone's attention, even if Ross's eyes looked a bit bleary in the firelight. Nodding acknowledgement to his audience, Laurence launched into a personal anecdote. "Maybe this can explain it. One afternoon I was walking down a packed earth street in a nearby town. Just ahead of me, three barefoot *!Kung* girls were strolling in the same direction. The girls' arms were linked and they were chatting and laughing like girls do." He gave a little nod toward me. "Suddenly the middle one jumped her feet apart, then went right on walking without even looking down. I was enjoying watching how their hips swayed as they walked." Laurence paused with a slightly guilty smile before continuing. "I clearly saw the spot where the girl had jumped and I went over to see what was there. The road was packed, really hard and dry, and I had to bend way over to see it. Imagine how surprised I was when I saw the tip of a scorpion's tail barely sticking up above the dirt! I couldn't think how she knew it was there, so I hurried to catch up and ask her." Laurence was a good storyteller. "They giggled," he said, giving a small laugh himself. "They exchanged embarrassed glances and just giggled. Finally, one of them said that it was not possible to explain this to a white person. But I pressed her further. '*!Nau*' she'd explained. 'It's *!nau.*' I was still puzzled, so I asked her to try to tell me what that is. 'Just knowing,' she replied. 'We just know. White people don't.'" Laurence said that his wife, Lorna, had interviewed many people, trying to comprehend their concept of *!nau*. "I guess I can't really explain it, but maybe you could read her articles."

The evening was just too perfect. The broadened sense of reality—and of connection—I'd gained on the airplane made me wonder what other phenomena I might experience if I remained open. Laurence Marshall was telling me that others were documenting the alternative realities in which Africa seemed to exist so easily. This conversation with the first multimillionaire I had ever known, in the middle of nowhere in Africa, was affirming my new way of understanding reality. Incredible.

Our glasses were empty and no one was seeking a refill. Laurence closed up his mobile bar and headed off amid our expressions of gratitude.

I stayed up late that night trying to document our conversation in my journal. As moths swarmed around my small light, I swore to my diary that I would seek out Lorna Marshall's works and learn all I could about *!nau*. Maybe I could return here and learn from her. This was a promising new direction for my anthropological career.

As we broke camp the next morning, we were all nursing hangovers. We continued on to Windhoek to spend a few days resupplying our expedition. This sweet, small city in the midst of deserts offered sumptuous amenities. Jacaranda trees rained lavender blossoms into residential yards, a respite for our sun-seared eyes. We camped in a private game park beside a small lake just outside town. With showers for genuine bathing, toilets to replace holes dug in the sand, and small, round, thatched-roofed rondovals to sleep in, we were in the lap of luxury.

Dawn seeped through the thatching of the rondoval Marty and I shared. I heard the soft, clicking sounds of a camera being loaded just outside my open window. Peering out, I saw Ross focused on a dry, grassy hill, the long lens of his camera now at the ready. My thin bedsheet barely swished as I slipped out and grabbed my own camera from the hut's one table. Creeping quietly, lest I scare what he was stalking, I caught Ross's eye. He pointed up the hill. Silhouetted against a carrot-hued morning sky stood the Clydesdales of the antelope world.

"Elands," Ross whispered. "They're the largest antelopes. F-5.6 at 125th, then bracket it on both sides."

I already knew that *National Geographic* partially funded Ross's expeditions, but I had increasingly come to appreciate what an excellent photographer he was. Despite his difficult side, I was grateful for his tutelage in all things relating to photography. With both of us shooting ASA 25 Kodachrome film, I trusted his judgement. I turned the lens aperture and shutter speed to the settings he advised. With their bodies contrasted against the rising sun, the elands would be silhouettes. Dramatic ones. Raising their thick necks, the herd wandered over the ridge and out of sight. My body tingled with the excitement of knowing I'd gotten a few "nuggets." Turning back toward the hut, I watched the waters of the lake slowly quench the orange flames of the sun's reflection. Africa offered itself always as a visual orgy; what other scenes were out there this morning? I stalked along the lake shore and did some more shutter-clicking before I returned the Pentax to its dust-proof case and started breakfast.

I lit briquettes (a luxury) in the camp's built-in grill (another luxury), and began stirring fresh eggs into flour and milk for the pancakes we'd have with our bacon (unheard-of luxuries, every one!). By the time coffee began to percolate in an aluminum pot, the smells of breakfast was wafting into the noses of those still sleeping. I spread our red-checked oilskin tablecloth across the cool, concrete picnic table, wishing I had a small bouquet for makeshift elegance.

Alan and Marty emerged and stumbled to the table. Marty poured coffee into the plastic mugs: green, red, blue, and yellow, each of us possessive of our own by now. Soon, all that remained of the stack of pancakes, platter of eggs, and pile of bacon strips was a dribble of egg yolk on Alan's chin.

As I gathered up the dishes, I slid them into soapy water warming on the dying coals. Carrying another dishpan to the faucet, I watched water flow freely, my fingers playing in the stream. Setting both tubs on the table, I laid a clean towel beside them. It was a joy to swish dishes in so much bubbly water. For the past month, each day I'd washed dishes, then myself, and then my underwear, all in the same half-gallon of water.

As I swiped my dishrag across the last of the plates, a long, very thin shadow fell across the table. Turning, I found myself nose-to-beak with an ostrich. Cocking its head, it kept one eye on me, then snatched at my dishcloth with its overgrown duck's beak. It missed its mark as I whipped it away. A woman's voice sounded from the neighboring camp. "You want to watch out for that fellow; he hassles all the campers. You don't want to make him too angry. He'll come after you. They stick out those chests and knock you down with that big breastbone. Then, they can tear you up right well with those big claws."

I stood looking down at the big claws she was warning me about, wondering what "watching out" for him might entail. I contemplated whether my new sense of being connected to all beings would keep me in the good graces of an ostrich. I tried radiating love.

The woman walked over to our camp, flapping her skirt at him and making shooing noises. He pulled his head back, puffed his wings, then strode off. It seemed like a risky maneuver on her part, given the advice she'd just finished doling out. Thanking my rescuer, I left the dishes to dry in the sun.

We were to have three days in camp to rest and clean up before heading back into the desert. Ross and Alan left right after breakfast to collect insects in the hills. Marty and I grabbed our swimsuits and went for an early morning swim in the lake. We had the water all to ourselves. Apparently, there wasn't much reason for locals to learn to swim in a desert.

The day felt lazy and relaxed. Lying side-by-side on towels, I felt a sense of camaraderie with Marty that surprised and pleased me. I rolled onto my stomach, propping myself up with my elbows. "I admit that it feels good not having the guys around."

"Uh-huh, my dad can be a real jerk." We made eye contact and both rolled our eyes. "I don't know why I came along on this trip." Marty turned onto her back and watched as a group of white-bellied, African crows flew over.

"Why did you? I know your dad is hopeful you'll learn to love Africa and science and bugs and all, but it really doesn't seem like it's your thing."

"You want to know the truth?"

"Sure."

"You know about Super Spade, don't you?"

"Yeah, I kinda heard about him."

"Well, you know that Super Spade was the main Marin County hippie drug dealer, right?"

"I'm pretty sure I smoked hash at his party once."

Marty turned toward me, seemingly more trusting, now that she knew I had a working knowledge of the San Francisco Bay area drug scene. "He was murdered just before we left for Africa."

My mouth dropped open. Everyone had said he was a good guy.

Marty went on. "He and two other Marin County dealers were murdered on the same night. His body was stuffed into a sleeping bag and dumped over a cliff near the Golden Gate." Marty paused, thoughtful. "He was a good friend." Another pause. Her face showed genuine sadness. "I worked for him. Distributed around south Marin. The Mafia came in. They're the ones who did the murders."

I rolled to my side to look at her directly. "Wow! How do you know?"

"Because they came to me and all the others and said we had to work for them now. Super Spade only dealt in psychedelics. You know, grass, hash, acid, mescaline. No hard drugs. It was pure. You knew what you were getting. The Mafia stuff is laced with all kinds of shit. They're dealing in hard stuff too. Heroin. All that. I wasn't going to work for them."

"And here you are." My voice was quiet, but my eyes were big.

"Yes, here I am." Her voice was quiet too.

A thousand questions bubbled in my head. I wanted more details. I wanted to know if she and Super Spade had been lovers. I wanted to know how many others were aware of what had gone down. I stayed silent, however, afraid that if I began interrogating her, she'd clam back up. This shit was serious!

Eventually she continued, "But I can't really deal with my dad. That was just crap what he did to you. And he's just so insecure. He always has to prove he's important. I don't think I can keep doing this." Marty closed her eyes. "I want to scream at him. You have no idea."

"What will you do?"

"Go home. I think I'm going to fly out before we leave Namibia."

I didn't know how to respond. Marty had seen things I'd scarcely even imagined. She must be afraid. How afraid? Afraid for her life? How dangerous were these people we generically referred to as "the Mafia?" She came to Africa to avoid them. Her dad would totally freak out if he knew.

And she was thinking of flying home. She'd be leaving me as the lone woman with her rather lecherous father and his sycophantic sidekick. Marty hadn't been much help to us around camp, but she definitely functioned as a buffer between me and testosterone. It'd be a different trip if she left.

"I hope you stay."

Marty gave a noncommittal grunt and rolled onto her side. Her freckled back clearly said our conversation had come to an end.

I gathered my towel and headed back to shower and dress, tucking all that Marty had shared with me into my brain somewhere it could be retrieved and reviewed later. At present, I had something new and rather exciting to think about.

An anthropology graduate student from the University of California at Berkeley had heard about our group, and Ross had given him directions to our camp. Anticipating the prospect of an intellectual discussion concerning people rather than insects, I cleaned myself up at our unaccustomed facilities, and was presentable when the student arrived that afternoon.

As he climbed out of his desert-dusty Jeep, Wade Pendleton's brown hair fell in a mop across his forehead. I immediately assessed him as good-looking in a preppy kind of way, but he lost points by wearing black socks with shorts and sandals, an especially bad fashion statement in a desert.

After some chit-chat and a beer or two with the group, Wade suggested he and I might take a walk around the lake.

He told me he was studying the perceived hierarchies among various cultural groups in Namibia. Terribly excited to encounter another anthropologist, I was interested to hear his findings. According to Wade, the three white groups—the English, German, and Afrikaners—attended different schools and spoke different languages. They remained nearly as distinct from each other as they did from the four Native African tribes. Not surprisingly, each of the seven groups perceived different hierarchies between the groups. Interesting.

By the end of our walk, Wade had invited me to dinner and more conversation at his apartment in town. I accepted without bothering to disguise my enthusiasm. Wade's invitation offered me a short escape from the forced intimacy of camp life.

We drove out to the "Tin City," a relocation area for tribal peoples. In the new rules of apartheid, native Africans were being forcibly moved from their own lands to live in "Townships" (huge, fenced compounds). Having established himself as a white person not aligned with the government, Wade had formed friendships within the town. He took me to a school where the children sang for us in their languages using beautiful harmonies. I marveled at the peoples' ability to find joy in the midst of such injustice. Wade also took me by a prison that still administered lashings as punishment. In order to satisfy legal requirements, each lash had to draw blood.

Shaken by what I'd been shown, I appreciated Wade's compassionate insights about the issue, while wondering at his ability to live and work around this system. Wade treated me to dinner and excellent conversation at a German restaurant before we drove to his apartment.

He lived on the second floor of a building that would easily fit into any mid-rent apartment complex in the San Francisco Bay area. We climbed the stairs, and after opening his off-white, metal door, Wade disappeared into his kitchen, and I settled onto a comfortable leather couch. Wade put two cups of coffee down on the glass-topped coffee table before joining me on the couch.

We chatted about several things before I told him about my airplane experience and my idea of a Tapestry that weaves together everything we know. To my surprise, he seemed to understand. Wade said that when we love another person, there's a dissolution of aloneness and we tap into that unity. I felt impressed and more than a little turned on. Wade then told me about his girlfriend back in Berkeley. Grateful for his honesty, I let the fact of his relationship back home keep the evening from evolving into something more than a satisfying friendship.

After a shared joint and homemade strawberry shortcake topped with a pile of whipped cream, Wade pulled out a record album. The Beatles stared out from the cover, decked out as an old-fashioned marching band. Having had no idea there was a new album out, I felt a pang of isolation from all the life I had known. Wade rolled another joint as *Sergeant Pepper's Lonely Hearts' Club Band* hoped that we'd enjoy their show. By the time we met Lucy in the Sky, her diamonds dazzled us both as we found ourselves somehow sitting beneath his coffee table. Wade told me that their song, "I Get by with a Little Help from My Friends," had to have been written just for him. A bolt of nostalgia stabbed through my enjoyment of the music: I was missing concerts at the Avalon Ballroom, in Golden Gate Park, and at the Fillmore West. I'd danced to Cream, the Chambers Brothers, and Janis. I'd heard Jimi Hendrix, BB King, and the Stones in the Oakland Coliseum; what was I now missing being so far away? The music revolution of the Monterey Pops Festival still had to be raging through California without me. I was missing out.

Stoned as I was, I started thinking about the lyrics of the songs. Janis didn't really want a Mercedes Benz; she was mocking the materialistic culture we'd grown up in. John and Paul admitted things were getting better, so much better, and all the time. I already knew Country Joe and the Fish strongly disagreed with the Vietnam war. Were others thinking about genuine love and a sense of unity too? When "Within You and Without You" came flooding into Wade's living room through his stereo's speakers, I bumped my head on the underside of his table. The words to the final verse nearly startled me into sobriety. It said that, when you look beyond your "self" you will find peace and see we're all one.

How did the Beatles know that? Had they been on the same plane to Africa? How had Wade Pendleton come to know that? Curiouser and Curiouser! I had lots to ponder. When Wade returned me to our camp, I crept into the thatched roof rondoval, managing not to wake Marty. Despite the late hour, I stared at the straw ceiling, contemplating the many-colored thoughts swirling behind my eyes.

During our final resupply visit to Windhoek before heading into Botswana, we took one last journey northward to visit Etosha Pan, a huge, usually dry, lakebed with water holes along its borders. We were told that all types of animals would gather there, one of the few places in Namibia that could support large mammals. All of us wanted to see more African animals.

We scarcely encountered another vehicle along the two-hundred-and-fifty miles of dirt "highway" leading to the game park. Ross flew along the rutted dirt road at his usual, breakneck, thirty-five miles-per-hour. Survival inside the truck required developing what I called the "Africa reflex." The instant the wheels bounced into a large hole and my body flew upward, my hands would shoot over my head to brace myself against the roof of the truck. It was a large truck with a tall cab, but if we didn't protect ourselves, we would commonly bang our heads.

I was singing to myself and watching the terrain change from grassy sand into greener scrubland when my body flew up simultaneously with the sound of an explosion. Ross wobbled the truck to a stop. Another tire blowout. Ross and Alan changed it to the spare, and once again, we limped along until we reached a tiny hamlet with a garage that would patch the tire or sell us a new one. We were grateful that Africa had as many garages as it did small stores. We left the truck and wandered around, bought a few supplies, then returned to the repair shop. As we pulled out of town with our newest tire in place, I looked beneath the front seat where I'd left

Du Toit in his little wooden cage. The cage was there, but our chameleon was not. I gave a cry of concern, but it was not something Ross deemed worthy of retracing our steps for. Besides, I wondered if having our "pet" in captivity might have been offensive and unacceptable to the man who changed our tire. Perhaps he had liberated the chameleon. I hoped that had been the case, and that Du Toit might find a comfortable new bush to live on.

Despite the series of tires we had left in our wake across Namibia, Ross accelerated down the dirt road, never slowing to accommodate rocks or potholes. Although I'd learned to brace myself against road hazards, I'd never succeeded in accustoming myself to the rifle shot of an exploding tire. Nor did I appreciate the fact that, once it was changed, we faced the unnerving experience of traveling through true wilderness without a spare. Annoyed at Ross' chosen speed, I knew we'd soon have another flat. Since the men changed the tires, it seemed wisest not to point out the obvious. Teeth clenched, I decided to forego the next battle.

In the late afternoon, Ross pulled the truck off the road. We drove a way through scattered thorn trees, choosing a good site for camp. As the men set up, I gathered sticks for a fire, built a circle of stones, and set the grill over flames I had coaxed to rise from one match and one bit of wadded paper. Fire-building had become a source of pride. We had few resources. Every bit of paper or match saved meant more for the future. We had just resupplied in Windhoek, so tonight's dinner would be special: cabbage salad, potatoes baked in the coals, and grilled steaks. Beef in Africa had a deep, bluish color, unlike meat we got at home. I had no idea what caused the difference, but the flavor was delicious. I even made us fudge for dessert. Ross mixed us some vodka cocktails, and we sat in our camp chairs, feasting in the lap of rural luxury.

Shadows lengthened across the sand as we lingered over our meal. I found myself cleaning up after the forest had grown dark. I turned on the light over the table, drawing in many uninvited insects. As I picked up a towel to begin drying the tin dishes I'd just washed, we saw a light bumping along the road. The vehicle drew even with us, then its headlights turned and it started moving directly toward us through the trees. Some yards off, the engine noises stopped and the lights went out. Minutes passed and no one approached us. With our truck lights blazing through the darkness, I suddenly felt like a sitting duck. We all waited silently, hearing only night sounds. We knew that north of the Etosha Pan, the park where we were heading, was an area of Namibia called Ovamboland, a section of the country that the white government mostly left under the control of the Ovambos, a strong tribe determined to keep its independence. Whites were not welcome, and few traveled there.

Our tension grew. I put away the last of the dinner dishes while we doused the lights and the fire and in hushed tones, discussed what might be going on. Finally, I stated firmly that I thought we should move camp. The males brushed off my comment with machismo, but they were clearly nervous as well. Choosing safety over toughness, I repeated my statement, willing to come off as the wimp of the group. Breaking camp and setting up again would involve effort on all our parts, but this situation felt too creepy for us to stay. "We're near Ovamboland. There's no one else around except this guy, and he's not showing himself. I really think we should leave."

The men grumbled about having to appease a nervous woman, but finally agreed. I collapsed the chairs and folded the table's legs, lifting it back onto the side of the truck by the storage cabinet door. The men untied and lowered the tent, then reformed the roof by sliding the aluminum side canopy up over top. Foregoing headlights, Ross crept out onto the road following only moonlight. We never saw the other vehicle, but continued north to the park entrance where we set up a hurried camp just outside the gate.

A ranger woke us in the morning and we recounted our story. I filled in dramatic details, expecting to gain kudos for being sensible and demanding we move camp. I wanted to have some back-up, some "I-told-you-so" retaliation. Much to my disappointment, the ranger smiled and shrugged his shoulders. "Undoubtedly some guy who was drunk and decided to choose a safe place to sleep it off before going home. He probably thought your lights were a farmhouse."

Ross and Alan refrained from chiding me about the incident making me think they had been just as nervous. Despite the ranger's words, I was still happy I'd made us move. I doubt any of us would have slept much that night.

We headed on into the park. Whirlwinds swirled like dervishes across the vast, dry lakebed. Water glistened from a pool surrounded by grass and a few trees. Ross parked the truck and set up his movie camera. The rest of us pulled out our longest lenses and extra film canisters. The hours we waited there rewarded us with visits by most of the animals residing in my mental picture of Africa: zebra, beautiful gemsbok, and many small antelope, which slowly found their way to the wide pool of water, a vital resource in this desert environment. A pride of lions ambled over to rest in the shade of some bushes, while their usual prey kept on drinking and mostly ignored them. Ross pointed out that research has shown local animals know when a pride of lions has recently fed and is thus less likely to attack.

A herd of elephants arrived, plodding their way into the pool. Even from across the water, their size astounded me. Maybe animals in zoos didn't grow as large as they did in the wild, or maybe having the magnificence of Africa as their natural backdrop made them more impressive, but those elephants were huge. Splashing and shooting fire hoses of water from their trunks, their antics turned the clear water muddy before they climbed onto the shore nearest us. A large bull faced our vehicle, flapping its magnificent ears in what we knew to be a threat, warning us to keep our distance. We remembered a man on crutches we had met in Cape Town who had been permanently crippled when an elephant stomped his Land Rover to pieces with him inside it. We weren't about to antagonize this not-so-gentle-looking giant. The elephant group stomped around on the dry earth, breaking it into a red powder. Sucking the dust up with their trunks, they reached back over their own heads to spray it in ribbons across their backs. Ross suggested that the dried mud crust probably helped deter insects, but I marveled at any diminutive life form that might sport mouth-parts capable of piercing an elephant's already-formidable leather skin.

As the elephants wandered off, three giraffes arrived, looking considerably warier than the other animals. I gaped at their heights. Their heads rose several feet higher than the backs of the elephants. They gave us a long look, but scarcely glanced at the apparently well-fed lions lying nearby under bushes. The giraffes turned and moved toward the water's edge. When they arrived, they slowly spread their front legs, carefully lifting and setting down one, and then the other. The awkward movement was repeated with all four legs until their heads could touch the water. Craning their long necks between sprawled legs, the oversized ungulates sucked up a drink. Their vulnerable positions looked like evolutionary design flaws.

The day proved to be a photographer's heaven. As the sun began its flame-colored descent behind scattered trees, we reluctantly packed up to leave. With our camera bellies full of visual diamonds, we headed back toward Windhoek.

That final trip to the city left our expedition greatly changed. Marty and I had spoken little since our revealing conversation. I feared she felt exposed and was avoiding me. She and Ross had several intense, low-voiced discussions. I had no idea what was said or even the topics they discussed.

The morning after we reestablished camp at our favorite little park outside Windhoek, I was cleaning the breakfast dishes when Marty dragged her suitcase out of our rondoval. Eyes fixed on the ground, she didn't meet my inquisitive gaze.

"She's going home." Ross spoke for her as Marty remained silent. "You two can stay here while I take her to the airport."

Marty turned and got into the truck.

"You aren't going to stay?" I called after her.

There was no response. Marty had been an enigma during the entire journey, but letting her leave silently, without even a goodbye, seemed crazy. I walked to her window. Peering inside, I saw tears rolling down her cheeks. She didn't look up. Seeing her crying, I stepped back. As Ross started the engine and steered the truck out through the park's entrance, I painfully realized that there were stories in life I had to leave to those living them. I might never know Marty's next chapters, and there was nothing I could do about that. Her life was not my business to judge or even understand. I couldn't help feeling I had failed to help her, whatever she had or had not asked for. Knowing her sulking presence would no longer be a damper on the trip did little to soften my sadness or sense of loss.

Now, after two months camping across sub-Saharan Africa, only three of us remained on the expedition. Marty flying home left the rest of us to reconfigure our roles. Since Marty had contributed little, things would mostly remain the same. Ross and Alan would continue capturing and euthanizing six-legged African wildlife for future study, while I would cook. I would also be navigating the path of a lone female traveling with two men. Ross was often annoying, but there had been no repeat of the fireside fiasco, so I didn't feel unsafe. And Alan was decidedly harmless.

Several days later—resupplied and rested—we set out to cross Botswana and the Kalahari Desert. After the Namib, with its huge, salmon-colored dunes, the thorn-tree-covered Kalahari scarcely seemed like a real desert. This land was home to the *!Kung* Bushmen I had just learned so much about. In anthropology classes, I had learned that they might be the oldest surviving culture on Earth. Since they were semi-nomadic, the chances of us encountering a group would be slim. But I had hopes.

One afternoon, as the truck bumped along through rocky scrubland, a family of four short, barefoot people walked onto the track. The man was clad only in a loincloth. He carried a bow slung over his shoulder, a quiver of arrows, and various gourds. His wife toted a lumpy, animal-hide bag. Their baby rode in a cloth tied around her back. A young boy walked between them, his short hair curled in tight black rings against his head. Stopping the truck, we all jumped out in great excitement. The group turned and walked toward us with open curiosity. Ross explained that we were a *National Geographic* expedition. Dumbfounded, I wondered how in the world Ross expected them to have any idea what that meant. The man answered in a beautiful Khoisan "click" language. Ross continued speaking, oblivious to what the man was saying. Our new acquaintance switched to another language, made clear by the lack of now-familiar clicks. When he got no response from us with this language, he seemed to try another one. Ross, meanwhile, continued trying to explain what *National Geographic* was. He opened a door in the back of the truck and pulled out the organization's flag. Seriously? The man looked at it with interest but no comprehension, at which point he switched languages one more time, trying out what I recognized as the Dutch-derived Afrikaans, the language of South African apartheid. Still, getting nothing more from us than Ross's flag-waving, the family nodded, turned, and disappeared back into the bush.

Three separate responses jostled my brain for priority, leaving me rooted to the sandy track. First, I had just seen genuine, living Bushmen, the people of anthropological legends! I'd read books on these folks, famous for the egalitarian nature of their culture. These were the people who had the concept of *!nau* that Laurence Marshall tried to explain to us. I felt incredibly lucky—excitement vibrated my whole being—but my second response was a flood of humility. The *!Kung* had tried four separate languages in order to communicate with us. Among the three of us, we had fluency in only one. Humbling, and more than a little bit embarrassing.

Lastly, and more personally, I couldn't believe what Ross had done. This man knew himself as a silver-haired entomologist, photographer, and writer for *National Geographic*. Did he fear that he had no self beyond those identities? I felt genuine pity for the insecurity that must underlie Ross's need to establish himself in exchange for accolades. He didn't seem able to meet the Bushmen as one person talking with other people. I thought about my experience of peeling away all my identities on the airplane, realizing what a gift it was to find that none of those "selves" were actually me. Ross seemed to lack that knowledge of himself, unfazed by our humbling encounter with the *!Kung*.

Resuming our journey, Ross chatted with excitement about the Kalahari. To him, being in a new ecology meant new insect populations to investigate and collect. Other than the Bushmen, I didn't see much to interest me in the Kalahari, but I did notice an abundance of scorpions. When I mentioned this to Alan one afternoon, we decided to do an unofficial survey. Our conclusion, after turning over many dozens of rocks: one in three rocks in Botswana hides a scorpion. I marveled that, in addition to being barefoot, the *!Kung* slept on open ground. The ubiquity of scorpions offered more evidence that *!nau* must be real. The Bushmen must have had some mysterious way of detecting and evading scorpions—unknown, or at least, undeveloped in our culture. Who would trust their "instincts" to keep their bare feet safe from the sting of a desert scorpion? In my culture, we wore sturdy boots.

As we continued on our one-lane sandy "road" across Botswana, I complained to my diary about the monotony of the land. Hour after hour, rocky plains with scrubby thorn trees filled my window's view. Scorpions, snakes, and beetles abounded, but we saw few large animals. I felt a bit bored, but I'm not an entomologist.

As we neared Maun, the town where we'd resupply, a wild-haired gnome appeared on the horizon.

"Baobab!" yelled Ross, awakening from his comatose drive through miles of sand.

"Huh?" Alan sounded befuddled, arousing from his own stupor.

The Little Prince! It's a baobab tree! My memory filled in the image from a famous children's book. The "Little Prince" had come from a very small planet. He'd taken great care of this planet, preventing any bad seeds from growing and making sure the planet was never overrun by baobab trees. I hadn't known they were real trees. Fifteen or twenty people could link hands and probably not reach all the way around this tree's leathery gray trunk. High up, its canopy of wild, jagged branches looked like they'd been poked inside an electrical outlet.

"Yikes! That thing is huge!" Alan's voice registered astonishment. I remembered that in the book, three baobab trees could have covered the Little Prince's entire planet. Now I believed it. One never forgets one's first baobab tree.

Huts appeared below the tree, and our trail turned into a proper road—not merely a game trail but one regularly used by cars. For the past few days, we had seen no other vehicles. The termite mounds we passed nearly equaled the unimaginable size of the baobab tree. Rising from the sand like monstrous, dripcastles, many of the mounds stood taller than our truck. With all of us gawking, Ross missed a rock and we crashed over it, the truck's engine quitting. Ross ground the starter a few times, but his efforts proved futile. He and Alan climbed out. The truck's hood squealed open on dusty, metal hinges. We'd recently passed a native village, so no one panicked. There were humans around and we could get help if we needed it.

Carol photographing insects.

I wandered away from the road and left the men to the mechanical tasks. Venturing into scrubby bushland, I heard and then saw a small grayish bird. It flew up to me, chattering like crazy, then landed on a branch directly in front of my nose. I grinned and chatted back. Seemingly pleased to have gotten my attention, the small bird flitted into the bushes, then returned, as if wanting me to follow. Obliging, I walked after it. The little guy repeated this performance several times. Amazed, I continued to follow. We proceeded with this bird-human communication until I began to worry about getting lost.

Oh my God, I thought, my sense of oneness had given me the ability to talk with birds! Ecstatic and anxious to share my wonder, I successfully retraced my steps, returning to the truck. Happily, the guys had managed to solve our vehicle problem. Ignoring the slightly impatient expressions on their faces, I babbled as loudly as the bird. "It led me! We were communicating!"

"A honeyguide." Ross loved a chance to educate, especially if it disabused me of some revelation. "Humans have been here so long that the behavior has evolved between the two species. The birds find a bees' nest, then go find a human and take him there to break open the hive. After the bees and humans are gone, the bird feasts on larvae."

As annoyed as I sometimes was with Ross, he did have an encyclopedic knowledge of all things wild in Africa. His explanation of my experience burst my psychic bubble concerning oneness with another species, but the honor of a honeyguide enlisting my assistance outweighed my loss. The small bird and I had, in fact, been communicating, but in a more Darwinian manner than I'd imagined.

One thought remained unspoken when we continued on toward Maun: what would have happened two days ago if the truck had broken down and we hadn't been able to fix it? The truck's tanks held a hundred gallons of water and sufficient gasoline to go about two-hundred-and-fifty miles, but because we were crossing many borders on this trip, we carried no firearms or other weapons that might be used for hunting. If we got lost or the truck broke down in a remote area, we would be in serious trouble. But those were the risks we'd signed on for with this journey. The danger now seemed more concrete than hypothetical, but I remained grateful for this experience. The silence inside the truck made me imagine everyone shared my sobering reflections.

Moist air plumped my desert-leathered cheeks as we drove into the city of Maun. It became clear that at last we'd left the harshest deserts behind. Ross knew a couple here who allowed us the comfort of their indoor plumbing while we set up camp in their backyard. The spreading branches of a mopani tree dropped a few butterfly-shaped leaves onto my pages as I wrote letters home and typed up notes under its shade. The clickety sound of our little machine hardly violated the stillness of the garden. This afternoon in Maun sweetened my assessment of Botswana.

After stocking up again on nonperishable staples, we headed north into the Okavango Delta. The Okavango River poured all of its water into a 15,000-square-mile swamp with no outlet. Our journey to the Moremi Game Reserve followed a scant track through several native villages. Men poled dugout canoes through the Okavango waterways. The Africa of travelogues and adventure stories delighted me throughout the day. Eventually, we reached the entrance to Moremi, where a guide joined us. Navigating the roadless, watery maze would have been impossible without his expertise.

Okavango Delta.

Our guide ate a tuna-and-rice dinner with us as the sun set, but mostly remained silent, since he spoke little English. Animals abounded. Sable antelope, hippos, and crocodiles added to our previous experiences with elephants, gemsbok, giraffes, and ostriches. As we climbed into our rooftop tent, Ross offered our guide the truck's front seat, which he accepted for his bed. I had barely drifted off when a deep-throated, cat-scream shattered the night. A lion was calling her pride right outside the truck, inviting them to feed on her freshly killed antelope. Despite our height above ground, I waited many hours for sleep to return. Mama Cat could certainly leap onto our tent if she sensed any danger from us. I imagine the guide was grateful to be sleeping inside the truck that night. In the morning, we saw no evidence of the kill, but then again, none of us ventured out into the deep grass looking for it.

A group of impalas grazed nearby as we enjoyed a breakfast of bacon and a dozen eggs fresh from Maun. We packed up camp and headed northeast, dropping our guide off with a generous tip for his much-needed knowledge of both animals and paths of solid ground through the swampy delta. On Ross's map, a dotted line indicated an oil truckers' route up to the Caprivi Strip—a thin corridor of Namibian land running along the northern border of Botswana—then eastward to the Zambezi River and Victoria Falls. The distance should have been well within the range of our gasoline supply, so we all felt excited to head through a new area of wild Africa. We discussed our only trepidation about this route: a battle currently existed between native Africans and the Rhodesian government. The Caprivi Strip was said to be used by the Ovambo—"freedom fighters" or "terrorists," depending on whose side you were on—who sought to reach Rhodesia and join the revolution. The danger of encountering one of these men seemed minimal, so we headed out.

We found the only track heading northeast, but after a few dozen miles it became obvious that few vehicles, and certainly no oil tankers, had recently used the road. Ross decided not to turn back. We forged ahead until we were stopped by an open-bedded truck filled with soldiers. Sitting on benches along each side of the truck's railings, the solemn-faced, uniformed men held their rifles beside them, ready to eliminate whoever they deemed their enemy. My skin turned cold, not knowing who they were or what they intended. A tall man clad in military green strode to Ross's window. Leaning on the truck, he informed us that they were looking for a "terrorist" thought to be in the area, and that we should be careful. Being white, it seemed, we were not suspected of being engaged in terrorism. We thanked him, regained our composure, and headed on.

Less than ten miles ahead, our road twisted through the savanna—its dense elephant grass rose higher than the truck. Suddenly, a man stepped out of the grass, walking onto our dirt track. Leather bands holding bullets crisscrossed his khaki-clad chest. A rifle hung from one shoulder. Our jaws dropped and our eyes sprung wide. The man's face mirrored our shock. Ducking forward, he dashed off the track and back into the grass. Ross continued driving. The whole incident happened faster than we had time to respond. Our mouths must have all stayed open until someone said, "Well, I guess that was the terrorist." I was glad the soldiers were headed in the other direction, and silently hoped they wouldn't find him. He'd looked every bit as frightened as we were.

The ruts we were following angled down a shallow embankment to end at a slow-moving stream. Anchored on each shore, two steel cables spanned the waterway, one about four feet directly above the other. A flat, wooden raft floated against the nearest bank. A man strolled over to us. His body was wiry-thin; his black skin glistened over stomach muscles rippling above his khaki shorts. Speaking in a language we couldn't understand, he gestured toward the square wooden platform resting below. Clearly, he expected us to drive the truck onto his questionable raft. Ross nodded and headed the truck down, following the man's hand directions. We drove onto the planks with trepidation. Ross offered some bills that appeared to be sufficient for the dubious crossing. Along one side of the craft, the cables passed through holes in vertical posts attached to the front and back of the raft. Our pilot stepped onto the lower cable, grasping the upper one with both hands. Bare toes gripping the woven metal, he leaned his body against the wooden upright and maneuvered the raft by sheer muscle-power as he walked along the cable, slowly pulling us across the stream. His thin arms bulged and sweat beaded on his back. His face remained calm, however, and soon we bumped against the other side. He held the raft to the shore as we drove off. I sat in amazement, pondering the various ways humans devised of making a living.

The sun was still climbing when we reached a place where elephants must have crossed the road during a rainstorm, leaving a trampled area of dried mud. Elephant-foot sized holes crisscrossed the area. Ross stopped so we could search out the road's exit beyond the hodgepodge of elephant tracks. Skirting around the area like bloodhounds after an escaped convict, we each tried to find a trampled area of grass heading off in a somewhat straight line. Laughing, I stopped to take some photos of the solidified, mashed mudhole, thinking of how I'd narrate this when I got home: "and this is where we lost the road."

Those words turned prophetic when all we found was a wide-ish trail of flattened grass that we hoped was our road, knowing it might merely be the place where the elephants left the mudhole to continue on their way. Everyone made an effort to sound brave as we drove on.

A half-hour or so had passed in silence when Alan suddenly cried out, "I don't care if I die! I don't care if I die right here! The trip has been worth it!"

Stunned, I knew we all were dealing with similar thoughts. In terms of the amount of fuel we carried, we'd passed the point of no return. Even if we turned around now, we no longer had sufficient gasoline to get us back to safety.

I started making up silly songs and poems so dumb they actually broke the tension for a while. The country around us was lush, beautiful, and filled with wildlife. I tried to let myself enjoy that fact, appreciating the many zebras that seemed to be headed in the same direction we were. As their numbers increased, I realized we had driven into the midst of a zebra migration. Black-and-white bodies surrounded us, stretching from horizon to horizon. All our cameras came out and we forgot about our predicament. Our truck flowed through a river of stripes. Mothers with babies leapt small gullies as though they'd melded into one, large, undulating organism. We continued with the animals for over an hour until eventually drawing ahead of their tide.

Peace filled our truck. Ross had to be pleased with the incredible film footage he had just captured. We were still in serious danger if our road didn't lead where we hoped, but sharing our journey with thousands of zebra left me with a sense of belonging. We were not just observers; we were animals too, a part of the life-stream of Africa.

A few hours later, the land ahead shimmered. Drawing closer, the moving carpet morphed into the gray-brown backs of wildebeests. Packed together like the zebra, they too moved as one. Their shaggy black manes and tails flared as they lumbered along. Soon we were surrounded by this second, migrating herd. Traveling alongside these ungainly animals, we witnessed their surprising grace when leaping over obstacles at full gallop.

I rolled down my window to photograph the moving sea. The musky odor of sweaty gnus entered the truck, along with dust and flies from swarms following the herd. Alan and Ross had their windows open too, clicking away with their cameras to record another serendipitous reward on an uncertain path.

As dusk neared, the track we followed began taking on more definition. A large river appeared to the left of our road. Ross let out the air he appeared to have been holding in for hours. "The Zambezi," he breathed—and we knew we'd made it.

ELEVEN

Never happier to see human habitation, we basked in relief as we bumped along beside the Zambezi River, soon entering a magical world. In the localized rainforest created by the mists of Victoria Falls, large, red globes of "fireball" flowers rose from the soft, damp earth. Huge trees offered a dense canopy, protecting the spot where we chose to set up camp. Strangler figs wound around a tree beside the firepit I began creating for cooking our evening meal. Ferns laced the area. A spotted gray salamander scuttled away when I lifted the stone hiding him from predatory eyes. I stopped gathering stones long enough to investigate the underside of one delicate leaf glowing a sulfurous yellow, almost emitting its own light. We ate a simple meal of tinned meat and rice, grateful just to be safely back in a known world. Emotionally exhausted, we fell asleep early after dinner to the muted roar of a thousand tons of water hurling over a vast cliff less than a mile away.

Crawling out of the tent before dawn the next morning, I followed a trail that led me toward the source of the water's roar. Ross had told us that natives called Victoria Falls *Mosi oa-Tunya*, the "Smoke that Thunders." The Zambezi River stretches more than a mile wide as it flings itself three hundred feet into a narrow gorge that turns immediately left, forcing all the water to surge wildly toward the next bend in the canyon. The unusual geologic formation allowed me to walk along the rim of the gorge opposite the world's largest curtain of water. Violent power ceaselessly tumbled down. Along my path, a point of land jutted out toward the falls. I walked carefully to its tip and stood, enchanted. Victoria Falls encapsulated me in fog and thunder. As the sun rose, I watched a double rainbow form around me, coloring the mists in a complete circle above and below. The people over whose traditional land *Mosi oa-Tunya* roared must have believed it to be the center of all Earth, and here I was, standing in its heart! Whatever else might happen in my life, everything would be worth it for that magical moment of mists and rainbows.

Returning to camp, I made breakfast as we eagerly anticipated playing tourist. I cleaned up the dishes while the men visited the falls. When they returned, we headed to a small dock above the falls, clambering aboard a wooden tour boat. Nothing disappointed us that day. As the boat headed upriver, we passed through a wide pool where hippos yawned their cavernous mouths. A scratchy-voiced P.A. system informed us that those mouths could snap a dugout canoe in half. A startled hippo sleeping on land, the voice continued, could trample any human who unwittingly came between it and the river, apparently the leading cause of death by animals in Africa. Gazing at the peg-shaped teeth looming beneath us, I felt grateful to be in the aged, but seemingly seaworthy, craft. Farther on, we watched a crocodile push itself into the river just below a wading elephant taking its morning bath. I could smell the elephant's musky breath when it exhaled a shower of water over its back.

Disembarking for lunch on an island, we chatted with two young men from South Africa while vervet monkeys dashed around, grabbing for our sandwiches and other unguarded morsels. Our lunchmates—the two-legged ones—encouraged Alan and me to join them that evening to explore the luxury casino frequented by jetsetters who flew in to view the falls and gamble away small fortunes. We agreed to meet them.

Back in camp, we rummaged through our duffels to find our most presentable clothes. Alan's short-sleeved, plaid shirt seemed a bit more upscale than my baggy Guatemalan cloth sundress, but it was the best I could do. Ross chose to stay in camp, perhaps feeling like he'd be a fifth wheel to the younger folks' adventure.

The sun set through the mist of Victoria Falls as Alan and I followed a trail away from camp. When the forest opened out, we stopped to gape at the largest building we'd seen in two months. A flashy casino loomed, more elaborate than I'd imagined, with manicured palms framing its entrance. Our friends were waiting by the door while I reluctantly parted with the five-dollar entry fee and the doorman eyed us with undisguised disdain.

The thick-carpeted room we entered dazzled us, resplendent in its luxury. Under cut-glass chandeliers hanging from high ceilings, the polished edges of wooden roulette tables shone beneath the leaning arms of formally attired guests. Money was a scarce commodity for me. I had no intention of risking it on games of chance, regardless of how enticing they appeared. I nevertheless felt eager to watch.

As the guys ventured farther, I moved toward the nearest table, positioning myself beside a tuxedoed gentleman. His lips smiled beneath a gray mustache as I sidled up near the roulette wheel. But a woman in a floor-length, satin gown sent me a look that would singe the eyelashes off a giraffe. Ignoring her gaze of disapproval, presumably regarding my appearance and position beside her husband, I watched the man stack piles of chips onto various numbers for each turn of the wheel. Time after time, he stood impassive as the attendant raked away his chips. Curious as to how much money he was losing so calmly, I peered closely at one of his chips: "$1,000" curved in print around its lower edge. An ice chunk seemed to lodge itself in my esophagus, despite having no drink beside me. Ten thousand dollars a pop and he wasn't batting an eyelash! Just one of those chips would totally change my life. I wondered if he'd trade me a chip for a kiss, but realized that would be like a mild form of prostitution. Besides, his wife was hovering nearby.

The couple obviously had no comprehension of—or interest in—the effect of one of those chips on my life. I thought about the man with the bare feet who powered the tiny raft carrying our truck across the Okavango swamp. I thought of all the Africans only miles away fighting to reclaim their country of Rhodesia from white domination. Imperialism, colonialism, and European exploitation, discussed in political science classes, stood before me, sipping pale liquor from a crystal glass.

I pushed back through the crowd, my sandaled feet sinking into the burgundy, fleur-de-lis-patterned carpet. The scent of wood polish laced with cigar smoke sapped the air of oxygen. Catching sight of Alan's red plaid shirt, I hurried to tell him I needed to return to camp, but could get there alone. I stumbled outside to breathe the cool evening air. The African night chorus comforted me along the dark trail following the stifling revelations in the casino. Vignettes of small, past experiences in which I'd always taken class and racial inequality for granted flashed through my brain: a progression of railroad cars pulled by a locomotive of injustice. How could I have known without comprehending? What did it mean to understand a sense of Oneness and the Tapestry if I accepted a world order that denied it? What was my role in all of this? Like an eddy along the shores of the Zambezi, these questions circled through my mind without end. Clearly, I needed time to sort these thoughts. I climbed into bed, sleep evading me long past the time I heard Alan stumble up the ladder.

Our destination had never been clear, but the unjelled plan was to travel through Zambia and Tanzania, and then spend time in Kenya, before completing the journey in Dar es Salaam. Leaving Victoria Falls the next morning, we headed into Zambia. Now that we were traveling through a wetter part of the continent, we'd be greeting new challenges. We spent a long day driving through misty rain in an undifferentiated scrub forest, affording plenty of time to mull over the events of the previous evening. Comparing the lives of two men I had so recently observed—the ferry man and the gambler—left me angry and unsure. Parts of the Tapestry were so divided that I visualized rents in its fibers, large rips with frayed ends proving nearly impossible to reconnect.

In a few months, our trip would end. I now knew I needed to do something with my life that reflected my altered worldview. Should I work to make the tuxedoed and satin-dressed humans of the casino comprehend the life of a man walking barefoot on a cable to feed his children? Should I work for those at home who faced daily social injustices, helping them reach past the barriers that entrapped them? Nothing resolved itself in my mind, but I couldn't stuff these thoughts into a category to be forgotten.

Alongside my mental quagmires, several muddy areas in the road nearly bogged us down during the day's tedious drive. After finally turning off the road for the night, we were forced to drive a long way before finding a dry area to set up camp. As was our usual routine, the men went off to see what new insects this area had to offer, while I began collecting wood for a fire. I gathered twigs and branches of various sizes. Everything dripped from the recent rain. I broke off parts of tree limbs from the most sheltered areas I could find, ignoring any wood lying on the soaked ground.

With paper and matches in limited supply, I had come to pride myself on creating a blaze using only one match. That night, ten matches, twenty curse words, and at least forty minutes later, a flame finally grew tall enough to resist sputtering out in dampness. Sighing in relief, I placed our grill over the stone circle I'd built, filled a large pan with water, and set it down to boil for spaghetti noodles. I nestled another pot beside it, filled it with meat sauce from a can, and sautéed a few chopped onions to add in. Satisfied that dinner would happen after all, I switched on the fluorescent light we hung over the table and began chopping cabbage for a salad. I heard the water start to boil at the fire and dropped a handful of dried noodles into the pot. As I whisked together oil, vinegar, and some herbs for a dressing, I realized that the conditions troubling my dinner preparation might be considered luxurious by local standards. How did the natives deal daily with damp wood and unlighted cooking areas? Even here, I was spoiled compared to most others.

My cogitations ceased when a tiny black beetle dropped into the dressing I was making. Letting loose a few more fine expletives, I fished out the beetle and checked on the salad. At least a dozen dark dots, lured by the light, inched around in the cabbage. Slapping a lid on the dressing jar, I picked little crawlies from the cabbage until I felt satisfied I'd unearthed them all. The fire flickered at the edge of a circle of light and I suddenly worried another invasion could be happening out there. I covered the salad, grabbed a potholder, and rescued the noodle pot from the grill. Sure enough, black dots drifted through the water, boiled to lifelessness. A hopeless exhaustion tried to paralyze me, but I knew the guys would be back soon, so I drained the noodles and picked out all the beetles I could. One pot remained over the fire. No part of me wanted to look at it. Without inspecting the dark sauce, I poured it over the noodles, camouflaging any beetles I might have missed.

As the men came into camp, I prayed two small prayers: that any crunchies be attributed to onions or bits of meat in the sauce, and that whatever species served as added protein would not prove to be poisonous. Too hungry and tired to worry, I served dinner. No one noticed anything peculiar. Flavored with exhaustion, the spaghetti tasted fine. I cleaned up after dinner and crawled into bed, acknowledging our status as seasoned campers—seasoned with salt, oregano, and unidentified beetles.

Soon the terrain began changing as we passed through. Scrub trees gave way to open savanna dotted with "fever trees," the flat-topped acacias that Europeans once thought caused yellow fever. One evening, as we crossed tall grasses to find a suitable campsite, we heard drums echoing through the trees. Others answered from somewhere off to our left. I felt certain their rhythms encoded some message about us. *Look out, there are Europeans!* Or, *Stay away from the grassland near the road tonight.* Or, perhaps, something more sinister. Who could blame them? I envisioned their villages. Thousands of years living in relative comfort before white-skinned people arrived wanting their land, offering enviable trade goods if they could capture members of neighboring tribes for the white men to sell as slaves. But here, far away from any city, perhaps the people had maintained their own language and their own culture. Yet, here we were again, the white invaders. Who would blame the natives if they decided to defend themselves tonight? I listened to the drums. Oddly, their sound seemed comfortable, reassuring. Those beats belonged here, among the fever trees. Perhaps they would just let us be for the night, but watch carefully to be certain we left in the morning.

At dawn we headed out, unmolested by unseen neighbors. We proceeded to bump, bump, and bump our way across Zambia, following rutted dirt roads that regularly punctured our tires. At one of our resupply stops near the town of Mkwamba, we waited in a tin-roofed tavern while a tire was repaired. I held a cold beer against my neck, relishing the dripping bottle's unfamiliar temperature. Ross brought out a map to point out that the Belgian Congo's border nearly touched the road we were on.

"It's just called the Congo now," a voice said from down the bar. "I came from there yesterday."

I turned to see a thirtyish white man wearing fatigues and an odd-shaped beret.

"It's pretty dangerous there, isn't it?" asked Ross, moving closer to the man.

"I'd say, mate! I was fighting there."

"The Congo's politics are confusing. Who do you fight for?"

The man gave a sardonic laugh and took a long pull of his beer. "I'm on R&R. When I go back in, I'll join up with the first group I meet. No one's sure anymore who's fighting who. You could say I'm a mercenary; I do it for the money."

I tried not to stare. I knew the U.S. had somehow been involved in the beginning of this war. Patrice Lumumba had been a leader in the liberation from Belgium, but then it seemed we'd turned against him—he was nationalizing the gold mines or something—and then he'd been assassinated. After my Peace Corps experience, I wondered in what way my country had been involved. Whose side should I be on? It seemed like the Congo's attempt to unify the country had been disrupted, perhaps with U.S. intervention, and now chaos reigned in the Congo.

I looked carefully at the man beside us. He appeared ordinary, not dangerous. An attractive face: I probably would have considered dating him if I'd met him somewhere else. But he killed people for a living.

I began using the edge of a fingernail to peel the damp label off my beer bottle. This world was proving more complex than I'd imagined. Did loyalty to my principles need to be stronger than loyalty to my country? Not a comfortable thought for a girl brought up during post-WWII patriotism. Had something changed in our country or was my perception changing? I chugged the rest of my beer and we headed back to retrieve the truck.

For more than a hundred miles of wilderness track, we saw no other humans. We were passing through a restricted tsetse-fly area; a permit had been necessary for us to enter. The government restricted access to this area because surveys showed that one in a hundred tsetse flies carried parasites causing trypanosomiasis (African encephalitis). No cure existed at the time for the African form of this brain disease, nearly always fatal. Death would occur within several weeks to a month. Choosing a different route would have involved hundreds of miles of detour, and despite the inherent dangers, we had all come to relish crossing untraveled land.

The open forest swarmed with a variety of unusual insects. In a grassy clearing where cicadas buzzed so loudly I thought my head would burst, Ross stopped to collect. As we climbed out of the truck, I was horrified to find tsetse flies swarming so thickly we nearly breathed them in. Not wanting to admit how nervous they made me, I worked for a while helping to collect specimens while cicadas screamed in the afternoon heat.

A tsetse fly is not a small, polite nipper. They are big, gray-brown, and decidedly ugly. Their bites were leaving red holes in my skin. I finally gave up and shut myself back inside the truck, attempting to escape the hordes of tsetse demons. The men endured longer than I did. But by the time we escaped the area, we had so many bites that we challenged the probabilities of infection. We headed out without further insect collection, except for those filling the truck's cab. Alan attempted to net and euthanize them, but I merely squashed them with a book.

After another few hours of bumping across a grassy tract, we were grateful when a small wooden building appeared up ahead. Uniformed guards waved us to a stop. Wielding miniature butterfly nets, they gestured us out of the truck and proceeded to explore every nook and cranny, hunting for and destroying any tsetse stowaways. Seeing how seriously they took the danger of these small beasties, I shivered at the exposure we'd just risked.

Eventually, we reached the Tanzanian border. Recently liberated from European rule, the country had just changed its name from Tanganyika and was said to be rallying behind a dynamic new socialistic government headed by Julius Nyerere. We didn't know what to expect.

When we approached the border, guards in berets held their rifles across the front of their rumpled uniforms, indicating our need to stop for an interrogation. At the beginning of our journey, Ross had decided that we would carry no firearms or anything else that might be deemed a weapon. He had been meticulous in keeping our papers together and procuring the necessary documents to make our many border crossings as easy as possible. Nevertheless, we sat beside the telephone-booth-sized border hut for several hours while three uniformed men chatted about our documents. No one else sought to cross into Tanzania while we waited. Nothing further was asked of us. They simply walked around, sat, and chatted, occasionally glancing our way. Despite the heat, we remained inside the truck, not wanting to appear in any way threatening or disrespectful. Ross remained very calm, telling us that this behavior, while annoying, could be expected. He felt certain they would eventually let us pass.

Late in the afternoon, Ross was proven right. The guards returned our papers without comment and gestured the truck through. We expressed our relief. Ross said he'd hoped to be farther along before camping, and that there was a town ahead where we might resupply if the ubiquitous Indian-run grocery stores of Africa weren't yet closed. We drove on for another hour or more through seemingly uninhabited open forests before seeing the town's first deteriorating buildings. Abandoned trucks, missing a wheel or fender, hunkered helter-skelter along the roadside. At the first corner we came to, a long-haired, swarthy, mustachioed man tilted back his chair on the veranda of a once-white Victorian home, feet resting on a wooden railing. Glaring at us from under thick brows, he pared his fingernails with a scythe-shaped sword, never once glancing down. Total silence. Ross kept the truck rolling, not turning onto what appeared to have once been the main street. Sweat prickled my arms. The air felt thickly unbreathable. Suddenly a group of children erupted from behind a building, yelling words we didn't need to know in order to understand. One smallish boy picked up a rock and hurled it at the truck. The others immediately followed suit. A large stone kicked up dust as it hit the road outside my window. Ross accelerated. I held my breath as we pulled away from the harassers following behind us.

Supply-less, we passed out of town with no further incidents. No one spoke for a while, each of us processing our emotions. Despite our various predicaments and adventures during the past few months, seeing hatred in the eyes of the man on the porch and hearing the cries of the children caused me to fear for our lives for the first time on the trip. We put the town as far behind us as possible before making camp that night. During the next several days, even Ross was willing to cut short the usual daily hours of insect-collecting. Southwestern Tanzania felt decidedly inhospitable.

The spookily derelict border town, however, did not reflect the general feeling of Tanzania. The further we drove into this new country, the more positive and optimistic its citizens appeared to be. Our accelerated pace had the benefit of shortening the time until our arrival at Serengeti National Park, a destination we anticipated with excitement.

We stopped to resupply in the picturesque town of Mwanza, where giant, sculpted rocks gathered on the shore of Lake Victoria, resembling a herd of elephants coming down to drink. In town, palms draped their fronds around roadside fruit stands like hens protecting their brood. Wandering through a spicy-sweet-smelling, open-air market, I bought limes, onions, avocados, and at least five kinds of bananas of various sizes and colors. Countless unfamiliar fruits and vegetables were carefully stacked on blankets laid out before smiling vendors wrapped in colorful African cloths.

We met up again for lunch in a shaded area outside a white stucco café, the three of us sitting down beside a man dressed in a park ranger's uniform.

"You're from the Serengeti?" Ross asked, noting the emblem on his olive-green shirt. "We're hoping to drive across." Entering the park from the west side, we would need to cross a hundred-and-fifty miles of savanna to reach Seronera, the usual tourist destination. We didn't know if the infrequently traveled road would be passable.

"Yes, I've just come from there. Not too bad. You know the rainy season is starting, right? The road is muddy, but you can probably make it through right now."

Grateful for the information, we finished our lunch, found the truck, and headed out.

Our road wandered the beautiful shores of Lake Victoria before turning inland, passing through forested hills before reaching the Serengeti's western border. Ross stopped the truck when the land dropped away. Plains stretched all the way to the eastern horizon. We had certainly seen and experienced plentiful wildlife on our trip, but the sight of the Serengeti, famous as a home to every type of African animal, still managed to send tingles down my spine. My spirits dampened when I noticed that our road disappeared into a wall of blackness reaching from the ground up to one of the widest, darkest stretch of cloud I'd ever seen. No one asked if we should proceed or not, because we had no options. We clambered back aboard and descended onto the savanna.

Reaching the edge of that storm was like driving straight into a waterfall. Our muddy little road turned into a very muddy river. Ross floored it, crashing through the deepest areas with varying, slithering success. Crossing an unusually wide puddle—more like a small lake—the truck lost momentum, miring down into mud. Alan and I slogged into the ankle-deep water, realizing shovels would prove worthless. For the first time on our journey, we were going to have to test out the winch and cable mounted on the front of the truck. Ross turned on the electric motor that unspooled the cable, waving for Alan and me to drag the hooked end over to the nearest and sturdiest tree. Our only option was a spindly-looking thorn tree. Looping the cable around the trunk, we hooked it onto itself and signaled Ross to reverse the cable. Standing well back, we watched the braided steel wire grow taut and respool. The truck moved tentatively forward, like a well-trained dog on its leash, before rolling onto passably firm ground. When Alan and I climbed back into the truck, thick, muddy water dribbled onto the floor.

At our next miring, the nearby trees stood less than twenty feet tall. We broke two of their trunks before one finally held long enough for us to winch ourselves free of the mud. We soon became experts, using the winch to pull the truck from one distant tree to another, with slippery driving in between. Eventually, we made our way out the far side of the storm, continuing to deal with mud left in its wake.

We traveled with increasing optimism until the truck slowed and sank once more into an expanse of reddish goop. Exhausted and discouraged, we breathed a collective sigh. The only available tree sat too far to the left, but it was our only choice. Alan trudged out to wrap the steel cable around its trunk while Ross worked the winch. As the truck began inching forward, an appalling grinding sound stopped our progress. Running to inspect the problem, we saw that the cable had jammed between the winch and its housing. Since the weight of the truck had wedged it in there, our puny human strength would not be enough to free it.

"There's nothing to be done. We're totally stuck." Ross slapped a tire, spraying bits of muck onto the three of us. Exhaustion appeared to drain any optimism that might have lingered in his mind.

"How far are we? How far do we have to go?" Alan slumped, equally discouraged.

"If there's a river ahead, at least we'll know we're still on the right road." Ross shrugged with wilted shoulders. "But we must be over fifty miles from Seronera."

And nothing was behind us for at least that many miles.

The men began discussing our dilemma, and I stayed quiet. Ross said he'd take a bag and start walking for help.

"Fifty miles?" I finally chimed in. "We have a saw. Why don't we saw through the cable?"

"A braided steel cable? No chance!" Ross dismissed my suggestion.

"Well, water can erode a rock, so eventually we should be able to cut through it, right?" My reasoning seemed ridiculously optimistic, even to me. But they agreed to try.

"We need to find out where we are. One of us should walk ahead to see if the river's there."

Since the men clearly had the strongest arms for sawing, I volunteered to head out as scout. The sun had come out and I found myself enjoying the freedom of slogging down the muddy track. Grasses waved beside me in the ozone-fresh air. This was the Africa of legends. The savanna gleamed fresh and new in the post-storm sunshine.

I'd probably walked less than a mile when I neared a thick copse to the right of my path. The trees cast dense shadows across the road. New thoughts jostled for control. *Lions lived in Africa. Lions lived in the Serengeti. I was small. I was gazelle-sized. I was the size of a lion's favorite prey.*

I slowed my pace. I peered into the trees. I stopped. I probed inside myself for some feeling of connection. This was the Serengeti, a beautiful part of the Tapestry. But I didn't want to become one with a lion from inside its stomach. Squaring my shoulders, every ounce of courage inside me formed the voices of my stalwart female ancestors: "Don't chicken out!"

Sunshine and shadows created every imaginable shape among the trees. I peered into the grove, trying to discern if any of those shapes resembled a large cat. It was impossible to tell. Dozens of lions could be hiding in there. My feet froze to the earth, refusing to move forward. I thought of going back, but how could I return with my tail between my legs, admitting I'd gotten too scared of hypothetical lions to go any farther? Alas, the voices in my head failed to get my feet moving forward again. Self-preservation took over. Keeping my eyes fixed on the cluster of trees, I turned around. I began moving back toward the truck, continually glancing over my shoulder, startling at every extra gust of wind shaking a branch.

My boots squished along the muddy track. I straightened my spine as the truck came into view, ready to confess my trepidations, preparing myself for inevitable mockery.

Both mud-caked men were kneeling beside the truck. Alan held the saw by his side; I feared they had given up. Holding my head high, I strode forward until they saw me.

"Look," Alan bubbled, triumphantly waving a grubby hand. "It's working!"

My jaw dropped in genuine surprise as I watched Ross pull and push the still-intact sawblade through a cut halfway into the braided steel cable.

"Wow! Super!" My excitement poured out, overshadowing my embarrassment at having failed my scouting assignment. "Well, I chickened out," I confessed, after a pause. "I started imagining a lion behind every tree, so I turned around before I ever saw a river."

"Don't worry. I'll head out. You can saw for a while." Ross nodded to me as he stood up.

The mocking I'd expected for abandoning my mission wasn't happening. Relieved, I took over sawing. Ross hefted a bag and headed down the road I'd just come from, still hoping to find the river.

Hours later, the sun had nearly set when Alan and I broke through the cable. Our joy was tempered by the fact that Ross hadn't returned. We'd freed the cable, but had no idea how to reattach the hook. Settling in for the night, we lifted the top off the truck, sliding it sideways to begin setting up camp, hoping for the best while trying not to worry about what had happened to Ross.

Spending the night mired in a giant mudhole qualified as the worst campsite yet, and there'd already been several notable runners-up. I gathered enough wood to begin cooking dinner on semi-dry ground when two figures appeared on the road, walking toward us, one of them pushing a bicycle. Ross plopped down onto a camp chair and gestured to his new friend to do the same. A native man wearing black trousers and a long-sleeved, white shirt sank into the chair beside Ross. Alan fished out a bottle of rum we'd kept for wee libations whenever they were warranted. Tonight, one was more than warranted. Alan poured drinks as I finished making dinner.

Speaking excellent English, our visitor told us that he'd ridden down the road a week ago to visit his sister and was just now returning. "On my journey there," he said between sips of our liquor, "somewhere near this very spot, I was treed by a lion. I was forced to remain in that tree for several hours before she finally moved away. I shall be happy if I may camp with you for this night."

Ross nodded. "Of course. We're happy to have run into you. We sleep on top of the truck; you're welcome to use the front seat."

Hearing the man's words, the hair on my arms stood at attention. Had I had a premonition? Could I have sensed the lion in those trees? Who knows? I was glad I had collected enough wood to keep the fire going far into the night. And I was thrilled that Ross, despite being annoying, had returned to us un-treed and uneaten.

The winch moved freely in the morning, and Ross managed to reattach the hook onto the end of the liberated cable. Bidding our new friend goodbye, we continued on, happy to find the puddles had receded during the night. We were still forced to dig and pull several times during the following hours, but we made relatively good progress and celebrated when the hoped-for river finally appeared on our right.

Just past midday, the road led into what can only be described as another small lake. Ross got out in the hope of finding a route around it, but the water had extended far into the grass on both sides.

"Well, do we go for it?"

I was happily surprised that Ross had included Alan and me in this decision.

"I don't see a lot of options," Alan replied, and I concurred.

Ross backed the truck up, shifted into first gear, and gunned it. We slithered and splashed, red water spraying everywhere, but slowly lost momentum as the tires spun deeper and deeper into the quagmire. Ten feet from the edge of the muddy water, we came to a soggy stop. No trees for winching stood in front of us. Wading out, we acknowledged that this would have to be our campsite for the night. Ross felt optimistic that the water would recede by morning. If not, we'd just have to wait it out.

I began setting up the table and chairs on a spot of dryish land. Since the day was fairly young, Ross and Alan decided to make the best of it and do some insect collecting. With the safety of the truck nearby, I felt no qualms about staying alone. I even used the relatively clear rainwater of a nearby, grassy puddle to do our laundry, since our clothes had all taken on a red-mud veneer. As I was hanging clean clothes across a handy bush, a smiling boy stepped out from behind nearby trees.

"Hellohowareyou," he beamed at me, speaking in what I assumed to be the Swahili language.

I smiled back.

"Hellohowareyou," he tried again.

It took three times before I realized that he was greeting me in English. "Oh, I'm fine! My name's Carol. How are you?"

"Iamfine." White teeth grinned from his small, dark face.

A man followed the boy, stepping quietly into the camp. Dressed in a white shirt and black trousers, like our visitor from yesterday, he appeared friendly and nonthreatening.

"Hello," he said, extending his hand. "My name is Francis."

I took his hand. "I'm Carol."

We chatted for a moment and I told him of our predicament. I said we were optimistic that the water would recede in the night. He agreed that without more rain, we should be able to free ourselves and continue on in the morning.

"I am a teacher in a nearby school. Would you like to come visit my classroom tomorrow?"

"Why, thank you," I replied, incredulous. "I would love to." Was this for real? An anthropologist's dream? Had local people just appeared out of the bush and invited me to visit their school? "I have hot water on. Would you like a cup of tea?"

The man nodded and sat. The boy continued to stand shyly behind him.

"There are two grades in my school. We have one other teacher. I would like if you come to visit my class. The students will show you what they learn."

We were sipping tea together when Ross and Alan returned to camp. I introduced Francis and his student and explained the situation, telling Ross that I'd accepted his invitation to visit the school in the morning. I feared that I might be rebuked for making a unilateral decision about our journey, but Ross was pleased at the thought and immediately invited himself to join us. Francis finished his tea and informed us he'd return to fetch us in the morning. Tanzania continued to defy the impressions from our frightening introduction. After that first creepy town, everyone had been relaxed and more than friendly.

When morning came, I was pleased that I could don my newly laundered clothes for the visit. Francis soon materialized from the bush. Alan opted out, so Ross and I, cameras and recorders in hand, followed our host through a winding path that led us to a rectangular, white stucco building. The two classrooms had wide openings serving as windows and doors. Inside, long boards spanned the rooms as tables, and fifteen or twenty students sat chattering on benches behind them.

Francis introduced us and began the class with an English lesson. Ross set up his tripod in a corner of the room, alternating between shooting movies and using his thirty-five-millimeter Nikon. I settled myself on the end of a bench beside the students.

It soon became clear that the children would rather sing for us than follow Francis' English lesson. He smiled at their excitement and allowed them to take over the agenda. With beautiful voices and overwhelming enthusiasm, they sang several songs before deciding to teach us the Tanzanian national anthem. The lively, haunting tune sounded totally African to my American ears. I eagerly tried to learn, repeating the unaccustomed syllables as best I could. Ross seemed pleased to merely film the interactions. The students laughed and were encouraged by my efforts. When they deemed my rendition of the anthem acceptable, they told me they wanted to teach me a dance. Without any appreciable embarrassment, Francis informed us that this was a fertility dance and the class had decided that, as a young woman, I must learn to dance it.

We formed a circle and the girls took my arms, leading me around as they sang a repetitive chant. The girl beside me dropped my hand and turned toward me, making eye contact and raising her eyebrows in an invitation to watch and follow her moves. As she faced me, her small hips began twisting back and forth. One knee and then the other turned in and out, sometimes bringing a foot up off the ground to waggle in the air. In America, the twist had recently become popular. I was dumbfounded at the similarity. The children appeared equally surprised and delighted that I could learn so quickly, but I just used the moves I'd practiced with Chubby Checker's songs at home. Looking at the small girl who had been most intent on teaching me, I felt warmth seep through my body. The rent in the Tapestry I had worried about, between the boatman and the gambler, seemed smaller and no longer central to the fabric's design. I could easily imagine my essence being identical to that of my new friend. I was her and she was me. As with the women in the Namib Desert, I felt woven into the universal fabric. The problem of injustice floated more distantly. Today was just a big dish of happiness.

We stayed all morning. Thanking our hosts and promising to write, we reluctantly headed back to camp. Before leaving, I took a portrait of Francis with his wife—who served as the other schoolteacher—and their baby, making certain I had their correct address to send him a copy. The idea that mail would be delivered to an address in the middle of the Serengeti seemed improbable, but I hoped it would work.

A despondent Alan greeted our return to camp. He noted that the pond had shrunk little, even with the day's warmth and sunshine. Buoyed by experiencing a photographic gold mine, Ross remained optimistic about our journey and directed us to pack up. I made sack lunches in case we managed to travel on. We had finished loading the truck and were again assessing our situation when we heard a commotion and the sound of a large vehicle coming down the road. After days of seeing no traffic other than a bicycle, we were astounded to see a bus approaching with passengers leaning from the windows and hanging onto chickens and livestock on its roof.

The bus stopped before the water hole and the driver slogged over to discuss our situation. Ross showed him the winch and cable. The man nodded happily, returned to the bus, and roared through the puddle. Stopping on the other side, he and Ross managed to attach the cable to something beneath the bus. The shouts of the passengers combined with the power of the bus managed to heave us out of the water and back onto dry land. With passengers laughing and waving and chickens squawking, the magic bus disappeared down the road.

For the rest of that day we pushed, winched, and ploughed our way through countless muddy miles. Covered in reddish muck, our truck and its equally filthy passengers rolled into Seronera, the tourist center of Serengeti National Park. Framed by low, sprawling buildings, Seronera's patio faced out onto the plains we had just crossed. Sipping their mint julips and whiskey sours on the patio, many clean and casually dressed tourists witnessed our arrival. We all stared at each other. I don't know who was more surprised, the elegant guests or the mud-covered campers. We ignored our disreputable condition enough to park the truck and head inside the building, bellying-up to a bamboo bar. A fake fringe of thatched roofing covered the impressive collections of bottles lined up behind an attentive bartender. People turned to watch us. Ross ordered whiskey, neat. Alan and I did the same. We were intrepid. We were survivors. We had slogged across more than one hundred miles of the Serengeti Plains. We were instant celebrities.

"Are you Americans?" a man beside us at the bar asked in a decidedly American accent.

We assured him that we were.

After introducing himself as a researcher from the Smithsonian, he extended us a surprising invitation. "Then you must join us tonight. I am leading a group from California. I have managed to procure for them all the fixings of a traditional American Thanksgiving dinner. You really must join us!"

Today was Thanksgiving! Who would have guessed? Grinning, we accepted.

We set up in the campground, gratefully utilized the nearby showers, then headed back into the restaurant where long tables had been set up for the researcher's group. Basking in the awe of white-haired, fellow Americans, we regaled them with stories of our trip. For the first time in months, I was relieved of cooking dinner. Instead, here in the heart of Africa, we replenished our weary bodies by gorging on turkey dinner with all the trimmings. What future Thanksgiving would ever measure up to learning fertility dances in a bush school, being rescued by an overloaded bus, and becoming celebrities at Seronera? By the time darkness fell on the African plains, I felt as sated as a lion cub whose mom had brought home a gazelle.

TWELVE

Despite the night's revelries, we arose at dawn the next morning to follow the retreating purple shadows eastward across the remainder of the Serengeti Plains. Ross agreed to my impulsive notion to spend the morning riding on top of the truck. I clambered over the windshield and onto the flat aluminum box that covered our Conestoga wagon tent. Freed from the human energies swirling around the truck's interior, I breathed in the wildness of Africa, trying to reclaim the feeling of connection I'd experienced on the airplane. If I were an inseparable part of the Universe, then were the vast grasslands stretching in every direction an inseparable part of me? Occasional acacia trees and rocky kopjes dotted the ocean of green. More numerous than the spread-limbed African trees, animals grazed or lazed around us. As the truck rumbled forward, hyenas rose from the muddy puddles where they slept away the morning after their nighttime hunts, complaining in eerie, cackling voices that we had disturbed their naps. I felt jubilant, brave, and free, amazed at the sweetness of such expansive energy.

Far off to my right, a heavy-bodied, hulky cat strode along a ridge in the dawn light. A leopard, rare and seldom observed! I felt nervous but privileged to see such a beautiful animal. As it angled more toward our road, I realized our courses were destined to intersect. Feeling totally exposed, I began pounding my heels on the windshield, trying to get Ross to stop and let me inside. No response. Leopards are dangerous, known to attack humans. I pounded some more. The wheels kept turning and the leopard kept pace with our truck, veering always toward our path. I continued kicking at the windshield. When a response still didn't come from inside the vehicle, eventually I froze, keeping dead still, hoping to escape the cat's attention as it crossed only yards in front of us.

When the truck finally stopped farther down the road, I leapt off and yelled my fury. "What in hell were you doing! Leopards kill people! You risked my life!"

Both men looked at me stupefied, but gave no response.

"What were you thinking, leaving me up there? I know we've had our differences, but I never imagined you wanted me dead!" My face burned with indignation.

"Leopard! That wasn't a leopard." Ross's forehead wrinkled, seemingly confused. "After all these months, why would you freak out over a cheetah?"

We'd seen lots of cheetahs. We'd photographed them up-close and personal, right outside the truck. I was certain the animal that crossed our path had not been a cheetah.

"Cheetahs are *not* dangerous animals, you know that," Ross lectured.

"Some people even keep cheetahs as pets," Alan chimed in. "Can't you tell a leopard from a cheetah?"

I was incredulous. Mouth gaping, I stared at the men. Was Alan in on this too? Was he siding with Ross in risking my life? Leopards are large and stocky; cheetahs are lithe and graceful, the greyhounds of the cat kingdom. I could *not* have confused them, but still, both men seemed genuinely surprised at my reaction.

"Just get in the truck," Ross said, trying to end my tirade as he restarted the vehicle.

My exposed, endangered brain clearly had seen a leopard; the truck-enclosed men swore they had seen only a cheetah. Two very different spotted cats, two very different perceptions. I had definitely seen a leopard. Had my subconscious mind morphed the cat into a more dangerous animal in order to get me into the truck? Because the two men were so adamant, I reluctantly accepted their verdict. But I remained angry they had left me exposed to any African cat. Ending my morning's liberated adventure, I climbed back inside the truck.[1]

Exiting the Serengeti, we turned north. For days, Ross had been telling me we would soon stop at Olduvai Gorge—the famed site of paleoanthropologists Louis and Mary Leakey's excavations. They'd unearthed fossils here that shifted the understanding of human evolution. Ross knew the Leakeys. Despite my morning's imagined brush with death, I was more than a little excited at the thought of meeting the person who, along with his wife, Mary, had inhabited my anthropology textbooks. I'd spent the past two summers working in archeology at Mesa Verde National Park in Colorado. Last year, I even headed the laboratory there. The thought crossed my mind that I might be able to get hired on as part of the Olduvai crew, but I hadn't shared my small dream with either of the men.

"You know, don't you, it was Leakey who got Jane Goodall into the field to work with the chimpanzees?" Ross's voice broke into my contemplations.

"Yes, but while the public loves her, primatologists have some concerns about her work," I replied. Jane had been in the field for seven years, starting her research center at Gombe. "My physical anthropology professors said she had no training in behavioral data collection when she went into the field. She lured the chimps to her by putting out bananas, and then interacted far too much for her data to be considered natural." It felt good to be able to tell Ross something scientific he probably hadn't known. We'd enjoyed sharing our knowledge in San Francisco. I thought these kinds of discussions were the reason he'd wanted to bring me along on the trip, but I'd probably been mistaken.

"Well, Leakey thinks we can learn something about early hominid evolution by studying the great apes, our closest primate relatives. He's looking for another woman now to study gorillas, and possibly a third one for orangutans in Indonesia. You might be interested."

---

[1] After we returned from Africa, Ross mailed me a photograph of the cat. It had, indeed, been a cheetah.

I had two thoughts: One, Ross would be rid of me and my slightly cantankerous behavior if he could leave me with Leakey, and two, I'd worked in archeology and couldn't really imagine spending years in the jungle traipsing after a bunch of gorillas. Since I did love animals, however, I let Ross's suggestion percolate.[2]

The land fell away before us and we headed down into Olduvai Gorge. Scrubby trees and brush carpeted the floor and walls of the canyon. We stopped by a tin-roofed building that appeared to serve as the archeological laboratory. One open-air side allowed us to see wide, flat boxes filled with chunks of stone resting on tall tables. Across the canyon, a white canopy protected what I assumed to be a current excavation site.

A pleasant-looking man walked over to greet us, his green shirt and shorts complemented shining, dark skin. He nodded a welcome, introducing himself as Stephen Mutuwa, the head of the camp. We were greatly disappointed to learn from him that Leakey had left that morning for London. But Olduvai Gorge stretched before us in all its fame and beauty, lessening the distress. After learning who Ross was, Stephen graciously offered to take us through the excavation sites, explaining the current finds. I climbed out of the truck, too excited to wait for Ross's reply.

Stephen led us on a dusty trail into the gorge. He stopped at a rectangular excavation on the side of the ravine. The archeologist in me was not surprised to note how perfectly flat the bottom of the trench was. Excavations require straight sides and smooth floors to expose soil changes, like the charcoal left by a firepit. Baseball-sized stones lay roughly around an excavated semicircle. Stephen told us they hoped this would turn out to be evidence of the first known house, probably dating back millions of years.

Returning to where we'd left the truck, Stephen let us browse through the field laboratory. I sat in Leakey's chair and held fossils still encrusted in their stony matrix, waiting to be freed by a dental pick. Sufficient hero

---

[2] Ironically, fifteen years later, Jane's work would be vindicated and I'd be doing my dissertation fieldwork traipsing after a group of rhesus monkeys. I'd also find out that by the time we had reached Olduvai Gorge in 1967, Leakey had already found his gorilla person in Dian Fossey.

worship coursed through my body to thrill and amaze me. *This is Olduvai! This is Leakey's lab and Leakey's chair!* Turning the ancient rock over in my hands, I wondered if the protruding bone fragment was the fossilized remains of an animal killed millions of years ago by a human ancestor. Maybe my own ancestor? If this antelope—or whatever it was—hadn't been killed, could the band have gone hungry and someone not gotten pregnant, and I wouldn't be here now? Wildly hypothetical, but an intriguing thought.

Louis Leakey's field lab.

We camped for the night beside the laboratory. I stayed up late batting away numerous moths attracted to the lights above the small table that folded down in front of my seat. I took out and reread the last letter my parents had sent, addressed to "Carol McMillan, c/o California Academy of Sciences Expedition, Poste Restante, Mwanza, Tanzania." Our friends and family had been asked to send us mail care of general delivery in several of the small cities we'd be passing through. I savored the letter, appreciating the goings-on in California, but especially basking in the simple feeling of connection. Everyone I knew was half a world away and sometimes I felt pretty lonely.

Using Ross' small typewriter, I wrote a long letter home, expounding on our recent adventures (I always omitted the scariest incidents). I told them we were camped at Olduvai Gorge and I'd held Leakey's fossils in my hands.

Continuing on another track, I asked my dad to let me know the price of a roll of Kodachrome film. *National Geographic* supplied Ross with more film than he could use and he sold the excess to Alan and me at what I thought were inflated prices. The whole deal annoyed me. After all, Alan and I had very little money and Ross was getting the film for free.

I sighed, sealed up the letter, turned out the light, and took a last look out over the starlit Olduvai Gorge before climbing up to bed.

We headed east the next day, leaving behind my hopes of working at Olduvai. Next stop, Ngorongoro Crater. We picked up a guide at the park entrance and descended the steep walls of the caldera. On the fifty-mile-wide volcano floor, African wildlife lived together in their own ecosystem. We watched eight lion cubs leap and tumble around their "sleeping" mothers, found our way through herds of antelope, and saw "George the Rhino" pee a torrent, the sight of which will stay locked in my brain forever. After spending a night surrounded by various animal voices and unfamiliar sounds, we continued on the next day.

The truck ground its way back up the four-wheel-drive track to the rainforest on the crater's narrow rim, then across to Lake Manyara in the Great Rift Valley. Winding down the impressive escarpment into the valley, we passed through tropical banana belts and coffee plantations, then on to the little gem of a town called Arusha.

While buying groceries at the largest store I'd seen in weeks, Ross struck up a conversation with a gray-haired couple. We were always a novelty. People often asked us who we were and what we were doing, and Ross never missed an opportunity to explain we were an entomology expedition from the California Academy of Sciences, and that he was a *National Geographic* photographer. The Thatchers—a couple from the Tanzanian Game Department—were suitably impressed, and invited us to camp at their house for the night.

After climbing the side of another tiny, volcanic crater, we parked the truck in the Thatchers' sweet garden overlooking a tiny caldera lake. A purple jacaranda tree's branches framed our first view of Mount

Kilimanjaro floating in clouds. Inviting us into their home, Mrs. Thatcher offered the greatest luxury possible: access to her bathroom. She let us know that due to the limitations of their hot water supply, we needed to take our baths in only a few inches of water. I accepted the female privilege offered to me: having the first bath. Lying back into five inches of hot water rivaled the most luxurious spa treatment ever!

That evening, while we enjoyed the non-camp food—fried chicken dinner—Mr. Thatcher began excitedly expressing his optimism for Tanzania's new government. Despite our rather unnerving experience of being stoned by children after entering the country, he assured us everything was getting better, and that Julius Nyerere was a brilliant, charismatic leader with high ideals. Rural border towns still suffered from the sudden loss of supporting businesses due to "white-flight" out of the country, but Mr. Thatcher said he, like other whites who'd decided to stay, were welcomed into the spirit of equality integral to a newly socialistic country. He talked with great optimism about new chicken farms being established to feed the population, and other such communal enterprises.

During my youth, communism had held a social standing akin to Satanism, and socialism followed in a close third place. Now I wrestled with this new-to-me idea of what a socialist form of government might look like. Thinking in terms of the interconnection of all life, I realized an egalitarian form of government fit my new worldview far better than the competitive capitalism America represented. The Thatchers' optimism and desire to join with others for the betterment of all seemed far more appealing than the precept that each person must climb his or her own way "up the corporate ladder," often stepping on the lives of others to better their own. I thought again of the barefoot man who had ferried us across the small river in Botswana compared to the fat-bellied millionaire who gambled away thousands so placidly at Victoria Falls. Much remained for me to ponder in terms of my future life. That night, lying in my sleeping bag, I wrote down many soul-searching thoughts and wondered what role I might play within them: politics? teaching? writing? social work? I preserved these ideas for future consideration.

We left the comfort of the Thatchers' home to journey to the twin craters of Ngurdoto. Winding past a lake that nearly filled the caldera of the first mini-volcano, we paused at the rim to photograph a herd of elephants grazing in the dripping rainforest. As we stood outside the truck, one annoyed mother turned toward us and flapped her huge African elephant ears, a sign of displeasure. Retreating into the truck, we drove away just as she decided to pursue us with a full, trumpeting charge. We bumped away as quickly as the road allowed. I thought again of the man we'd met in Cape Town who'd been crippled by the elephant that trampled his Land Rover. A truck offered little security against an enraged elephant.

The road wound up through a dense forest to the rim of the sister Ngurdoto crater. We clambered out of the truck, appreciating its four-wheel drive slithering us to the end of the road. In the inaccessible caldera far below, animals appeared as if on a stage. Seemingly miniature giraffes, zebras, and antelope dotted the grasses. A rainbow of butterflies fluttered around us. The guys set off to collect, and I followed a black-and-white colobus monkey, trying to get an artsy photograph as it leapt between trees above me. The monkey's long tail ended in a clump of feathery white fur that sailed behind it with every leap. After nearly an hour traipsing after it, I gave up, only having captured a blurry shot through a gap in the branches.

Following the monkey through a true jungle, I felt like a fairy sprite in a magical land. I thought of Sausalito, when I'd smoked hashish at Super Spade's house. I felt just as high, but instead of detachment from others, I felt connected. The threads of Tapestry wove ancient patterns in this untouched section of the planet, and I was a part of those patterns.

After a few hours, I was still reluctant to return to the truck. My joy slid from my chest to lodge itself somewhere in my lower body, morphing slowly into resignation as I caught sight of the two men swinging their butterfly nets. Winged jewels were swept from the forest to be spread between cotton layers inside cardboard cigar boxes, then stored in a chamber in the back of the truck, waiting to be analyzed, studied, and classified by academy scientists in California, or, perhaps, left to gather dust and be forgotten in the museum's basement. I wrapped my fairy wonderland experience around my heart, smiled past the guys, and found my journal, writing down the afternoon's experiences before they, too, were forgotten like a butterfly's dusty corpse.

When the sun was nearing the horizon, we headed back the way we'd come, past where we'd encountered the elephant herd, but we saw no sign of them. I was riding in the seat behind Ross and looking out the window, mentally reliving my stroll through the forest. We were passing along a roadcut about the same height as our truck. I suddenly saw gray legs pounding along, just a few yards from the top of my window. The still-angry mama-elephant was running above us at full speed. She hadn't forgotten us.

"Floor it!" I screamed.

Luckily, Ross responded to the imperative in my voice and jammed the accelerator to the floor. One elephant leap would have landed her ponderous body squarely on top of our roof. Despite the rutty track we raced along, Ross managed to hold the truck steady until we outdistanced her.

Sighing in mutual relief, we began winding down the inside wall of the first crater. The road curved around the small lake on the floor of the caldera. Ross chose a grassy beach for our campsite.

During dinner, we discussed our two near-misses dealing with an angry African elephant. Ross pulled out our nearly empty gin bottle, and I found a withering lemon. Mixing a bit of both, we toasted to our escapes.

Just as light faded and I had finished washing the last of the dinner dishes, Alan stood, pointing out elephants on the far side of the lake. Ambling down for a drink came the herd we had twice escaped! Ross threw more wood on the fire as they waded into the water. A ranger had told us to keep a fire burning when elephants were near, and to remain quiet since they might charge if startled. While the animals drank and splashed on the far side of the lake, we all began quietly gathering more firewood to pile beside the truck. Moonlight reflections played across the water as my anxiety increased. The lake was shallow; the elephants were wading across toward our side. I grabbed my bedding and tape recorder and announced I would be sleeping inside the cab that night. The herd communicated with a wide repertoire of noises. I hoped I could at least get some interesting recordings out of this experience. Ross piled wood on the fire. The elephants drew closer. Ross and Alan retreated up the ladder and into the tent. I began recording elephant noises. The pachyderms huffed out of the water and started grazing around us. Shuffling and munching sounds imprinted onto my turning tapes. Eventually, as the night quieted, I turned off the recorder and tried to sleep.

Morning light angled through the windshield when I slowly opened my eyes. Bird and frog sounds greeted my ears, but I strained to hear anything *elephantish* beneath them. Not daring to sit up until I felt certain I wouldn't be eye-to-eye with something enormous and gray, I lay still. A leathery, slapping sound came from nearby. Elephant ears? Flapping against insects on elephant bodies? The herd must still be right outside. Frozen, I listened for movement from the tent above me, hoping the men would have sense enough to stay put, but also hoping my bladder would hold out until the animals decided to move on. All stayed quiet above.

After what seemed like hours, the huffing and slapping grew more distant, and I prayed the elephants had finally ambled off. Human footsteps sounded on the ladder, tentatively coming down from the tent. "All clear." Alan's voice was a stage whisper. I gave a prayer of thanks for the strength of my bladder as I rose up slowly from the front seat and scrambled outside to relieve myself and begin making breakfast.

We packed up and headed north toward Amboseli Park, following another small, dirt track. Where our road crossed into Kenya, we were surprised to find that instead of a border guard station, a homemade banner stretched over the road declaring, "Welcome Home Our President Mzee Jomo Kenyatta." Kenyatta was the first president of Kenya after the Mau Mau Rebellion that liberated their country from the British. Kenyatta was a Kikuyu, but was known to have been successful in uniting the country's various tribes. We gathered he must be about to return from a visit to Tanzania.

We drove under the banner, slowly passing spear-carrying Maasai moran warriors lining the left side of the road. Red sarongs covered the men's ochre-painted bodies. Powerful chanting accompanied their high, stiff-legged leaps.

On the opposite side of the road, a line of Kikuyu, clad with elaborate beadwork, shuffled along in a narrow ellipse, singing a song of their own. We crept along between the two groups and parked the truck a small distance from the dancing.

The two tribes were not friendly companions. Maasai herd cattle: we'd been told they believed all the cattle on Earth belonged to them. During raids on neighboring Kikuyu villages, they consider the "reclaimed" cattle rightfully theirs. This practice in no way endeared them to the Kikuyu. The dueling dancing going on along the road felt like high-tension challenges, not at all like a joyful celebration.

Although our white skin must have glowed like a neon sign, we tried to remain inconspicuous at the edges of the crowd. A safari-jacket-clad white couple appeared at my elbow and spoke into my ear.

"You mustn't take pictures."

Startled, I turned toward the woman.

"Don't let anyone see you with that camera," she continued whispering, inches from my ear. "Just last week, a Maasai moran—a warrior—thrust his spear through the arm of an American girl who took his picture without permission." She looked at me with wide eyes, nodding toward my tape recorder too. Whispering back my thanks, I turned to pass the information on to Ross and Alan, before quickly scuttling all my recording devices back into the truck.

Just as we were returning, two motorcycles sped under the banner, followed by a long, black limousine flying flags over each of its headlights. Pulling to a stop in the center of the street, a car door opened and Jomo Kenyatta stepped out, looking dignified and presidential in his black suit. Short and somewhat stocky like the other Kikuyu, he paused for a minute, observing both groups of dancers. Quietly turning, he walked, not to his fellow Kikuyu, but to the line of tall, thin Maasai on the opposite side of the road. After nodding his head in rhythm to their chant, he began leaping alongside the men. Almost immediately, the groups dissolved, everyone pouring into the street, cheering Kenyatta and dancing together. All tension drained away, transforming the scene into an ecstatic celebration. Dancers mixed in a colorful melee of joy. My heart filled. I felt privileged to be able to observe such a powerful example of the leadership this man brought to his country.

Africa's political awakenings were beginning to impress me: Julius Nyerere in Tanzania and Jomo Kenyatta in Kenya. Two new charismatic leaders who were uniting their countries. Maybe others were experimenting with less hierarchical systems before my own country did. I knew from anthropology that Africa had a history of thousands of years—maybe tens of thousands of years—where many tribes had sustainable, egalitarian cultures. Should this be my cause in life? Should I try to bring a more equitable social system to my own country? I felt I had so much more to learn from Africa.

That night, we camped at beautiful Amboseli. Bugs of all kinds flew around our lights as I finished washing the dishes. I had a bad headache and was disgusted with so many bugs, so I headed up to bed early while Ross and Alan draped a white tarp on the side of the truck under the lights, intentionally attracting as many bugs as they could.

During my breakfast preparations the next morning, I felt honored to be in the company of at least two dozen colorful birds pecking their way through last night's layers of insects piled on the tarp. So intent were they on their feast that I had to shoo them out of my workspace. Ross and Alan happily filled numerous collecting bottles with bugs of every shape and size before shaking out the tarp and loading up the truck. Around noon that day, my headache returned, full-blast. Alan felt my forehead and declared I had quite a fever. I began to worry about sleeping sickness from my multitudinous tsetse-fly bites. Encephalitis had a recurring fever as one of its symptoms. It was almost always fatal. I thought I had come to terms with death during the airplane flight, but had I really? That was my imagined death, but what if this were my real death? What if some little parasite had taken up residence in my body and was eating its way through my tissues until my body gave out? The possibility gave me the creepy-crawlies. Now I would have to look the prospect of this corporeal death squarely in the face.

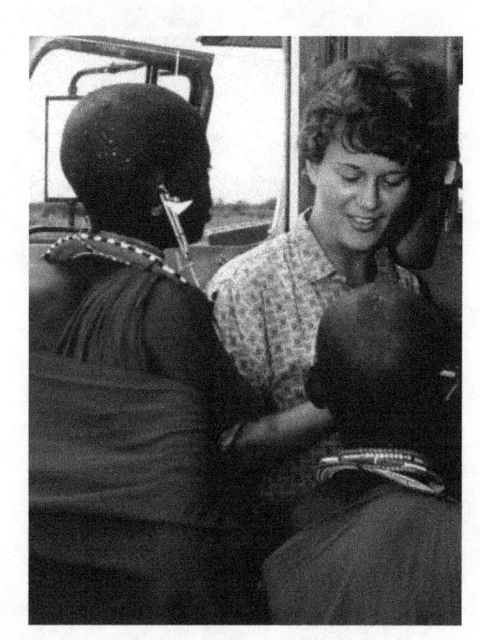

Carol with Maasai girls.

A pattern had developed by the time we camped a few miles outside Nairobi. I would feel relatively normal for a while, but then my head seemed to grow into a monstrous balloon. I would hold it with both hands when I stood, convinced it had become too huge to balance on my shoulders. Ross said my fever cycles were consistent with parasite infections. He explained that one's immune system would kick in when they'd used our bodies to produce a new generation of offspring. After a die-off, the parasites built up again at a rate specific to that particular species. We were all relieved my illness did not have the four-hour cycle typical of encephalitis. Days would pass before I'd begin to feel normal, then the fever would hit again. We determined that whatever the disease was, it had about a four-day cycle.

When the fevers came, Alan had to take over my duties as camp chef. I could do little more than lie on my mattress in our tent. I was trying to detach from the pain one evening when voices drifted up to me.

"You don't cut cabbage that way!" Ross's voice rose into my fogged brain.

"But that's how you cut it for coleslaw." Alan attempted to defend his salad-making skills.

"Squares! Small squares! Here. Cut it like this into small squares."

Even though my head was surely going to explode, I couldn't help giggling to hear Alan experiencing firsthand what I'd been putting up with for four months. In Ross's opinion, there was only one way to do almost anything, and he had never shied from letting me know exactly what that was. Alan had never been unkind, but he also never stood up for me when Ross attacked. He undoubtedly hadn't been immune to Ross's directives either, but I quietly enjoyed hearing Alan getting reprimanded in what previously had been my domain. I rolled onto my side, careful to bring my head along with the rest of my body, and tried to shut out their voices and fall asleep.

A few days later, Ross drove me to the hospital in Nairobi where I was examined, blood was taken, and I was given some pills for vitamin-C deficiency. None of us believed my problem could be that simple, and when the fever hit again at noon, everybody was on edge. Fearing the worst, we all agreed I should book a ticket home. I loved Africa and had made countless plans to stay, but I now had the prospect of possibly never making it back home. We found a travel agent and I booked a flight through Rome to San Francisco for the following Thursday.

During my good periods, we all tried to believe the fevers were gone. We decided to camp near a Maasai village outside Nairobi. I was excited about visiting this village. Perhaps I could compensate for my lack of data collection in the Namib by learning something of these people.

A dusty car drove up to where we were camped. Two women and a gray-haired man got out to greet us. They introduced themselves as professors from the University of Nairobi: John and Betty Hemmingway, a biochemist and his wife, and to my great joy, Jean Brown, a woman doing anthropological fieldwork. They had come out to spend several days in the village and they agreed to let me accompany them.

The Maasai were not known to be friendly to outsiders, so I had some trepidation as I followed Jean into their village. I listened eagerly to everything she shared with me about the Maasai culture. Fences made of tangled thorn bushes enclosed their living compounds, or "bomas." Jean was already known in this village and welcomed with a conversation in what I recognized as Swahili.

"They've invited us into their home," she translated for me.

Crouching to almost a crawl, I tried not to breathe too deeply as we entered a circular dome made of mud mixed with cow dung. We semi-crawled through a tunnel that spiraled into the interior room of a large, round hut. In a niche along the way, a sick calf watched us pass. When we reached the center room, a grandmother holding an infant looked up at us with startled eyes. The young man who had led us in quickly spoke to her. She grunted her acceptance. There was little to see in the dim light, so we turned to make our way back out.

To my great relief, no one offered us a drink from the hollow gourds our hosts wore hanging from their shoulders. The stench of their main food, a curdled yogurt of milk and blood from their cows, would have challenged my cultural politeness. The Maasai felt foreign and peculiar to my American sensibilities, and I was glad I had spent a month in a Nama village, not in one of theirs. Finding a place of universal commonality might have eluded me here.

Outside the hut, we sat down with several women under a copse of acacia trees. They wore wide, beaded collars and earrings that hung beneath their elongated earlobes. Flies buzzed everywhere. Even with months on the expedition, I still could not ignore so many insects landing on me. The Maasai women seemed unperturbed. Flies walked unmolested across their naked legs as they sat chatting.

Jean Brown translated their Swahili conversation for me: they were stringing beads to make necklaces for a young girl's wedding. The barely pubescent bride-to-be joined us. I guessed she must not be more than twelve or thirteen. The older women teased her and she glowed and giggled with happiness.

In the few hours we spent with those women, I again felt a connection. Some of their customs were difficult for me, but our similarities outweighed those differences. I didn't understand their words, but surmised that the elder women were affectionately teasing the young bride and offering advice for her upcoming marriage, a custom at our own bridal showers. Preparations for weddings might take many forms, but the excitement and expectations seemed to be cultural universals.

As we headed over to another compound, Jean told me about a position for an anthropologist opening in Nairobi, encouraging me to apply. We were discussing

Maasai bride, Kenya.

that possibility when my head began to ache again. I hoped it was merely from the heat, but soon my fever returned full force, making us cut the visit short and putting a huge damper on my anthropological hopes.

Apologizing to Jean and thanking her for the extraordinary visit, I returned to the truck and climbed onto my mattress while Alan started a fire to make dinner. John and Betty Hemmingway, the biochemist and his wife, appeared in our camp. They told Ross that since I was obviously sick, they would take me home with them and make certain I got to the airport for my flight back to the States. Ross readily agreed. Perhaps too readily? Before I had a chance to understand what was happening, Alan gave me a hug and wished me well. Ross and I exchanged formal, cool goodbyes. Semi-delirious, I let everyone else make decisions about my life. My new guardians helped me gather up my meager possessions and leave the expedition to take me to their home in Nairobi. It was such an odd ending to our expedition that I wondered if everyone believed my death was imminent.

In and out of a raging fever, I remember little of the conversation I sought to carry on during the journey in the comfortable backseat of the Hemmingways' beige Peugeot. Arriving at their suburban Nairobi home, I followed Betty through a tidy front garden. Cradling my painful, cotton-candy head, I gratefully accepted the offer of a warm bath and clean, fluffy towels. The luxury of a steaming bathtub filled to the brim with clear hot water penetrated my jumbled, incoherent mind. Betty probably offered the bath in self-defense. Other than my one shallow bath in Arusha, the months of occasional wipe-downs with rinsed underwear must have left me smelling like something other than a rose. I soaked in that tub so long the water turned cold and my fever began to abate. I reached for a downy towel before donning the terrycloth robe Betty had hung for me on the bathroom door. I vowed to never again take hot, running water for granted.

Padding out of the bathroom, I learned that all my clothing were following the same sequence of events as my body. Betty had dumped the lot into her washing machine: safari pants, khaki shirts, and the sleeveless, purple, Guatemala cloth shift that I wore in every town.

John Hemmingway was sitting cross-legged on a cushion in their living room. Having had only my father and his friends as models for chemists' behaviors, I thought his position odd. He gestured to a cushion opposite him. I sank down and made myself comfortable, while Betty brought me strong, hot tea, generously laced with sugar and real cream. I felt certain I must have died of the fever, and having led a sufficiently saintly life, ascended into heaven.

To my surprise and with no preamble, John leaned forward and began speaking to me about my life. "You've encountered a new understanding of reality," John asserted, blue eyes calm but penetrating beneath his bushy brows.

I didn't recall having told the Hemmingways about my airplane experience. I couldn't contradict him, because what he said was true, however odd it was to hear it from him. Unable to question his assertion, I nodded in agreement. "I am calling it the 'Tapestry'," I responded.

John leaned back and smiled his approval. "Ah, yes. Perhaps you might call it the 'Cosmic Tapestry,' right?"

I nodded again and he continued. "Sitting like this, speaking from the place of all connection you recently discovered, we are surrounded by Light."

I knew he didn't mean sunlight. There did seem to be a peaceful energy cocooning the space we occupied together. He continued into a discussion of "light" and reincarnation.

"I have studied Eastern philosophies for many years. Although you've only recently come to terms with death, you will soon learn the reality of reincarnation."

Reincarnation a reality? I was not ready to embrace that idea. My airplane experience left me ecstatic about uniting my consciousness with the rest of the Universe. I wasn't pleased about the possibility of reentering life as a returning human.

John rebutted my unspoken thoughts. "Although you don't yet know the truth of this, you will struggle with it for quite a while and will come to understand."

Was he reading my mind? How did he know so much about me?

"You have had a glimpse into Nirvana, the final ending we all hope for, but it's not so easy to get there. I'll send you a list of books you could read. First, you might want to read *Autobiography of a Yogi* by Yogananda. In case you find you can't believe his book, I assure you that what's in it does happen."

I stayed silent. As we faced each other on cushions in a middle-class African home, the remnants of my fever kept me from wondering at the strangeness of a science professor interpreting the meaning behind my recent revelations. This man might be sharing deep truths with me, and I feared there was no way I'd remember them. I hoped he would follow through and send me his list of books.

"Functioning in your newfound world of unity here in Africa is easy for you," Mr. Hemmingway continued. "The trick will be doing the same back home. You were born in the United States for a reason, and carrying this new knowledge back with you may be that reason." He leaned forward and looked into the soul lurking behind my eyes. "The comprehension of the unity of all will remain a gift that has changed your life forever."

By the next day, my fever had not recurred. The Hemmingways packaged me up and put me on a plane to Rome, where I would catch another plane to San Francisco. From the moment of my abduction outside the Maasai village, I'd willingly allowed my life to be governed by these generous benefactors. Boarding the plane at the Nairobi airport, I waved goodbye, wondering at the nature of a Universe that just supplied me, however improbably, with precisely the people I needed.

I buckled myself into a window seat on the Qantas jet. Night had fallen on the continent of Africa. Nairobi's lights twinkled outside as the plane taxied down the runway and began its ascent. The book I laid on the tray table slid into my lap, so steeply were we rising. I closed my eyes, wondering if I'd ever return to Africa, hoping I might do so someday with a congenial partner who would share my wonder at this vast and incredible continent. Every part of our bumping, four-month journey across the barely existent roads of sub-Saharan Africa had held unexpected gems. From elephant charges to drum-filled nights, thousands of experiences had awed, terrified, delighted, amused, educated, and thrilled me. When I stood on that point overlooking Victoria Falls, when rainbows completely encircled me, Africa's antiquity poured over me, as soothing and comforting as an exotic oil from Cleopatra's bath. My Universe had been altered. I was living in a newfound, yet ancient, reality.

After I got home, would I be cured of whatever was happening to my body? Feeling certain my fevers would reoccur, my greatest concern—with my death no longer hypothetical or distant—was whether I'd make it home while still able to function. I carried with me my imagined death on the airplane when flying to Africa; the memory of it served to lessen the emotional trauma of my illness. Maybe my fever was simply a trick the Universe was using to make sure I didn't back out, that I returned home and put my newfound worldview to use. My life might still be scriptless. But Africa had given me a foundation upon which my personal script could be written.

To my surprise, as the plane ascended and Africa shrunk below me, I found that flying was now easy, perhaps even enjoyable. I experienced a sense of comfort contemplating my body's inevitable mortality. My brain realigned with feelings of belonging, with an acceptance of my consciousness as indivisible from the rest of the Universe.

THIRTEEN

After stopping in Athens and changing planes in Rome, I peered out the window as Pan American's Boeing 707 jetliner began its descent over San Francisco Bay. My mind swirled; how would I reenter this world I called "home?" I watched Oakland and San Jose sparkle beneath me while the plane circled in for a landing. Minutes later, after skimming over choppy waves, the plane thumped safely onto the ground, officially ending my four-month-long adventure into another world and another worldview. I exited the airport gate and stumbled into the arms of my waiting parents.

I'd telegraphed Mom and Dad the time of my flight, but hadn't mentioned anything about the illness that precipitated my return. Since we'd never had a definite date for the end of the trip, they had no questions about my arrival. Luckily, I was in one of my states of remission, so I had no headache or fever. To them, I appeared normal and healthy.

"Are you hungry? What kind of food have you missed the most? Where would you like to eat?" Although my mother's concerns and joys often focused on meals and restaurants, the empathy in that simple question surprised me. I felt a surge of warmth for my mother.

"A salad! With blue cheese dressing!" The image of fresh, crispy lettuce with creamy chunks of blue cheese seemed a tonic after months and months of heat-tolerant, durable cabbage being our only fresh green vegetable.

We headed to baggage claim, where Dad grabbed my African-dust-covered, once-white, Samsonite suitcase.

We found a restaurant, and I savored each crunch of lettuce, happily licking blue cheese dressing off my lips. The meal passed easily with small talk concerning events in each of our lives. Theirs a bit less exotic than mine, but no less important in our individual minds.

Sitting in the backseat of their pale-yellow Pontiac, I looked at the familiar back of my dad's head as he piloted the car through the streets of San Francisco. He had been the confident leader of all the family's expeditions throughout my childhood. Last time I'd looked at that head from the car's backseat, I'd had no understanding of the Tapestry. My dad was a scientist, a research chemist. All my life I'd been blessed with the opportunity to share any questions I had concerning the nature of this world with a brilliant man who enjoyed scientific inquiry. After my arrival in Africa, I had written a letter trying to explain my airplane experience and the powerful shift in my worldview. Dad's reply, in a letter that we picked up at *poste restante* in Windhoek, had sounded skeptical at best. Although both Dad and John Hemmingway were chemists, the two men's views of reality couldn't have contrasted more. Twenty-four hours, twelve thousand miles, and entire mental universes separated these two men. What should I do now? Drop the whole subject?

I watched the rectangular towers of the San Francisco-Oakland Bay Bridge slip past outside my window. The Tapestry messed with the ideas I'd had for my future. We all had more or less assumed that one day I would return to a university and pursue a graduate degree in anthropology. Now I felt a more pressing need to do something more direct to help change the inequities of our country. How would my parents respond to a change in the direction of my life path?

Riding along on the smooth, rut-free, elevated freeway across Oakland and Alameda, there was no need to brace my hands against the roof in anticipation of the next bump. I marveled at the substantial houses we passed that weren't made of straw and dung. Even though each house might be a mansion compared to those in the villages of Africa, these houses were nothing like my parents' home in Orinda. Inequities separated the two sides of the Berkeley Hills. What if I did something like teach in an inner-city school? That might be a place where I could make a difference. Inner-city kids needed a positive start in academic life, and they weren't being offered that in Oakland's underfunded, understaffed schools. Maybe I should look into teaching programs available at the University of California.

I sighed and leaned my head against the seat as we entered the Caldecott Tunnel, emerging a mile later on the wealthier side of the east-bay hills. During my childhood, Orinda had been a small town sprawling through rolling hills dotted with spreading oaks. But now it had become a wealthy bedroom community, insulated from Oakland and "others" by the mass of the Berkeley Hills. Dad drove us past the business section of Orinda, still referred to as "the Crossroads" it once had been, onto Tara Road, and up the driveway of my parents' adobe-brick house.

Dad carried my suitcase into a pink-and-white bedroom. I said my goodnights and climbed into a welcoming bed. I'd tell everyone about my illness and deal with any future decisions in the morning. For now, I simply felt a bubbling gratitude to have made it home, still alive, and hopefully, still with a chance for a future, whatever that turned out to be.

When I managed to rouse my body from bed the next morning, everyone looked up at my rumpled form shuffling into the kitchen. Two glass walls revealed a patio where birds clustered around several feeders. The kitchen smelled like a bakery: coffee and something wonderful. My sister sat in her bathrobe, sipping coffee at the glass-topped kitchen table.

Jean recently had begun working at Fly Oakland, a kind of travel agency for flights out of Oakland Airport. Her husband, Bob, was deployed in Vietnam, and for the first time in almost ten years, both Jean and I would be sharing a room in the home of our parents. I strongly objected to the war; my understanding of the Cosmic Tapestry left no room for dropping burning petroleum on people halfway around the world. Although Bob was in the signal corps and not directly killing anybody, sharing a bedroom with my sister, nevertheless, would have to be handled with conscious control and compassion.

"Guess I'm the only one missing breakfast," I muttered, walking around the table to give my sister a hug. "I never even heard you come in last night."

"You looked pretty out of it," she replied, returning my hug with an extra squeeze. Her brown eyes looked me up and down for a moment. "So, I see no elephants trampled you."

"Nope, I lucked out. Sorry about Bob. Have you heard anything recently?"

"Yeah, I sent him a 'care package' full of socks and a few artichokes, because they're his favorite thing. Of course, the box sat on a dock in the sun, so he said he got artichoke-rotted socks that weren't quite salvageable."

I gave a poignant laugh.

"Your dad's making pancakes," my mom informed me. "We were waiting for you. We hoped you'd be up before your sister had to go to work. How're you feeling?"

"Jet-lagged, but okay." I plopped down onto a white, wrought-iron chair and leaned my elbows onto the tabletop, resting my chin in my palms. "Your birds seem happy."

Dad handed me a plate: blueberry compote drizzled down a stack of small pancakes. Mom gave me coffee in a Franciscan Ware cup matching the apple-patterned dishes I'd grown up with. I took a sip and speared a bite of pancake. Since I had all of the family together, I figured now would be the time to tell them about the fever.

"I guess that I'm not really okay. I have a fever that comes back every few days. It's pretty bad."

Forks stopped midair and everyone looked over at me.

"Ross thinks it's from some kind of parasite, but he ruled out African sleeping sickness because it's not on the right cycle."

"Have you been to a doctor?" my dad asked. Concern laced his voice.

"Yep, in Nairobi. But he didn't really diagnose it."

"Well, I'll call Dr. Bulware. I bet he would squeeze you in today." Mother seemed surprisingly unfazed.

I smiled to see that no one was panicking. They hadn't seen me with the fever yet, so there was no visible cause for concern. To them, it probably seemed about the equivalent of my announcing I had strep throat or the flu. "Thanks. That would be good. I'd love to have someone figure out what this is."

Jean left for work as I finished breakfast. The appointment with my parents' doctor was made, and I marveled at how normal it all seemed. Where were the moths and mosquitoes and zebras and mud and baobab trees? Could I really just step back into an old reality and have it fit? Would all I learned in Africa quietly slip beneath the puffy, emotional comforter of familiarity?

"I think I'll go soak in the bathtub. If you don't see me for a few days, come in and see if I've drowned. Just know that if I die today in a tub of hot water, it will feel like a bit of paradise has come down to retrieve my soul." I disappeared down the hall and failed to resurface until my mother called through the bathroom door that we needed to leave soon for my appointment.

Dr. Bulware's private office at the Crossroads greeted us with the not-unpleasant smell of disinfectants. Yellow walls, a nurse with a starched cap, and a cold stethoscope pressed to my back gave me a comforting feeling of being in competent hands. I hoped this handsome-yet-fatherly man would be able to cure me. After the usual poking and prodding, when I lay back on the examination table, Dr. Bulware told me to put my hand on my stomach.

"Push there, above your navel," he suggested, prodding me himself to show where. "Feel that?"

I did. There seemed to be a large, unfamiliar bulge.

"That's your liver. It's enlarged. I think it's full of spirochetes."

"Spirochetes? That doesn't sound too good."

"They're little corkscrew-shaped bacteria. What you have is called 're-lapsing fever'."

It made sense, since my fever did keep coming back. Mom and I both must have looked confused and concerned.

"Don't worry, we can treat it. The periodicity of the fevers is due to the reproduction of the parasites. Your immune system is triggered into a strong reaction that kills a lot of them off, but the remainder build back up until your body responds again."

That sounded like what Ross had said.

"After you take the medicine, be sure to drink lots of water to flush everything out."

I sat up, putting my shirt back on as Dr. Bulware scribbled out a prescription, handing it to me as we left.

Perhaps I should have found it creepy to be hosting a bevy of wormy things in my liver, but all I heard was the part about him being able to cure me. I thanked him profusely and left with Mom to pick up the prescription at Bill's Drugs nearby. I swallowed two capsules, and Mom drove us home.

To my utter joy, the pills proved effective. My family was spared from having to watch me become semi-delirious. They never had to know the seriousness of my illness or how afraid we all had been in Africa. I suffered only one more episode of fever, far less severe than any I'd had in Africa. Lying in a comfy bed in my parents' home, I thought it ironic that after all I'd been through crossing the "dark continent," my seemingly fatal illness had been cured by a small-town physician in an American suburb. Within two weeks, I felt well enough to begin the application process for an inner-city teaching program at U.C. Berkeley and start hunting for an interim job to begin paying off my debt to Dad.

Since my return from Africa, I had stayed in touch with Steve and Libby, now apparently living comfortably together in an apartment just north of Sausalito. Libby and Steve's baby had been born, and I hoped Steve had never confessed the final words he'd said to me before their wedding. There would be no reason to, especially since they both now sounded madly in love with their new daughter. Continuing their rather surprising effort to keep me part of their lives, they had offered to make me the godmother of Tina, the baby whose creation had resulted in our strange relationship. I gratefully accepted their offer, despite the fact that throughout Libby's pregnancy I'd had a niggling, not-quite-conscious, hugely ungracious thought that Libby would probably die in childbirth. I'd found it impossible to believe that a universe might exist where Steve would be married to someone other than me, regardless of whether or not I ever decided to marry him. I accepted a dinner invitation for the next day.

Rain pelted my windshield as Dad and I picked up a fellow chemist friend in Berkeley. They were going together on a business trip to Europe to do research for the book my dad was writing. Mostly memoir, he called it *The Chain Straighteners*, a history of polymer chemistry (the invention of plastics). I dropped them at the San Francisco Airport, then headed down the peninsula for a job interview at Stanford Research Center. Dad had been working part-time there since his retirement from Shell Chemical, so I figured he had probably pulled some strings to get me the interview. I wasn't sufficiently qualified for the job they'd advertised. The people who greeted me kindly performed a perfunctory interview, but as I had suspected, made it fairly clear that I wouldn't be in contention for the position.

The Democratic presidential convention was going be taking place at the end of the summer, and one of the candidates would be speaking that day on the Stanford campus. Making my way among the neatly laid-out, red sandstone buildings, I discovered that the auditorium was already full. As an antiwar candidate, Eugene McCarthy was generating quite a bit of interest among students. Loudspeakers and extra seats had been set up in the center of the quad. Passing under one of the archways, I found a seat and settled in to listen to his speech. McCarthy sounded decidedly human, not pretentious or *politicianish*. Compared to Johnson and Nixon, he was an honest breath of fresh air. This would be the first election in which I'd be able to vote. For the moment, McCarthy had gained himself one vote.

I'd accepted the dinner invitation from Steve and Libby and headed north to meet my new goddaughter. I felt excited to hear what they thought of the widening field of presidential candidates, but was anxious as I rang the doorbell of a nondescript apartment building. I started climbing the stairs after being buzzed in. I liked Libby, and knew I would just have to adjust to this strange situation.

The door opened to reveal the blue eyes I knew so very well. "Carol's here," he called over his shoulder to an unseen Libby.

Steve had never called me Carol. Ever. His name for me was "Babe." I could not recall a time when I was anything else to him.

Libby arrived with something small, soft, and rather adorable on her shoulder. Steve's face melted into a semblance of mush as he turned to look at them.

"This is Tina." He lifted her from Libby's shoulder and looked at me with unabashed, fatherly pride.

"Adorable!" Speaking the truth required no effort on my part. This Universe where Steve and Libby lived together and fawned over a very-much-alive, adorable baby girl didn't seem so bad after all.

We sat down for a spaghetti dinner laced with surprisingly easy conversation. Later, in the living room, Tina was passed around among us like a newfound treasure, which I guessed she was. Captivated by her sweet-cheeked grins and those miniscule fingers wrapping themselves around my gargantuan thumb, I decided that this was, indeed, a totally acceptable world to be living in. I still loved Steve, Steve still loved me, but we would no longer act on that love in any physical way. Libby and I surprisingly connected on many things, not the least of which was our shared love for Tina and her dad. *Better Homes and Gardens* would never carry an article on this melding of our lives, but it seemed we might actually find it acceptable and comfortable. The situation fit into my concept of connection and Oneness far better than the old high school image of females backbiting and fighting each other over a man. Perhaps old girlfriends no longer needed to disappear from one's life. I knew that Libby, having once broken up with Steve, probably did not consider him to be the love of her life she had imagined, but the three of us were accepting and fitting into a new concept of *what is*, instead of clinging to fantasies of *what might have been*. And a sweet new life existed for all three of us to care about. Odd as it was, everything felt right about it, despite the fact that my parents could not seem to wrap their brains around why Steve and I would still be seeing each other. But my mom asked few questions after I returned from my evening in Sausalito.

Two months later, I was sitting behind the counter of Herrick Hospital's nurses' station. A gurney's wheels squeaked along the linoleum hallway as an orderly rolled a surgical patient back to his room. After my body had become free from the unwanted guests stowed away in my liver, and after a long and frustrating job search all across the Bay Area, I'd consulted an employment agency who'd found me this job as a ward clerk at the hospital in Berkeley where both my sister and I had been born. The pay was acceptable, and for the first few months, I appreciated how much I was learning. I enjoyed the sincerity and commitment of most of the people I worked with. Saving lives and healing people attracted many caring folks with great empathy for others. Even if they didn't use my words for it, they were functioning as a positive part of the Tapestry.

After I had finished training at the rehabilitation ward and been transferred to the surgery ward, however, the job circumstances had become humiliating. Nurse Zeller craned her wattle-neck over my shoulder, surveilling the way I divided out the doctor's orders onto appropriate forms. Her medicinal smell always suffocated any creative thoughts. Numbed by her ceaseless scrutiny, I felt my cerebral cortex shutting down, deciding to go on strike rather than feed me possible misinformation she would pounce on immediately. I found myself scarcely able to remember if the blue form went to the lab and the yellow form should list medications, or if it were the other way around. I grabbed a pink form, knowing it was the right one for ordering x-rays, quietly filling it out while my brain scanned itself for the solution to the blue-yellow problem. Minted, sour breath exhaled by my left ear.

An urgent loudspeaker voice echoed down the hospital corridor, pulling Nurse Zeller away from my back.

"Code blue, Room 24, Three West. Code blue, Room 24, Three West." It was the hospital's call for staff to attend a patient in cardiac arrest. My wing was Three North, surgery ward, so this call didn't require my response. Thankfully, "Heller Zeller," as the nursing staff called her, scurried off to investigate the call.

It was 2:45 p.m., an hour-and-fifteen more minutes until I could be out of there. Without the white, looming presence behind me, my brain resumed its normal functioning. I pulled out the proper forms to copy the doctor's orders, put the finished requests into the outgoing baskets, and clipped the original orders into each patient's chart folder. Just as I slipped the last one into the wheeled cart holding the folders, a semi-famous heart surgeon dressed in pale green scrubs strode down the hall.

"You must be new," he huffed, leaning across the desk and peering at the charts. "*My* patients' names are always written in red so I can easily pick them out."

I considered the cart. Each patient's name stood out in black, bold marker so the physicians could recognize their own when they arrived for rounds. He wanted his to be in red? What about the other doctors? His tone of voice clearly indicated he considered himself more important than the others. I lifted his patients' charts and handed them to him. Irritated with his arrogance, an admittedly petty idea occurred to me on how to begin my rebellion against privilege and hierarchy. When he returned the charts, I carefully removed all his patients' large nametags written in bold, black Magic Marker and replaced them with tiny-lettered tags written in a regular red pen, much too small for him to read across the counter. He probably would never "get it," but my small rebellion made me smile.

Eventually, the clock clicked its minute hand to a vertical position, signaling my release. Grabbing my gray raincoat and handwoven African bag, I made my way through a misty Bay Area rain to the brown Tempest station wagon my parents were lending me. The car was boring but reliable. I called it "Charlie Brown," and felt grateful for the use of it. Driving east, I decided to wind up through the dripping eucalyptus forests of the Berkeley Hills, trying to calm down before returning to my parents' home.

Life was running surprisingly smoothly in our reunited family. My sister and I shared a bedroom easily and respectfully. By tacit mutual consent, conversation in the house mostly stayed on noncontroversial topics. I refrained from attending any antiwar protests for the time being. Bob was stationed in Saigon, far from the front lines, which kept Jean's anxiety mostly to a minimum. Life in the McMillans' reunited family felt reasonably comfortable.

I sorted through my slides and the boxes of rocks and other collectables I'd shipped home. Everyone "oohed" and "aahed" appropriately over carved masks, desert-scavenged semiprecious stones, African cloths, jewelry, drums, and other memorabilia. As I held each object, part of me was back on salmon-colored Namibian sand, or standing under a dripping palm tree bargaining with a native craftsperson. Some of my enduring souvenirs were scattered white dots on my otherwise tanned arms—scars from tsetse-fly bites! It felt kind of exotic to be the only person in Orinda who had tsetse- bite scars.

We spent hours in the evenings watching each of the thirteen separate slide shows documenting sections of my trip. Slide shows, where a humming projector cast enlarged photos onto a beaded glass, roll-down screen, had been a tradition in our family all my life, and now the slides were not of family vacations, but my life-changing African adventure. Hornbills took flight, turquoise beetles nibbled the petals of yellow protea, and gazelles danced across my parents' living room. Neighbors and old family friends came to watch and some invited me to speak at various organizations around the area.

What about the airplane experience, the Cosmic Tapestry? I omitted any discussion of my life-altering thoughts concerning Oneness, but I began to silently obsess about the injustices in our country and the rest of the world. Forgetting about such uncomfortable topics could have been easy in the upper-middle-class comfort of isolated white Orinda. The only faces browner than my own belonged to the maids who cleaned Orinda houses. Other than the blatant inequality of the service professions, one had to venture to the other side of the hills to find even the slightest human diversity or visible hardships. The geological land masses pushed upward by the Hayward "strike-slip" fault created more than separate watersheds; the cultural divides were as powerful socially as the earthquake zones were geologically. Herrick Hospital was situated on the western side of the Berkeley Hills. Each day I drove my mother's borrowed car back and forth across the cultural/geological divisions between contrasting worlds.

I'd been accepted into the teaching certification program at U.C. Berkeley designed to create much-needed, inner-city elementary school teachers. The internship program seemed an appropriate direction for my life. Not having been considered the nurturing type as a child—I had hated dolls and playing "house"—I'd never imagined myself as a schoolteacher. Africa had given me a different perspective. By teaching in inner-city Oakland, I could try to give children of diverse backgrounds a leg up into the society in which we were required to function. I wanted them to gain essential tools. But as an anthropologist, I also wanted them to honor and carry on the cultural systems they had been born into.

The job at Herrick Hospital felt stifling; my small rebellion with the charts did little to fill my need to advocate for change. Nurse Zeller's constantly nagging presence was draining my brain of its ability to function. Although I needed the money, I also needed out.

Passing a monster roadcut where winter rains caused mud to slide across the highway every year, I gripped the steering wheel. Sighing deeply, I made a decision. I had just enough money to limp along for a few months, and living in my parents' house, I could get by. Heller Zeller was going to be history. Hopefully I could find more useful and stimulating employment.

The front doorbell chimed as I reached to peg a pair of shorts onto the wire clothesline in my parents' backyard. Hurrying inside, I crossed the mustard-yellow Navajo rug I'd bought while working in the southwest two summers before. Pulling open the front door, I smiled to see Dorothy

Williams, one of my parents' best friends. Graying, permed hair bobbed with her usual little head tic, accompanied by pursed lips and a tight smile that always preceded her speech.

"Hello, Carol. It's so good to see you healthy."

It had been quite a while since the fevers had gone. I stepped aside to welcome her in.

"I can only stay a moment, but it was you I wanted to see anyway." Dorothy perched her skinny body on the edge of the brown-plaid living room sofa as my mom came in from the kitchen. "Your mother told me you were no longer working at the hospital, and I wanted to tell you about a position at the church."

Dorothy snapped open the clasp of the purse she was balancing on her knees. Rummaging, she pulled out a many-folded square of paper and held it toward me with a slight hand tremor.

I undid several folds of the proffered document before it opened out and I could see an advertisement for a summer children's program.

"Project F.O.C.U.S.," it read, "Fruitvale-Orinda Christian Unity Summer."

"They're looking for an assistant director. The director has been hired already, but they need an assistant who will start organizing the program until he's done with his classes at Berkeley this spring. It's only for the summer, but the pay is good."

A summer church camp? Still looking at Dorothy, I tried not to screw up my face. Although a maroon Bible with "Carol Ann McMillan" printed in gold letters on the cover sat on a shelf in the bedroom—my reward for perfect attendance in Sunday school at the Orinda Community Church—I hadn't attended a service there in more than ten years. The job she described sounded like it would fit me about as well as a three-fingered glove.

"Where is Fruitvale?" I asked, trying to be innocuously polite.

"In Oakland. It's a district. Central Oakland, but more toward San Leandro. We're partnering with a Fruitvale church. We have a grant to bus kids between the sites. We'll offer different activities and try to integrate the children. Fruitvale has mostly Negro families."

And Orinda is all white, I finished for her in my mind. This was interesting. Dorothy Williams was trying to do something to integrate Orinda, to brown-up its whiteness, perhaps? We had all suffered the recent shock of Dr. Martin Luther King Jr. being assassinated. Maybe even isolated suburbanites were starting to pay attention to the civil rights movement. Now, I was intrigued.

"When does it start?"

"If you meet with the churches and want to take the position, you probably could start right away."

Knowing the open, non-doctrine of the Community Church, I realized that there would be no proselytizing; nobody would be running this program in order to convert children to a particular religion. I would have a chance to become more familiar with inner-city Oakland, and let's face it, I needed a job.

"Thanks, Dorothy. That does sound interesting. I'll check it out tomorrow." I hoped my shocked surprise at the church's attempt at integration didn't carry through in the tone of my voice.

Dorothy licked her lips and squeezed them together as she made a jerky little turn toward my mother. "Frances, I won't stay for tea or anything. I was just coming back from the church and I thought I'd drop this off for Carol. Will you and Frank be at the Pollaczeks' tomorrow?"

I let Mom lead Dorothy to the door while I settled down to look at the flyer. Teenagers from both areas would serve as counselors. There would be arts and crafts, hiking, and sports. Apparently, several Orinda families were offering their swimming pools. I had to smile at a mental image of inner-city Black teenagers serving as lifeguards in the manicured backyards of Orinda matrons. There might be more than a little culture shock taking place from both sides. Did the organizers realize they will be showing Oakland children everything that their families didn't have? But the intention seemed good-hearted. I would certainly check this out.

The next day, I became the acting director of the Fruitvale Orinda Christian Unity Summer program. Everyone I met who was involved with the program seemed genuinely committed to doing something, however small, to follow the lead and words of Martin Luther King. For several weeks, we planned the program, hired staff, organized volunteers, arranged for busses, and lined up locations for activities.

Every day, someone reminded me that I only held the position of *acting* director, and that we were lucky to have hired Peter Feuille as the new director. Peter Feuille was a PhD student in the industrial relations department at U.C. Berkeley. His exams were almost over. He'd join us soon! Everyone assured me he would be excellent at organizing and structuring our program. Meanwhile, I continued to organize and structure the program. None of us had met the mysterious Peter Feuille.

A bit of resentment began prickling its way through my body. Who had hired this guy, and had they signed some kind of contract with him? Wasn't he a bit late? I'd done almost all the organizing; why hand it to him on a silver platter? Couldn't he come in as *my* assistant? I knew the real answer: he was male and I was female. In 1968, organizations needed a man in charge; a woman would not be the boss of a man.

Finally, the day came for the first all-staff meeting. Everyone involved with the program was gathered at a large hall in Oakland. I arrived a bit late since I'd run into traffic on my way from Orinda. Conversation and milling bodies already filled the room when I climbed the gray stone steps and pushed my way inside the double doors. Draping my coat over a chair, I began chatting with the program's secretary.

"Have you met him yet?" she asked, almost giggling.

"Who?"

"Peter Feuille, of course!"

"Is he here?" I craned my neck to look around for some face I'd not seen before.

"Right over there. The blonde guy with the mustache."

I let my gaze follow the line of her pointing finger. Blonde, athletic, blue-eyed, somewhat resembling Robert Redford: Peter Feuille stood slightly taller than the Oakland director he was chatting with.

My body responded much faster than my brain. Nearly a year had passed since I had been anything other than celibate. Several of my internal organs petitioned the rest of my body to end that condition.

I lowered my gaze and began winding my way through the bodies impeding my mission. My hormones boiled away conflicting professional thoughts as I snaked across the room to meet my new boss. Peter would be my boss only for the next three months, and any other role for him waited to be determined.

"Hi, I'm Carol. Acting commander until this moment." I reached out a hand to shake his.

Peter Feuille.

Deep-set blue eyes smiled back at me. "Peter Feuille."

"I know." I tried to ignore the color I felt pinking my cheeks. "We've been waiting for you. But things are pretty well on track. I think it's going to be a good program." Did that sound inane?

"I actually have one more exam tomorrow morning, but then we'll have to have a long meeting so you can fill me in on what's what."

"Excellent." A long meeting might be delightful.

We turned away from each other as the meeting was called to order.

There was a small conference at the Orinda Church the next morning. Five of us shared our first impressions of the new director (well, I didn't share all of mine), and discussed how we would bring him up to speed. They said he and I would have to be joint directors until Peter gained sufficient knowledge to take over completely. I had no objections to that plan. I refrained from pointing out that things could be much simpler if *I* just remained in charge, but was disappointed that no one else thought to point that out. As the meeting broke up, one woman held up a blue binder.

"Peter left one of his class notebooks at the hall yesterday. I bet he might need it."

My lie came swifter than a lion could pounce. "I have to go into Oakland anyway today. I'll take it to him. Does anyone have his address?"

My hormone-laden claws were out and my prey was unsuspecting.

FOURTEEN

Telegraph Avenue ran from the University of California campus in Berkeley all the way into downtown Oakland. Peter's address was on Telegraph, but I wasn't sure which direction to turn as I came down the freeway from the Caldecott Tunnel. Guessing that a graduate student would find cheaper housing in Oakland, I turned south into that city.

I drove along a not-very-residential section of Telegraph, peering at street numbers in an attempt to find Peter's apartment building. When I reached what had to be the right block, I turned onto a side street. A small sign stood beside the alley leading into a parking lot; its numbers matched the address I'd been given. The dirty, peach-yellow building to my right looked more like a 1950s motel than a residence. A large black numeral "6" on the corner door identified Peter's apartment.

This is it. Peter's apartment. Am I really doing this? A cautious part of my brain queried the more adventurous side that had brought me here.

Unannounced. He has no idea I'm coming. He might be making out with his girlfriend right now. He might be smoking marijuana. Heck, he might not even remember meeting me! I'll have to reintroduce myself, give him context if he opens the door. Could meeting Peter be scarier than lions, elephants, and tsetse flies? Get a grip, woman! Go for it!

Seeing no doorbell, I banged my knuckles loudly against the door, compensating for the chicken-shit conversation going on in my head. My heart did a little jitterbug when the door opened to reveal Peter in a white T-shirt and torn blue jeans. My eyes fell to the ripped fabric across the top of his left thigh, a most interesting tear. I quickly moved my gaze up to meet the smiling blue eyes about half a foot above my own.

"Hi, I'm Carol. From FOCUS."

"Right. Come in." No hesitation. He even seemed pleased to see me.

Formica-topped table on the left. A dribble of stains leading across the lentil-soup-colored carpet to a utilitarian kitchen.

Peter gestured toward a boxy couch, the color reminiscent of partially digested brussels sprouts.

Yep, definitely a graduate-student apartment. I felt seriously overdressed in the blue-and-white minidress I'd chosen for its sex appeal.

"You left this notebook in Orinda. I was coming into Berkeley anyway, so I thought I'd just drop it off." Never mind that this was Oakland. I was several miles south of Berkeley, but hey, it was still Telegraph Avenue, not too much of a stretch.

Peter took the proffered papers, plopping down into an overstuffed chair with cat-frayed edges. His legs spread wide, revealing the origins of that tear in his jeans. I tried even harder not to look.

"Thanks," he said, as a wiry, black-and-white cat jumped into his lap. "This is Fred. Small but undaunted. We're proud of him. Gutsy little guy. The other night he went straight through the window screen going after a German shepherd outside."

Who is the "we" who're proud of, Fred? Is Peter talking too fast? Could he be nervous too?

Fred looked friendly. I offered my hand and he jumped down to rub it.

Peter's curly, blonde hair curved below his ears. I thought I'd like to trace my finger around one of those ears. His eyes were not particularly gentle, more like inquisitive. Hard to read. Looking down at Fred, I noticed Peter's bare feet. Kind of bony—male-shaped feet. Male toes just weren't the sexiest part of a man. Time to look back up, except that my gaze was bound to recross that dangerous territory.

Peter was grinning at me. Did he know? That grin looked as if the tear in his jeans had been deliberate and was now serving its intended purpose. Maybe I felt manipulated. Maybe I didn't like this guy. Or maybe I was just less honest than he was.

"You know, I was going to head out to a party. If you finished what you were doing in Berkeley and you aren't doing anything now, would you want to come along?"

So, the "we" alluded to must not be the girlfriend I'd imagined him making out with behind the closed front door. Go with him to a party? Maybe this wasn't really a date, but maybe there wasn't a current girlfriend who might get pissed.

"Sure. That sounds cool."

"I'll change and then we'll go."

Thank all the heavens and deities that may prevail! Yes! Please put on some crotch-protecting clothing! How long could I have gone on with my conscientious gaze avoidance?

Peter reappeared in a blue denim shirt, and sufficiently unified lower wear to spare me an evening of complicated eye-moves.

"Can you ride a motorcycle?"

What? You're kidding me! I'd never even been close enough to touch a motorcycle. "Sure."

I swung my leg across the rear seat of the red Yamaha 250—I knew what it was because it said so on the side of the fuel tank—as Peter donned his helmet (none for me), and kicked the engine into a throaty roar. He walked us around in a tight circle, engaged a gear, and out we sped onto the streets of Oakland.

Scared? A bit. It felt reckless and sexy and thrilling to have my arms wrapped around his denim jacket. My hands laced across some rather tight abs that undulated whenever he shifted gears. With my nose in his neck, I breathed deeply, inhaling some seriously sexy male pheromones into my overly celibate body. Peter-molecules found their way into whatever gland it was that controlled the moistness of my nether-parts.

Yes, this evening was going very well indeed!

We drove a bit too quickly back up Telegraph toward Berkeley, Peter weaving us in and out of traffic. He peeled around the UC campus and took Euclid Avenue into the Berkeley Hills. We wound along the one-car-wide streets that suited motorcycles better than automobiles. Eucalyptus branches hung over our road, scenting the darkening air. The cities below began twinkling in the dusk; the bridges seemed strung with fairy lights spanning the blackness of San Francisco Bay. This view had always felt like home to me, as cozy as my grandmother's quilt. A quilt now infused with adventure.

Peter braked the bike at a carport that also served as the roof of a typical Berkeley Hills house, the kind that layered itself down the hillside. The cedar shingles covering its sides had weathered to near blackness. We followed the sounds of voices down a wooden staircase that wound around the outside of the house, arriving at a large deck overlooking the bay. Peter looked around, then grabbed us each a beer from the cooler. An African-cloth-covered table was laden with hummus, veggies, salsa, cheeses, and bottles of red wine. The array was noticeably different from the canapes, cheeseballs, sour-cream dips, and various alcohol mixers usually seen at Orinda parties.

Following Peter to a group of his friends leaning against the railing, I once more felt inappropriately dressed. While my minidress fitted perfectly with current fashion, these people seemed to have a fashion of their own, or perhaps, a non-fashion of their own. Shoulder-length hair on both men and women did what its internal genetics dictated it should. What was now being called an Afro was the shortest style, probably having started from a place of very close-cropped hair a year or so ago. Other hair hung straight and silky down women's backs. Frizzy curls flew around when Aretha belted out her demand for R-E-S-P-E-C-T!, while everyone swung to the music coming from an indoor stereo system.

Billowing harem pants and skirts of various lengths, made of fabrics from all over the globe, swirled around the bodies of dancing women. The men were clad in cut-off jeans, tie-dyed shirts, or nothing much at all. Peter's and my attire raised no eyebrows or caused any slightly-longer-than-necessary glances. The group of Peter's friends we joined had more of a navy-blue sweatshirt-and-blue-jeans attire than most of the others. People made eye contact and smiled in an open and welcoming way. A distinctive whiff of marijuana replaced the woodsy, evening smell I'd noted on the road.

"This is Carol. We're working together on that Oakland program this summer," Peter said as he introduced me.

"Good to meet you. That's some kind of summer camp for kids? Well, good for you, Pete. Don't know why they'd want some industrial relations guy to run it, though." The guy teased Peter with a smile in his voice.

I'd actually been wondering the same thing.

"Just sounded like a good thing to do to pay the bills. Kinda fell into my lap." Peter shrugged.

*Yeah, and maybe **my** lap is where it should have stayed.* But I let the thought go. I was enjoying myself.

"So, did you hear about Colombia University? What a fucked president!" said a guy in granny glasses with a long mustache.

"What?"

"He's not going to give the commencement address. 'Cause the students have threatened to pull some shit unless they release the guys arrested during the sit-in last month."

"Sounds like he's just too chicken-shit to risk getting something thrown at him."

"Yeah, but it's cool that the Establishment is starting to shit their pants a bit." Laughter.

A stocky guy with curly, brown hair joined the group.

"Carol, this is John, my roommate. Graduating from Boalt." This from Peter as he put his arm around me. It felt good and warmed more than my shoulders.

Ah, this is the "we" of Fred-the-cat's window incident. "Hi, John."

"Good to meet you." John chugged half his beer before going on. "Fuckin'-A, man. Damn right! Just got into the California Law Review!" He chugged the other half of the bottle.

Peter and the others raised their beers, clinking bottles and cans.

"Guess you must be pretty smart for a fucker!" One of them laughed.

The conversation continued on in this rather disquieting mixture of political activism and raunchy language. A joint appeared and was passed from hand to hand. When it got to me, I took a toke and let it relax me.

After a bit, I excused myself to get something to eat. A breath of eucalyptus air seemed necessary to process this strange party. I gathered a plate of munchies and poured myself some wine before wandering to an empty edge of the deck. With my elbows propped on the railing, I watched strings of red lights flow along paths that defined the Bay Area freeways. Coit Tower glowed small and white across the bay.

"You here by yourself?" A pixie-like waif appeared at my elbow, beads woven into her braided hair.

"No, Peter Feuille brought me."

"Are you balling him?"

"Huh?" *Did she really just ask what I thought she did!*

"Are you screwing him? No offense. You just look a little bit uptight. Thought you might need a good lay. If you haven't screwed him, you probably should. It might do you good." Smiling broadly, she raised her left hand and offered me the twisted cigarette she held. I ignored my surprise and mild offense at her bluntness and took a hit. Her face shone with youthful enthusiasm. At a newly minted twenty-four, I felt old and out of date.

"Peter and I just met. Nothing's progressed that far."

"Well, first-date sex has its advantages. You haven't had to deal with any conflicts yet. I can just tune in to the soul of the person without having to get all hung up on ego trips or anything. You know, just pure soul to pure soul. It's kinda the best, if he's there too. Later you both get back into your egos and you worry about whether he leaves the toilet seat up or whether or not he's got athlete's foot and you might catch it when you're walking around naked together. Do you know what I mean?"

Surprised, I turned to look right at her. Was she talking about sex as a form of spiritual connection? Like sex as an experience of the Tapestry?

"I do know what you mean, but I honestly have never thought about it that way."

"Have you ever dropped acid? Sex on acid really puts you there. That is, if you can be in your body enough to want to have sex. Sometimes I like it just when you're starting to come down."

I hadn't ever dropped acid. Timothy Leary and others had been talking about it for a while. How it dissolves your ego and shows you a whole different level of reality. Could it be real? Could a drug induce the same experience of being unified with everything that the airplane flight had done for me?

"I've never tried anything more than alcohol and weed."

"No reason. I don't think you have to. But if you don't get how we're all connected, then it's a quick way to understand. I've only done it a few times. It's like you don't have to keep learning what it shows you. I don't think you can forget it, maybe even if you try. But who would? Try, that is?"

She was so positive, so earnest.

"My name's Carol. What you're saying is cool. It sounds like the same thing that I just realized when I was in Africa."

"Wow! Far-fuckin' out! In Africa!"

"Yeah, it was pretty amazing. I haven't had sex since. I'm really thinking about what you're saying. Makes sense."

"But you've got to be sure that the guy is in the same place. Or the woman. I've gotten it on with a couple of girls, though I like penises better. But some guys just sort of pretend so that they can fuck you. If you pay attention at all, you can see where they're at."

"I agree. It's sort of like another reality and you can tell the ones who see it from the ones who don't."

"Uh-huh. Some of us are trying to put together a commune. You know, a group of us living together and sharing stuff and not doing ego trips on each other. We're really into it, but we haven't found a place to live yet."

"That sounds amazing—if you could pull it off."

"Maybe we'll see each other around. I'll let you know what's happening. Maybe you'll want to join us. If it's meant to be, it'll happen. I'm Sunjoy." She hugged me. My hands jingled little bells in her braids when I reached around her back.

"I think three-month affairs are about the best. After three months, you kind of lose some of the connection and get caught in the material. Just sayin'. Thinking about that Peter dude. He's the blonde guy over there, right? He may be too much into the material plane for you, but what the heck, a good screw is a good screw!" She giggled and drifted away.

Watching her go, I saw Peter at the food table. He looked over at me, raising a beer and one eyebrow. I nodded, and he made his way over.

"John's a bit of a trip," Peter said semi-apologetically, then handed me an icy Coors. "You doing okay?"

I nodded and sipped the beer.

Peter continued his train of thought. "When Mario Savio sat on the steps of Sproul Hall at Berkeley and held up that sign saying 'FUCK,' John thought it was cool. They're calling it the 'Free Speech Movement' now. Liberate the word 'fuck' and all that. It's funny. John's really into it."

I'd heard about it and didn't much care one way or the other. But Peter was right, John would take some getting used to. "It's okay; I haven't been known for having the cleanest mouth on the planet." I laughed.

Peter put his arm around me again and we both leaned back on the railing, watching the assortment of humans moving around on the deck.

"Where are you living? I haven't asked you anything at all about yourself. What have you been doing? Why did you get involved in FOCUS?"

I gave Peter a brief summary of anthropology, Africa, tsetse flies, and the nightmare job at Herrick Hospital. He told me he'd gone to USC. (Cal Berkeley students more or less universally disparaged the University of Southern California as the school of choice for blonde-haired, surfer types. I tried to resist categorizing this man, but he might have been fitting the stereotype rather well.) Peter had been at Berkeley for the past five years or so. He'd accepted the summer job with FOCUS simply for the money. He had no interest in any church teachings, but the idea of trying to physically integrate kids—usually so separated by hills and cultures—also appealed to him.

Okay, so he was no longer a southern Californian. There might be hope; he'd seen the light.

"I drank a lot in college. I got expelled from USC, but then they let me finish. I applied to graduate school at Cal, because I didn't know if they'd accept me back at USC again. Besides, Berkeley does have the best Industrial Relations school."

He was a blonde, party animal. And Industrial Relations, isn't that in the business school? *Hmmm*. He was *so* not my type.

"Do you surf?" I asked, thinking I'd get further proof.

"Oh yeah, all the time down there. But I don't care enough about it to surf here! I ski instead, now."

The water temperature off the coast of San Francisco averaged around fifty degrees or so. Surfing was done in wet suits. Not enticing to a beach boy. Well, I skied like crazy as an undergraduate in Colorado, offering some hope for a connection.

Our introductory chitchat carried on. During a lull in the conversation, Peter turned to face the bay, choosing scenery over people-watching. I followed suit, leaning my elbows on the railing. Then, reaching over, Peter took my chin in one hand, gently turning my face toward him. With one eyebrow raised inquisitively, head tipped, he leaned in and gave me a gentle kiss, pulling back slowly with his eyebrow still raised, seemingly asking for my response or permission or both. I smiled into those aquamarine eyes, so he leaned forward, this time pulling my whole body into his and giving me a longer and seriously satisfying kiss. Satisfying for the lips and the mind, but leaving my body craving much more satisfaction.

The evening moved into night and our stances became more of a cuddle, without further kisses. It seemed that something had been established that was delightfully undefined, but nevertheless acknowledged. Not hurrying to move into a definition felt sensual.

As the night chilled, Peter guided us through our goodbyes and back up to his waiting bike. Donning his helmet, he offered me his jacket, an act sufficiently chivalrous to leave the warm, squishy feeling undisturbed inside me. I climbed on the bike behind him—after letting him turn it around on his own this time, demonstrating an acceptable learning curve in "all things motorcycle"—and felt a sense of rightness in enjoying the tensing of his stomach muscles beneath my fingers. Perhaps those muscles weren't responding only to the demands of bike-driving; maybe the pressure of my fingers elicited its own response.

We wound down out of the hills at a slower pace than we'd ascended. Perhaps both of us were enjoying the hand-abs juxtaposition from either side. I thought about my conversation with Sunjoy. (*Really? Sun Joy? Did she name herself that? Surely her parents hadn't.*) Her understanding of universal connection seemed genuine, as though she'd been thinking about it longer than I had and had followed its implications into various realms. Sex to experience Oneness? Sex to celebrate Oneness? Where had this come from? These were not concepts my family would likely comprehend, let alone conclude for themselves. I had to experience the perception of my own death on an airplane to gain an awareness of the Tapestry. How had this young girl gotten there? Acid? Could LSD really do that for people? And what about the others she spoke of? The ones who wanted to live together without clashing egos and try to make a material reality of what to me seemed a spiritual concept. Did all the flower children know this? Had the ones I met and danced with and played with in Sausalito before I'd gone to Africa already understood this? Was this what being a flower child demonstrated? Wow, food for a lot of thought. Potentially the basis of much conversation. Were there really people here I could talk with openly about this?

Meanwhile, my fingers felt the rise and fall of Peter's breathing. All of me enjoyed the sensation. Warm honey flowed from my fingertips into every corner of me. *Mmm*, I'd missed this feeling. Too long of a dry spell. But did I like this man? Did I have a clue who he really was? My body argued strongly against any intellectual concerns. Do I let my body win? Sunjoy said I needed some good sex. The kissing ability of this man, the compatibility of our pheromones, indicated I might be able to have some decidedly good sex. *Mmm*. I leaned in to test the hypothesis again, drinking in a deep inhalation of Peter-scent. Yes, yes, yes. Body responded. Body was craving. Body was very, very happy with the sense of anticipation.

We rolled to a stop in his driveway. Decision time. That was, of course, if he were to ask. I swung my leg off the bike first, disappointed he couldn't see the enticing length of bare leg exposed in my maneuver. My hands separated themselves from those stomach muscles. *Ah Carol, you wanton woman! Yes, I'm wantin' some! I'm wantin' him.*

"Do you want to come in? John's car isn't here. He probably won't be back tonight."

Not much pretense in this invitation.

Peter reached around and clasped his hands behind my back. Pulling me against him, I had more proof of his intent and interest. Meeting his lips willingly, my intent and interest began to match nicely with his.

But my parents. Jumping, green, shit-filled lizards! I was living with my parents, and we hadn't updated any expectations in that relationship. My mother was a devoted, born-again worrier. She had a PhD in worry. Probably even a post-doc achieved while tending to her four siblings at an early age. I pushed back gently and reluctantly. "I'd best not." Damn! I should have added, "tonight."

"You're going to drive all the way back to Orinda? Are you sure you won't fall asleep? I do have a tolerable couch you could stay on."

Yeah! Ha! Fat chance! If he didn't crawl onto my couch in the night, I'd sure as heck jump his bones and make room for two in his bed!

"I'll be all right. I had a great time."

"I have your number. I'll call you. Actually, I'll see you Monday anyway!" Peter laughed. Neither of us had been thinking of FOCUS or the fact that we now worked together. *Screw that! A summer job together was not going to impede a summer fling together. Not if our bodies had their way!*

I laughed too. "Yes, I'd like that. And, yes, I guess we'll see each other on Monday."

One last, long, deep, groin-hugging kiss. Twice as difficult now to keep my resolve. I pushed back again and we looked at each other for a long moment. Yep, we'd established something implicit.

He released my body and we walked down the alley to my car. I unlocked the door and turned to slide in. Peter turned me back toward him and, *ah*—one more. This man could kiss. This time, he was the one who pulled away. He kissed my nose and slid his hand across my hip to be certain my dress was tucked in before closing the door. *Mmm* and *mmm*.

"Drive safely. See you Monday."

FIFTEEN

The next morning, my dogpaddle back up into consciousness was greeted with some sumptuous sensations. My lips held memories of something soft and delightful. I was still lying in bed, reviewing the previous night's deeds, when I heard my mother answer the ringing phone.

"I'll see if she's up." Slippered footsteps headed to our room where Jean still slept. "It's for you. Sounds like a young man." Inflection rose at the end of Mom's sentence. Curiosity. She wanted to know who. I wanted to know who too. I hoped.

I swung my feet onto the plush white carpet, wiggling them into my flip-flops. Pulling on a robe, I flushed like an overexcited schoolgirl who'd just been asked to the prom. I couldn't imagine that it would be any man other than Peter calling me at my parents' house on that Saturday morning. I kept my face lowered as I passed my mom in the hall, hoping she wouldn't pick up on my crimson shade.

The receiver felt large and clunky in my sweaty hand.

"It looks like a beautiful day. Thought I'd take the bike for a drive out Wildcat Canyon Road. Wanna come along? If you tell me how to find your parents' house, I'll pick you up."

"Sounds good. It's 99 Tara Road. Turn off Overhill about a mile after coming out of the Crossroads."

"Yeah, I can find that. In about an hour?"

"Fine. See you then."

Holy moly! I had done it. Peter and I were going to be an item. I'd conquered my fear of snakes, poisonous insects, and blue-eyed, surfer men. Go, Carol!

"Who was that?" My mother's simple inquiry came across the kitchen counter as I set the phone receiver back into its cradle.

"Peter Feuille, the guy I'll be working with this summer. The director of FOCUS He's coming out to pick me up in a bit." I left it at that and went to get dressed.

As I showered, I considered all the ways the upcoming encounter with Peter might be interesting for my folks. Motorcycles were not a favored form of transportation. Had they ever ridden or ever even known anyone who'd ridden a motorcycle? Hell's Angels about summed up motorcycle riders for them. *Please, Peter, don't roar up the driveway. Just roll in sort of quietly. And please, please, please, Peter, do* not *wear the jeans with that tear!*

I pulled on my own pair of jeans, sans any revealing tears, and found a scooped-neck T-shirt to wear with them. Coral-colored. I looked good in coral.

My ears strained until I heard the roar of Peter's Yamaha cresting the hill perhaps a quarter mile away. Not too many motorcycles raced around Orinda. I grabbed my denim jacket and headed toward the living room, hoping for a short parental interrogation with minimal disclosures.

Oh, God. I'm twenty-four years old, but I feel sixteen!

Just as the roar grew loud enough for my folks to hear it, the sound stopped. Clever man. He must have cut the engine just in time to let his momentum carry him up the driveway. Peter, no doubt, had middle-class parents too, probably with values similar to my folks'. Was he trying to make a good impression with my family? I hoped so.

The living room window faced away from the driveway. The motorcycle might go undetected. I slowed my walk toward the front door, not wanting to appear overanxious. When the bell rang, I took a moment to check myself in the hall mirror before opening the door. His wide, white-toothed grin met my gaze before my eyes slid downward, checking for possible rips in his thigh-tight, blue jeans. All was well.

"Come on in and meet my folks."

My dad set his newspaper down and rose to shake Peter's hand as Mom came out of the kitchen. My sister was still sleeping, so she lost out on meeting Peter. I'd have to wait for her evaluation. Fifteen minutes of ordinary small talk followed before I could disengage us from the situation.

Mounting the bike proved way more comfortable in jeans than it had in a miniskirt two nights before. Peter let the motorcycle roll silently down the driveway before kicking it into gear. This guy did have some commonsense smarts as well as academic smarts.

My parents remained blissfully unaware that right outside their home, I was relishing some rippling, male, abdominal muscles while riding, helmetless, on the back of a motorcycle. Sometimes ignorance is bliss, especially when it's someone else's ignorance.

My hair had grown long enough since its pre-African shearing for me to enjoy the wind whipping it about as we picked up speed heading out of Orinda. I allowed myself to inhale the back of Peter's neck.

A slight hint of aftershave? Not the usual prep for a bike ride? Nice!

Peter rotated the hand grip and roared through the gears after we turned off Camino Pablo onto Wildcat Canyon road. Clutching his waist tighter, I felt free and daring as we flew through grassy hills on the deserted road. Huge oak trees twisted their gnarly limbs as we passed.

I remembered a joke I'd heard recently: *How can you tell a happy motorcyclist? Count the bugs on his teeth.* I pulled my lips together but could not suppress a shit-eating grin.

I happily glued myself to Peter's body as he leaned the bike into the curves. As our speed continued to increase, I peered over his shoulder to glimpse the speedometer. Eighty miles an hour! I started to feel exposed in my thin denim clothing and lack of a helmet. Scarcely slowing for the next turn, Peter leaned us so far over that I felt the bike's foot peg scrape the ground.

My enthusiasm waning for this ride, I simply held on and closed my eyes. We finally slowed to a stop in Tilden Park at the intersection beside the botanical gardens. I was annoyed at the danger he'd put me in.

"That was just a bit much for me," I yelled into Peter's helmet-covered ear.

"Sorry. Don't worry. I'll take it slower through the park."

True to his word, we progressed safely along the ridge of the Berkeley Hills. Sun glinted off the bay through small breaks in the eucalyptus forest. Gray-green, sickle-shaped leaves littered the roadside, giving off the aroma of Vicks VapoRub. I felt grateful that millions (billions?) of tiny spirochetes had not managed to do in my liver and me. Foot pegs aside, this was a good day to be alive. My life was taking a most interesting turn.

Peter guided the bike into the parking lot of a wooded picnic area adjacent to a wide, green field. Blankets dotted the nearest grassy area. Assorted groups spread their blankets, coolers, toys, and pets across the field. Children threw balls that dogs raced after. Moms sorted through picnic baskets, offering sandwiches to their families. Dads pulled dripping bottles of Coke and 7-Up from icy coolers. I watched a nearby young man trace the outline of tree shadows down his girlfriend's arm.

Peter and I climbed off the bike and plopped onto the bench of an empty picnic table. I brushed off some knobby eucalyptus pods as Peter unzipped his jacket and pulled out a small, paper bag. Pretzels and four Chunky candy bars rolled out.

"Here, I've got these too." He reached into his bulging side pockets. "They're probably too warm and not quite legal in the park, but what the heck?" Two cans of Coors joined the snacks on the table. He tapped the top of one a few times then stuck his finger through the pull-tab's ring, opening the beer and handing it across to me. As he did the same for his own, I took a small sip from the can, glancing around to see if anyone was noticing our contraband beer. Everyone seemed involved in their own afternoon activities, having little interest in a couple on a motorcycle, once the roar that violated the peace of the park had ended. I munched a pretzel and took a larger swallow of beer.

Peter came around beside me, sitting backwards on the bench. He leaned back, elbows on the table, spreading his legs out toward a couple batting a shuttlecock back and forth between badminton rackets.

"So, where did you say you went to college?" he asked, turning his head to look at me.

"Colorado. We'd moved from Orinda to New York when I was in high school, and I wanted to come back west. It ended up feeling pretty weird at first. My sister was at Cal and my folks were in New York, and I realized that I didn't know a soul for a thousand miles in any direction. But it ended up being cool. I love Colorado. Majored in anthropology. How about you? You went to USC?"

"I went to USC. I was born in Little Rock, but my folks weren't from there. My mom hated it, so they moved back to southern California. I grew up in San Pedro."

He pronounced it "San Peedro." My five years of Spanish language classes cringed inside me.

"USC kicked me out for a short time, but let me back in. So I graduated and then came to Cal for grad school."

"What for? Did they kick you out?" I'd wondered about that since he'd mentioned it at the party. My curiosity overrode politeness.

"Indecent urination. I peed off a balcony at a girls' dorm when I was drunk."

I laughed inside. Sounded like "indiscretion" to me. Did Peter and I have checkered pasts in common? I decided not to share my Peace Corps' exploits with him for now.

We watched people enjoying the park sunshine for a while, nibbling food and drinking our beers in companionable silence. The square Chunky bars were melty, so I finished chewing peanuts and raisins and licked milk chocolate off my hands. Chunkys were one of my favorite treats. The fact that Peter had chosen them for our picnic placed a check in the "positive" column for a potential relationship.

Suddenly, Peter jumped up and walked over to four young people near us who had just flopped onto their blanket following a spirited game of frisbee. After a brief discussion, Peter returned, their frisbee in hand.

"Catch this," he said, twirling it to me from about ten feet away.

I reached with both hands and clasped it to my chest, trapping it in my arms. I laughed. Clumsy, but successful. "I've seen these but never thrown one."

As I stood up, Peter came behind me. He put his right arm along mine and adjusted my grip on the plastic disc. "You have to fling it with a twist of your wrist at the end. Just whip it so it spins." He led my arm and hand in a slow-motion approximation.

We walked a distance from the other folks on the grass. Peter gestured for me to stay there and kept on walking.

"Are you kidding? That's far enough!"

He halted obligingly. I whipped my hand around, watching the Frisbee sail sideways into the ground no more than fifteen feet away. We laughed. I retrieved the Frisbee. Peter coached and I persevered. After a half-hour of laughter, encouragement, and occasional apologies when our projectile landed in the midst of someone else's game or gathering, I had mastered the art of getting the thing to ride on the air, sometimes landing close enough that Peter could actually catch it. We declared me to be an official frisbee-player. Our benefactors began packing up their picnic, and we returned their toy.

After discarding the remains of our snacks, we climbed back onto the red Yamaha. Holding onto Peter's waist felt more companionable now, less uncertain than it had. Peter was turning into a three-dimensional person for me, not just a sexy fantasy. I leaned my head against the back of his shoulders as we began winding down toward Berkeley. The white-domed cupola of the Claremont Hotel rose into view between the trees on our left.

When I was four, Shell Chemical was in the process of transferring my father's job, and we were supposed to be moving to England for a year. We'd spent our last California night at the Claremont. We'd left the hotel in the morning and gotten on the brand-new, California Zephyr at the Emeryville Station, when Jean realized she'd left her Vicky doll at the Claremont. As the gleaming silver train rolled through Berkeley, blue-uniformed "Zephyrettes" tending to the needs of passengers helped calm her. When the train made its first stop in Sacramento, Dad got off and called the hotel. Three days later, when we reached our grandparents house in Chicago, my sister's doll was waiting. As Jean danced with joy and cuddled her doll, I beamed at my parents, expecting them to be as happy as we were. But, instead, I watched my mother's hands clench into fists as Dad relayed the message awaiting our arrival: my father's transfer had been cancelled and we'd have to return to Berkeley. No England. Sweat covered Mom's forehead and her knees wobbled as Dad hurried her into the bedroom.

Later, they told us that our mother had collapsed with a "nervous breakdown." I didn't know what that meant, but even at four, I already understood that one of my jobs was keeping my mother from being too upset.

Mom's parents kept us for a few weeks while she and Dad went for a "recovery trip" to New York City. As Peter and I passed that looming white turn-of-the-century Berkeley landmark, the confusion I felt about my parents' long-ago, whispered conversations twisted in my mind, braiding itself uncomfortably into the memory of how much I'd loved the Claremont's rescue of my sister's most precious doll. I squeezed Peter's waist a little tighter and wondered if I could let go of the responsibility I'd always felt for keeping life as smooth as possible around Mom. *Sure*, I thought, *why not?* Breathing in a whiff of Peter's aftershave, mingling pleasantly with the scent of eucalyptus leaves, I felt liberated. Today, the world was a pretty good place.

We turned down Telegraph Avenue to Peter's place, even though we hadn't talked about what would happen after the ride. My heartbeat rose steadily as we parked the bike. Peter didn't ask me if I wanted to go in. Actually, he didn't ask me anything at all. We both knew what was happening and it seemed right. After half a year of celibacy, I didn't let my brain ponder this being our first official date, or what my own "rules" were. I merely followed him inside.

Peter dropped his jacket on the ugly, green chair and turned to face me. Heat seemed to rise from the depths of the Earth, fighting gravity as it flowed up my body. With one hand, Peter cupped the back of my windblown hair, while pressing me against him with the other. He leaned in to kiss me. Moist lips and tongues intertwined. He smelled like sunny hills and healthy sweat. His hands met behind me to unhook my bra, then he stepped back to hold my gaze. I smiled and nodded, then closed my eyes as his hands began a gentle exploration of my body. He pulled my T-shirt over my head and helped my bra slip to the floor.

Shit, this man knew what he was doing, and that was fine with me and every part of my increasingly aroused body. More clothes fell away, leaving a Hansel-and-Gretel trail for me to follow, should I ever decide to find my way back out of the deep and delicious woods. When he'd backed my legs against his bed, I let my knees give way.

Our lovemaking was slow and deliberate. Afterward, I lay nestled beside him, my head resting against his shoulder.

"I think we need to make certain to do that again someday." There was a smile in Peter's voice.

I traced my fingers among the curly strands of his bronze chest hair. "I'll check my calendar."

Thirty-six hours later, Monday morning came to Orinda, Oakland, and the Orinda Community Church, where the roles of director, co-director, lover, and co-lover rushed to weave themselves into a workable, two-person whole. I was not optimistic. This job didn't rank as any kind of career move; it only served as summer employment. But still, I wondered how anybody working in the program would feel if they knew what had occurred between their leaders. *Ah, well*, as Scarlet would have said, *I'll think about that tomorrow*. I tried to calm myself as I drove up the hill and into the church's parking lot. Peter's motorcycle shone red and smug beside the chapel doors.

He didn't look up as I took a seat in the wood-paneled conference room. He was deep into an animated conversation about the lack of sufficient busses to move children back and forth in all of our planned activities. Maybe it was a good thing he'd taken over as director. There were going to be endless headaches that I would no longer be in charge of soothing.

When Peter looked up, our eyes met, smiling at each other without our lips giving us away. "Hi, Carol." He nodded, then turned to address the rest of the group. I released a lungful of air that I hadn't realized was growing stale. He'd be professional. No worries.

The meeting progressed in the way of all planning meetings: issues, proposals, solutions, potential problems, and then a repeat of all of the above until it was time for lunch. With a week to go, things actually looked pretty good. The meeting had taken my mind away from weekend reminiscences and returned it to Project FOCUS. My role as daily go-between for the two districts had formed into something reasonable and seemingly manageable. I was to check in daily with groups on both sides of the hills to find out what was working well and what was not. If everything ran as smoothly as we all hoped, I'd scarcely have any work beyond being an available ear for people's daily stories. If things didn't go well, I'd be able to call in the reinforcements and guide them to the situations needing help.

After our lunch break, the conversation moved on to issues that had little to do with me or my job description. I looked up at the patterns of tiny black holes in the dingy, white, acoustic ceiling tile and let my mind wander. Here I sat, back from Africa, seemingly fitting right back into that American lifestyle in which I'd grown up. Obviously, there were some differences. I was older and things were changing. But what about the most important thing I'd found in Africa, that feeling of total connection I'd experienced on the airplane? Could I recover the knowledge here that I'd responded to so strongly on another continent?

The understanding seemed spiritual: the essence of what I'd experienced was pure love, and it seemed to me that this same essence of pure love was what religious prophets had been talking about. Is what we call "God," pure love, and what we call "pure love," God? I'd been to Sunday school for years in this same building during my childhood. I'd memorized countless Bible verses. I now let some of them trickle through my consciousness. Wasn't there a whole lot that Jesus said that supported my theory? "As you do it unto the least of these, you do it unto me." Didn't that refer to the fact that all is Oneness. How about ". . . and of all these, the greatest is love"? I knew I wasn't quoting these verses right, but I was getting their essences. Christ, Buddha, maybe even Muhammed—weren't they all trying to explain this concept that God really was love, a concept we struggled to comprehend?

When I'd tried to share some of my airplane experiences with my scientist-father, it had sounded too spiritual to his atheist ears. He hadn't accepted my logic that we couldn't die and not exist, because, in fact, we were part of this Universe and we *did* exist. Yes, it sounded circular, but I knew it was true. What sense would it make for us to just pop into and out of existence? Science tells us that matter and energy can neither be created nor destroyed; why would we think consciousness could? After being so joyously aware that I was an integral part of a cosmic, intelligent, entirety, that argument made sense to me. But it had left my dad cold.

Now, here I was, sitting in the heart of the opposite camp from my dad's atheism. What did the minister think about these things? I suddenly felt anxious to find out. Tuning back into the meeting, I saw that Peter was winding the discussion down. Should I hang out afterwards and see if he wanted to make plans? But, heck, he had my folks' number, and my mother always said I should never look too anxious or available to a man. Besides, the concepts rolling around in my neural networks seemed weightier than the bodies that had rolled around on Peter's bed. As people began rising, I suppressed my corporeal longings and sought out the minister.

"Do you have a minute?" I asked. I didn't know this man. The minister I had known here during my childhood had long gone to other places.

His eyes looked tired but questioning.

"It's not about FOCUS. It's a personal issue," I replied to his unspoken query. "We could talk another time if you want. It's already been a long day." I felt myself chickening out of our potential discussion, offering him a means of escape.

"No, that's okay. Let's go to my office."

I followed him into a pleasant office. Somber-colored books filled shelves that lined the walls. He gestured me to an aged but comfortable sofa.

"What can I do for you, Carol?"

"I think this is going to sound strange, but I recently got back from Africa and I think I had a spiritual epiphany."

He took off his glasses and began cleaning them with a cloth as he perched himself upon his desk, one leg braced against the floor. "Yes?" He did not sound enthusiastic, nor did he look up.

"Well, it's just that I totally got it that there's the Universe and that consciousness is a part of that Universe and we're part of consciousness and I felt like my boundary of self just disappeared and I got reunited into that conscious wholeness. Does that make sense? I think that wholeness is what God is."

"Some mystics think that. Maybe the Eastern philosophies that some people call religions."

"But if we're all a part of God, then God's a part of us, and there's no way to determine how large that part is. If we just let go of our egos, we can be God. All of us just merging into a universal Oneness that is everything."

"Yes, a philosophically interesting concept."

"But I felt it as more than a concept. It happened to me when I accepted my death. I've never felt so much love and inclusion. It was like coming home, to a real home I'd forgotten I had, after being away for a really long time!"

"Many of the people who find Christ feel they have come home."

"Well, I think Christ knew about this. Lots of what he's supposed to have said fits with everything I experienced. Didn't he tell people to heal themselves at one point? Like if you let yourself be the part of you that is God, you can heal yourself just as well as Jesus did?" My pitch had risen with excitement. I wanted to know that he agreed. I wanted to know that he already knew and understood everything I was trying to get across.

"I think you had a very interesting experience. I'm pleased it makes you happy. I know you'll do an excellent job of leadership in FOCUS this summer. It was very nice chatting." He raised himself off his desk and extended his hand.

I was definitely being patronized. Our Orinda Community Church never preached a specific doctrine when I was young. Maybe it didn't really have one, now. This church was a gathering place, which was a nice thing to be, but it didn't have much need for, or interest in, spiritual epiphanies. What had happened on the plane may have been the most important experience of my life, but there didn't seem to be anyone I could really talk to about it. I wanted to go out and preach about my revelation, but how would I get anyone to listen? Would this important memory fade if I never spoke of it?

As I left the building, a sigh rose up from somewhere near my bellybutton and slid from my mouth across the overly long grass of the church lawn. Obviously, conversations concerning the Tapestry would not come in the guise of an Orinda Community Church minister. He didn't get it, and yet he got paid to preach it.

A further disappointment greeted me when I saw that the parking lot no longer held any sign of Peter's presence. The shiny motorcycle that should have dazzled me, that would have reflected the sun's reddest rays straight into my eyes, that could have raised my spirits, was missing. My chest heaved with a second sigh.

Heading back to my parents' house, I felt deflated. I'd struck out trying to find any confirmation of my African experiences with the minister, and I'd missed a chance to confirm with Peter our mutual joy at more corporeal experiences. Loneliness wound its snaky body through my heart.

I remained silent through our family dinner, giving only the necessary responses to confirm that Project FOCUS seemed to be on schedule and would be ready to begin its program next week. Jean talked about her day at Fly Oakland, the Oakland Airport's travel service for booking flights. Inexplicably, my sister had always loved airplanes just as much as I had feared them. She verbally painted pictures for us of the women she worked with and the handsome pilots who flirted with them. She missed her husband, so the harmless male energy being sent her way tended to buoy her spirits.

The phone rang as I covered the remainder of my mom's Gravenstein apple pie and began wrestling space for it in the refrigerator. I hurried to grab the telephone before anyone else came into the kitchen. The voice that greeted me raised my spirits at least as much as a dose of pilot flirtations had raised my sister's.

"You weren't avoiding me today, were you?" Peter's voice came through the line.

"Definitely not! I had something I needed to discuss with the minister. You were gone when I came out."

"Good. I didn't think you were." The smile was back in his voice. "There's a peace march in the city on Saturday. Wanna go?"

Peter and I had never yet discussed politics. In fact, we really hadn't discussed much of anything. Our relationship had advanced on a less-than-intellectual level. I felt pleased to know he opposed the war, although nearly all Berkeley students did. I was more pleased, however, that he wanted to be active in its opposition.

"I'd heard about that. Yes, I'd love to go. Shall I meet you at your apartment?"

After we'd settled the time and place, I said goodbye and stepped out into the coolness of the patio. Frogs croaked out their affections from a little pond beside the house.

A deer bounded away up the hill, startled when I closed the door behind me. The lonely feeling I'd carried with me from the church flitted off like fireflies in the gathering night. I looked forward to the march and to sharing it with Peter. But what about after the march? I wondered. I was pretty certain that Peter and I shared a common expectation for what would happen Saturday night. But what were the unspoken understandings my family had with a twenty-four-year-old daughter living in their home? They'd worry, of course, if I didn't come back that night. But what should I tell them? Excuse me, but I might be making love with Peter all night? They were still adjusting to what had happened or, I should say, not happened with Steve, whom they'd always loved. And here I was, sleeping with some guy they'd hardly met. My parents had been good to take Jean and me back into their home after each of our lives had taken unusual turns, but no ground rules had been laid out. Without men in either of our lives, Jean and I had fit neatly back into patterns we'd developed in high school. Now, as a sexually active adult, I didn't want to create uncomfortable situations for anyone.

I headed back inside to get ready for bed, hoping that the night might bring some delicious dreams. Perhaps it was time to move back across the hills.

SIXTEEN

After a week of FOCUS issues and solutions, Saturday arrived. I drove into Oakland to pick up Peter. Unlike my experiences with Steve, whom I'd known and loved for eight years but hadn't slept with for the past five, Peter immediately elicited an uncontrollable sexual response, despite my knowing him for less than a month. I was in lust with him, not yet in love. But for now, lust felt pretty good. The grin he gave me when he got into the car looked a bit lustful too, which felt intoxicating.

I drove us into the city where we managed to find the rally and ditch the car. Peter and I joined the throng. We were surrounded by thousands of chanting, dancing, sign-carrying, anti-war activists. Peter grabbed one of my hands, and I used the other to hold up the sign I had made: "Make Love, Not War," in bold black letters with hearts around the border. Mine wasn't as creative as the one carried by the paisley-shirted man beside me: "Suppose they gave a war and nobody came?" The harshest and most poignant sign I saw suggested one might:

Join the Army
Travel the World
Meet fascinating people
And kill them.

As the group began moving, we joined in, shouting, "One, two, three, four. We don't want your fucking war!" I felt as if my chest were opening wider each time I hollered those words, so liberating for my Orinda-raised self.

The crowd ahead of us parted around someone in military uniform. I'd seen "Veterans for Peace" signs earlier, so I assumed he must be with that group. But as I drew closer, I saw plastic jet planes sewn randomly onto his dress uniform around his hat and shoulders. He turned from side to side, showing everyone the headline of a newspaper he carried. In bold letters, it read, "War is in Very Bad Taste," and, beneath that, "General Waste-More-Land." General Westmorland was the top general in the Vietnam war, and this man satirizing him regaled us with his commentary on the war. Odd-looking medals were pinned across his uniform. He pulled on one attached to an elastic ribbon. Stretching the ribbon a foot or more from his chest, he told his audience, "This is the longest medal given by the American Congress."

After walking more than a mile, we neared the top of a San Francisco hill. The march snaked its way around a corner. I stopped, looking back down Geary Street toward the bay. Ten abreast, marchers filled the street as far as I could see. Dazzling sunshine spread the spirit of the day. Although the war we protested was bloody and brutal, a sense of determined optimism flowed from the marchers, entwined in the chants that echoed off aging brick buildings.

As the protesters bunched up to round the corner, warm bodies jostled me over to the edge of the street. I stepped onto the sidewalk in front of a bar, being careful to move around a man sleeping against its dirty, brick wall. One of the fellow's hands held a paper-bag-covered bottle. As I passed, the other hand lifted a stick with a sign attached. I leaned over to read it. "Winos for Peace." When I burst out laughing, he opened his eyes and winked at me.

We shared the connection of that private, humorous moment. As children, Jean and I would have given him a wide berth and been scuttled past. Perhaps we would even have crossed the street to avoid any imagined odors or insects coming from his unwashed body. But today I had seen him. I had felt his "self." Something warm and knowing had passed between us.

I hurried to catch up with Peter, who had already rounded the corner, but my thoughts stayed with the figure slouched against the bar.

I knew him. He knew me. What did that mean?

I turned back around to look at him once more. He was setting his sign down again and lifting the bottle.

I am him. He is me.

I thought about all the aspects of myself I had released mentally on the airplane, all those parts of me that I'd realized weren't really me. The essence of existence that I'd been reduced to was the same essence of existence in him. His disheveled body and clothing were no more him than my ability to sing was me. I looked at the people around me in the march, protesting against the killing of people we'd never met. Each of the marchers had identical, essential selves. Each one of the Vietnamese that the U.S. military murdered had that essential self. Each soldier sent over to do the killing, each one who was killed or wounded, shared that place of pure existence.

This is what love is. And they all feel it too. That's why we're marching.

I had to find out. I hurried up to the long-skirted, halter-topped woman marching beside Peter and looked into her face. She met my gaze with warmth in her eyes. Smiling, she put her hand on my arm. I felt the connection with her just as I had with the Wino for Peace.

Turning to Peter, I looked up into those blue eyes that held so much attraction for me. They met my searching gaze with a quizzical expression.

Peter doesn't know. It's intellectual for him. He's here, because he thinks it's right. But he doesn't really feel it.

Odd. The man my body lusted after, whose company I increasingly enjoyed, wouldn't understand what I was feeling. But Sunjoy would. It's exactly what she had been talking about. I reached for Peter's hand and he took mine willingly. But it felt more like a conscious gesture on his part than a sharing of warmth. Peter held himself contained.

Had the American individualism of the 1950s simply dissolved for those being called the "flower children?" We were understanding a communal consciousness. How had the others come to know this thing? Obviously, everyone hadn't. Peter wasn't less of a person for not understanding. He just hadn't found that place.

I squeezed his hand, not wanting to judge him. But should I judge myself? Here I was, falling for this man who was finishing a PhD in business school. Studying a discipline based on getting the most one can for oneself. Compassion and connection with others had little place in the world of finance. To his credit, his area of interest was public sector bargaining, unions for government employees, giving people a voice in their professions they hadn't had previously. Steve, on the other hand, had just finished a Master of Business Administration and planned to go into banking. Which should I judge as a more compassionate profession? But then I reprimanded myself for making mental comparisons between them.

I leaned my head against Peter's shoulder. Everything felt a bit confusing. The world seemed to be making a major shift and I didn't understand how it was happening. The ramifications of this new movement would transform our entire capitalist system, wouldn't they? Obviously, perceptions of the military had already changed greatly, and we were here, marching together by the tens of thousands, on a glorious San Francisco day, trying to spread the message that we couldn't kill people half a world away without damaging a piece of ourselves. Wasn't that the message?

Later that evening as we drove home from the march, I accelerated onto the Oakland Bay Bridge. The East Bay unfolded in a carpet of lights as the road arched across the water. Berkeley twinkled beneath the rising quarter-moon. Looking at the cities spreading out before me, I saw networks of reciprocity. A new culture existed all around. Focusing my attention on separate spots of light, I realized that there, and there, and over there, we might find a person's door where we could knock, where we would be given food if we said we were hungry, where we might even be asked to stay if we had no other place. It felt spiritual, an understanding that something more essential existed beneath the material world in which most of us had been raised. The self-protective individualism taught to us in childhood had shifted, been replaced by something magical. I looked over at the man beside me. He may not be consciously thinking about this, but he was surely a part of it.

I dropped Peter off at his apartment. He walked around to open my door when I didn't get out of the car. I rolled down the window.

"It's pretty late. I haven't told my parents about anything between us yet. I'll figure something out soon. Maybe look for a place over here."

Peter leaned over and found my lips inside the car.

Not fair! Most of the cells of my body responded.

He drew back and smiled. "A loss tonight, but we can make up for it later."

I nodded, shifting into reverse before my resolve faltered.

"Thanks. See you."

The next night, the smell of Lil's "porcupine balls"—rice-speckled meatballs in a rich tomato sauce—greeted my parents and me as Tom opened the Mikas' front door.

I had joined Mom and Dad again in accepting an invitation to dinner with their best friends. Jean was working that night and couldn't join us. After encouraging me to go to Africa months before, Lil said she'd be excited to hear about the trip.

Heading straight into the kitchen, I wrapped my arms around Lil's generous body.

"Porcupine balls! You remembered how I love them!"

"Well, you didn't have gourmet tastes as a child, but we all still like 'em." Lil smiled at me. It was typical of her to remember someone's favorite dish and to make it again more than a decade later. "I think there's a trivet on the table you can put them on." I grabbed potholders and picked up the casserole dish. I carried the dish of rice sticking out of tomato-y meatballs from oven to table. My mom's voice greeted me even before I reentered the dining room, where everyone already sat around the glossy, Danish Modern table. "We got to see the Niosis yesterday. They're both doing well." Mom liked keeping everyone up to date on the lives of mutual friends. I couldn't help mentally contrasting her polite garden lunch of the previous day with the march up Geary Street that had occupied my own.

"Are you still working at Herrick Hospital?" Tom asked, ignoring the direction of my mother's conversation. I wasn't certain that his comment implied I lacked self-sufficiency at twenty-four, but I suspected he already knew I'd quit the job.

"I'm working for a summer program that Dorothy Williams set me up with. Through her church. Working with kids here and in Oakland. Trying to mix them up a little, give them some shared experiences. And I've been accepted into an inner-city teaching program for a master's at Berkeley."

"But you're abandoning your anthropology?" Lil sounded dubious. She'd been a strong advocate for my trip to Africa. Her advice, "If you don't go now, you'll probably never have an opportunity like this again," had been a major factor in my decision to go. But I think her image would have had me coming away determined to get an advanced degree in anthropology, rather than being an elementary school teacher.

"No, I don't think so. I'm sure I'll use my anthropology a lot teaching in Oakland." Oakland served as the landing point for immigrants from everywhere. The city had a majority of African Americans, but walking down a street you could hear nearly as many languages as were spoken at the United Nations.

"Well, if it pays enough to live on, it would at least be different. I'm sure Oakland needs teachers." Lil always had my back and was able to roll with different scenarios.

"The Niosis said that Rosemary's coming home this summer. She's majored in voice and appears to be doing well." My mom was holding to her train of thought, despite the directions of others.

"Would you stay in Orinda when you are going to Cal and teaching in Oakland?" Dad wondered, ignoring Mom the same way Tom had. The question seemed only for information. I didn't think he was planning to kick me out.

Tom sipped his sparkling rosé. "It might be dangerous to go to school there right now. I'm not sure you should be on the Berkeley campus. There are too many protests, too much antiwar activity."

"Actually, that would be a good reason for me to move to Berkeley. I'm getting active in the protests in San Francisco. I just went on the peace march yesterday."

"War protests! You kids need to have more respect for your country."

I didn't realize the danger this conversation might hold. I knew my dad, at least, had fairly liberal politics, and I assumed Tom, as his best friend, did too. "But we have to stop the Vietnam War," I argued.

"How do you know?" was Tom's instantaneous response. "Are you privy to government intelligence? We don't know all the reasons we're sending troops over there."

"It just seems to me that killing a bunch of people half a world away can't be justified. Bobby Kennedy has decided to run for president, because he thinks we should get out of Vietnam."

"Humphrey is a much better candidate. He understands the need for a strong military," Tom insisted.

"I feel sorry for anyone who would be president now," my father put in. Always a faithful Democrat, he added, "Don't you think Lyndon Johnson would give anything to be out of the war?"

"Well then, why doesn't he simply get out? He could bring everybody home. He has the power, but he's too tied into the military-industrial complex to go against them. This war is making somebody rich." I held my own, surprised that the Mikas and my liberal father didn't see this clearly.

Tom straightened. "Where has patriotism gone? How can you be so unappreciative of all your government has done for you?" His voice was rising.

Their generation had lived through World War Two and believed we had a benevolent government. I knew this, but felt compelled to help them see how different Vietnam was from WWII, or perhaps even Korea. My passion about the issue kept me arguing, although I could feel my mother's discomfort pulling at my skin. "Even Martin Luther King has started speaking out against the war. Have you read his book, *Where Do We Go from Here?* He's not only talking about civil rights, he was laying out plans for a more egalitarian, socialistic society."

"Well then, he was going too far. He has incited the Negroes."

"Incited? How can you call an attempt to peacefully end hundreds of years of racism 'inciting'?"

"Just look at that militant group, the Black Panthers. They're picking up arms and threatening all whites!"

"Bullshit! The media makes them sound bad when they're just trying to stand up for all . . ."

Tom's hand slammed onto the table as he stood up, nearly toppling the wine. He leaned across, glowering down at me. "You will NOT use language like that in my home! If you want to speak like that you can just leave!"

No voice spoke. Four human statues riveted on his scarlet face. The room's oxygen exited through a hole made by the sudden force of his words. Silence stunned our ears. Tom dropped back onto his chair. One by one, each person tested a breath, seeing if life continued. In over twenty years of friendship, no one had indulged in such an outburst. If life were anything at all in Orinda, it had always been quiet and polite.

After time had stretched thin, my mother's voice ventured into the vacancy.

"The Pollaczeks' thirtieth anniversary is coming up. I think they're planning a party at the Moraga Country Club."

Moving with the grace of a crippled caterpillar, the conversation stumbled fitfully on.

Lil sat quietly when she wasn't bringing food or clearing dishes. I recognized that she was taking in everything but holding her tongue. It wasn't until years later that I understood her night's silence. After Tom died, she told me that her Lithuanian immigrant father had worked as a meatpacker in Chicago in the 1920s. As a young woman, she had been a member of the Young Communists League, not a fact one would voice in Orinda. If she hadn't been married into the Orinda community, I imagine Lil would have joined the protesters.

We gathered our coats and said appropriate goodbyes. I longed to just head across the hills to a different reality. My brain felt as scrambled as a flock of crows caught in a dust devil. Separate aspects of my life had accelerated along a collision course.

When we got to my parents' house, the weight of silent disapproval added fifty pounds to my body. Each step felt like I was wading through molasses. Somehow, I had caused a crisis. I'd rocked the carefully constructed, post-WWII, suburban happy-boat. The emperor may have been clothed, but I'd pointed out the transparency of his raiment. The shards of the bubble I had just burst lay around us like a broken dream. Suburbia had been created to move middle-class, white families away from the less fortunate who might cause them discomfort. Indians on reservations. Blacks confined to inner cities. Latinos living in orchards. All were safely out of view. People of color entered the scene only as gardeners and housekeepers. We, the light-skinned, postwar offspring had also been carefully scripted and crafted. Puffy-sleeved, pastel Easter dresses, curls by Tonette, white-lace-topped socks inside our black patent leather Mary Janes. The boys were dressed as cowboys, but we girls had been dressed as dolls. We were asked to display appreciation for birthday parties full of ribbons, cakes, balloons, friends, and party favors. Our parents had created the insulated world of Orinda, protected from another reality. The Caldecott Tunnel drilled through the Berkeley Hills provided the only leak in the geographical barricade used to keep out all forms of discomfort. My evening's sin had carried that discomfort across those hills. The slap of Tom's hand attempted to ward off the reality of Oakland. A slap meant to shore up the mythical families portrayed in 1950s TV sitcoms. To ward off knowledge that the tickets to the American Dream were only sold to whites and that the price for our country was Black servitude, reservation poverty, poisoned farm workers, and now the lives of Asians half a world away—their body count buoying up the endangered suburban myth.

The price for my traitorous tongue would be ostracism. The air of Orinda had become too thick for me to breathe. The oxygen sucked from the lungs of non-white humanity lay too heavy in the valley. That night, I felt stifled under a blanket of persistent illusions. The bedroom walls of my childhood revealed themselves to be my unwitting prison.

The contrast between my mother's and my own Saturday activities, and between dinners at friends' homes on opposite sides of the bay—Steve and Libby's versus Lil and Tom's—reinforced my need to flee Orinda. If I remained in my parents' home, the serenity I had gained in Africa now threatened to melt away like an elegant candle set down too near a familiar but overly warm furnace.

In the morning after the Mikas' dinner, my parents and I adhered to the proscribed script: eggshells to be carefully trod upon, the incident never to be mentioned. How many other Orinda children were contemplating fleeing? How many children were breathing air liberated by reality? I flopped onto the living room couch and picked up the neatly folded pages of the *Sunday Oakland Tribune* lying on the coffee table. Turning to the classified ads for rentals, I came across some possibilities.

Jean stumbled out of the kitchen with two cups of coffee, unaware of the previous night's difficulties. "You take milk, right?"

Relieving her of the extended cup, I smiled up at her. "Look, I found a couple of apartments that sound pretty good in Berkeley; want to live there together?"

Jean laughed. Orinda life fitted her easily. Already having found herself a "good" husband, her goal now was to remain and raise children in the same place we'd grown up, hopefully not living far from our parents. It was probably a good thing that she didn't take my housemate suggestion seriously.

I called the next day in response to an ad for an inexpensive room in a shared house in downtown Berkeley. Again, borrowing the car that my parents graciously put at my disposal, I drove through the tunnel to the other side of the hills to check out my potential housing.

The old building on Durant Avenue near the Cal campus hulked beneath cedar shakes, aged to blackness by decades of Berkeley weather. A lively young man, apparently in his late teens, showed me the five-bedroom house and its overgrown yard. Three of its four inhabitants, he told me, were currently students. The other was over thirty and had had his legs crushed in a motorcycle accident; he survived on disability payments. I'd have the fifth bedroom and a bath shared by two others. Dinners were communal: each one took a turn cooking, but for weekends and all other meals, we were on our own. I liked the place immediately and said so. Everyone gathered to interview me, and finding me an acceptable housemate, told me the room would be available at the beginning of July. I would have to continue as an Orinda resident for a while.

My shaking bed rattled away whatever dream I tried to hold onto, but consciousness won on a sunny June morning. Earthquake!

"Wake up to a beautiful day!" Jean was shaking my bed. It wasn't an earthquake.

"Is it snowing?" I wondered if it were snowing; something that had happened only once during my Orinda childhood.

But as my awakening brain realized it was early June, I figured snow wasn't it. Besides, her tone didn't match her implied sentiment. I squinted my eyes open and peered up at my sister's silhouette against the bedroom window. I couldn't see her face, but her next words dripped with anger. "They shot Robert Kennedy!"

RFK was our political hope. He was running for president, telling it like it is. Declaring war on organized crime, not Asian countries.

Before JFK's assassination, none of us really believed a U.S. president could be shot. And then, just a couple of months ago, Martin Luther King

Jr.'s death had left us reeling. The United States was slipping away from the post-WWII, "I like Ike" world in which my sister and I had grown up.

"How?" When I'd gone to sleep the night before, Kennedy had just been declared the winner of California's presidential primary election.

"After he spoke in L.A., someone just shot him. Just point-blank shot him." Jean's voice was laced with anger. The assassination shook her emotionally as hard as she had been shaking my bed.

"This country is fucked." I startled Jean as I let slip the word that had been liberated on Berkeley's campus by the Free Speech Movement.

We headed to the kitchen where our folks were watching the tiny black-and-white TV set by the table. Numb, no one spoke. Even my mother let the fact of the news settle into our house, not trying to scuttle it beneath her rug of prattle.

America reeled. The country was spinning a chrysalis for some type of metamorphosis, but none of us knew what creature might emerge.

SEVENTEEN

Project FOCUS bumbled its way through the summer like an inebriated, tight-rope walker, often teetering on heart-stopping verges of imminent disaster, but somehow making it through. No one cracked a single skull trying backflips into a backyard swimming pool, no serious fights broke out, and no children were misplaced for longer than an hour. Peter and I generally oversaw different areas on any given day, so we seldom worried about job/romance conflicts.

In the week before the program began, we had to dismiss two of our Neighborhood Youth Corps counselors for inappropriate conduct, but after that, the group proved pretty amazing. Several Orinda families hosted our teenage counselors and the ten children under each one's supervision. Backyard pools turned into raucous, splashing playgrounds for a few hours each weekday during the program's six weeks. Trim, tanned Orinda matrons interacted with Afroed young men, perhaps secretly enjoying the scantily clad view of one another. I watched for any signs of discomfort or misunderstanding where I might need to intervene, but was surprised to see almost none. The high school students we had chosen proved capable of handling both the children and their Orinda hosts.

Painting, clay sculpture, games, and outdoor sports at both the Orinda and Fruitvale churches occupied the children when they weren't at the pools, but of course, the pools were what they most hoped for each day. We tried to integrate each group equally, but since more Oakland than Orinda children signed up for the program, it never worked out perfectly. Throughout the summer, Orinda children still tended to clump with Orinda children, and Oakland with Oakland. But a few friendships were forged that to continue past the end of summer. Certainly, all the children involved came to know that the humans living on the opposite side of the hills from them were also just humans, with similar giggles, pouts, exuberances, frustrations, and joys.

In the final evaluation, our pilot program was deemed a success. The churches decided to repeat Project FOCUS the following summer, validating Peter's and my assessment that we hadn't screwed up anything too badly. This summer job had been a good start toward a life that aligned well with my new worldview.

When the program was almost finished, I left my parents' home and moved into the Berkeley house on Durant Street. By then, my family had figured out Peter's and my relationship and we were all functioning on a tacit, don't-ask-don't-tell agreement. My parents would have much preferred Steve be the one I rode with into the hills, and that the ride be in a midsized Ford Tempest instead of straddling the back seat of a red Yamaha motorcycle. On the sparkling July morning when I reversed a journey begun months ago, I felt freer to live out my increasingly active sex life, and also to align my life with the spirit of my African revelations. One motive for my escape tasted far less noble than the other.

On moving day, as I parked in front of the old brown house on Durant Street and began carrying boxes across its dandelion-filled lawn, the youngest member of the household came out to help me. His neatly trimmed brown hair and plaid shirt did nothing to adjust my guess about his age, not moving it upward, toward something that might allow him to drive a car or drink beer legally. He scarcely looked sixteen, but I chose not to question him.

The oldest member of the group sat on the couch smoking something that neither looked nor smelled like a cigarette. He nodded with a slight smile, but went back to his book. I recalled that he'd crushed his legs in a motorcycle accident several years before, so I didn't expect any offer of help. However, I would have enjoyed more of a greeting.

Dust motes danced through rays of sunlight streaming into the room I'd been given. I plopped a suitcase onto the bed and asked that my boxes be left where the ceiling slanted to meet the floor. The room wasn't large, but it was sufficient. I didn't plan to spend a lot of time in it, or in the rest of the house. During my interview, I'd gathered that each person more or less did their own thing. Household members appeared to know each other well, but I hoped they didn't expect me to become part of their collective "family." I was open to new friendships, but my emotional energies were focused elsewhere.

After filling the small closet with the clothes I'd brought, I clattered down the wooden stairs to find the living room deserted. So much for a welcoming party. Somewhat relieved, I drove down Telegraph Avenue to Peter's apartment.

Our relationship's rapid progression left me confused and uncomfortable about where we were headed and whether or not it was a great idea. Since our summer jobs had required minimal homework, Peter and I fled the city every weekend: camping and hiking in the Sierras, floating down lazy streams on air mattresses, or if we got stuck in town, swimming at the Olympic-sized pool at his parents' Oakland hills condo. We proved to be great playmates, both in and out of the bedroom. But I wondered how well our relationship aligned with my new values. How did Peter fit into the culture evolving around the country?

Many evenings (and nights) spent at Peter's apartment left me well acquainted with roommate John and the infamous cat Fred (named after Peter's annoying father). John was first in his class at Boalt Law School at Cal (no small accomplishment), often railed against the Vietnam War, and supported nearly all humanitarian causes. But those attributes contrasted with his verbal irreverence for any and all things dear to other humans. He'd taken the Free Speech Movement to heart, and "fuck" appeared at least once in any sentence he uttered. I struggled not to dislike him, or at least not to disapprove of his general nature.

Peter admired his cat and had told me several Fred stories, but I eventually got to witness one myself. Their apartment's Formica-topped kitchen table sat against the wall beside a wide, sliding window. One evening, three of us were eating barbecued ribs brought home from our favorite eatery. Small and wiry, Fred sat nearby with his eyes fixed on our dinner. John leaned forward, dripping barbecue sauce onto his plate. Fred leapt onto the table and swiped the rib from John's hand, making off with it into the living room, leaving a trail of sauce across the already-stained rug. Both Peter and John found that hilarious. Fred ate the rib and John cleaned up the mess on the rug.

Such a scene would never have unfolded in any of our parents' suburban homes. Admiring Fred's acts of spunky self-expression, the guys saw the cat more like a roommate than a pet. Was that an example of having a wider definition of "us," a more encompassing worldview? Or was I trying to stretch an explanation of the silly antics of male college students?

Peter played no instrument and didn't sing, but he immersed himself in the new music that accompanied the revolution. I loved dancing with abandon at the Filmore West or the Avalon Ballroom, but having been trained in classical music all my life, I was skeptical of the quality of some of the screeching and yowling currently being called "music."

Finishing the breakfast dishes one morning after both of the guys had left, I allowed my voice to soar at full volume with "What's the Use of Wonderin'" from *Carousel*. In high school, when we lived in New York, singing and musical plays had been my life. I'd starred opposite Kenny Howard in a local production of *Oklahoma*, and had played Nettie Fowler with him in *Carousel*. Kenny was going on to a professional career and had just opened on Broadway in *Promises, Promises*. I was happy for him, and possibly a tad envious of what he'd chosen to pursue. Now it felt good to exercise my vocal cords, and the Roger-and-Hammerstein lyrics advised me to stop worrying so much about who Peter was, but to just enjoy him. Maybe that was good advice.

We had recently gone to see Janis (now the second time for me) at the Filmore West, an intimate setting where bunches of grapes and smoldering joints had passed among the dancers. Janis, mere feet away from us, poured out every molecule of her emotional being to the audience. By the end, I imagined each of us felt we'd spent hours making love with Janis Joplin.

Leaving the dishes to dry themselves, I rubbed Fred's ears, then went over to Peter's record collection to search for something by Janis. I picked *Cheap Thrills* out of a brown packing box holding a few dozen LPs. I pulled the large vinyl disk out of its cardboard sleeve, cradling it by the edges so as not to touch the grooves with my fingers. Carefully sliding it over the metal peg on the stereo's Gerard turntable, I lifted the needle, gently placing it onto the record's outside edge, pleased that it made no scratchy sound. As the music began, I smiled at the album's cover, cartoons of Janis posed to introduce each song. In the center, "Ball and Chain" went with a drawing of Janis in a zebra-striped dress, slouched forward, dragging a black ball and chain behind her. The song had been number one on the charts for several weeks. I waited for it to come on, wanting to listen again, more carefully, to the song I'd first heard her sing in Golden Gate Park.

Her band, Big Brother and the Holding Company, began the number with a high, piercing, screechy guitar solo, dropping to a scratchy bass guitar. Strange as they sounded to me, the notes were musically perfect. The scratchiness sounded much like me inadvertently sliding the needle across the record grooves. But then, Janis' voice came in sweet and soft and gentle, telling us she was sitting by the window lookin' out at the rain. The band hushed, smooth and gentle behind her voice. She told us she was grabbed by something that felt like a ball and chain. Her voice grew loud and painful. Sandpaper rasped as she cried out, "why! why! why!" things go so wrong. Jarring. Janis risked damaging her vocal cords with that sound. My throat hurt for her. The song's emotional pain translated into physical pain. Then her lyrics softened and her voice smoothed out. She just wanted to hold and love, until her lyrics flowed on notes held long and gently, with perfect vibrato. When I'd sung with my trained voice throughout high school in New York, I could hold all the notes smoothly, keeping my vocal cords from scratching, keeping the air moving, steady and unshaking through my upper sinuses. Perfect control when I performed well. But this woman, this free and creative woman, played with her voice! Gentle as flowing water when singing of love, but wild and scratchy when telling of pain and confusion. Janis' voice lived every emotion of the song. At the end, she slipped around the entire scale as she held onto the final "ball and chain," hitting amazing intervals between notes.

Though I had been trained by an opera coach, I couldn't begin to do with my voice anything close to what I'd just listened to. I could, perhaps, hold my own next to Shirley Jones playing Laurey in *Oklahoma*, but I saw that was pitiful compared to the awesome creativity of this woman. Janis' free experimentation with her songs seemed to be the vocal equivalent of the Movement: ideals encouraging you to bust loose from conventions and be your own person. We were marching with Caesar Chavez and boycotting grapes to support the farmworkers, learning to speak Spanish, hoisting backpacks and hitchhiking around the globe, and these new artists were writing the music—the soundtrack to our lives and dreams. Joan Baez, Joni Mitchell, and other folk singers sang into the hearts of the flower children, while the rock groups danced us into action.

I thumbed through the rest of Peter's albums: Cream, The Rolling Stones, The Chambers Brothers, BB King. We were seeing all these people live. I wouldn't have experienced half of this if Peter weren't such a fan. Did he understand these concepts musically? Did he pay attention to the messages held for us in some of the songs? The man might be more complex than I was giving him credit for. I realized what a privilege it was to be in the midst of everything going on. The times, they definitely were a-changin'!

Spending more and more time at Peter's, I seldom returned to Durant Street to eat the meals cooked by my housemates. Making dinner for everyone once a week eventually became an annoying obligation. They complained that I wasn't being creative enough (maybe I did make tuna casserole a bit too often), but I felt that the main problem lay more with the fact that I hadn't really integrated into their communal living situation. Marijuana was certainly not unknown at Peter's place, but the Durant house seemed to emit a permanent haze. The sweetish odor permeated the furniture and carpets. Most of the time, I was willing to take a hit if a joint was passed around, but I didn't share the same commitment as the others.

After I had fed us homemade lasagna with Italian salad—an improvement over tuna casserole—three of us were sitting in the living room late one evening when a house member who had missed dinner tore through the front door.

"There's a raid coming. Flush everything!"

The others flew through the house. Doors banged. Toilets flushed.

"Wait, are those his allergy pills!" echoed down the stairs.

"I don't know; just flush everything."

I felt strange simply sitting on the couch, but I had nothing to contribute to the drug cleansing, and had no idea how to help dispose of whatever they had. With a sweaty forehead, I stayed curled on the overstuffed couch, reading Erich von Däniken's *Chariots of the Gods*, a semi-scientific bestseller questioning visits to Earth by alien astronauts. Interesting though it was, I found myself rereading the same paragraph over and over.

Eventually the others trickled back into the living room and we waited for what was to come, but the warning proved to be a false alarm. I wondered what types of drugs had been flushed, and hoped my housemate's allergies wouldn't be too bad that night. I thought about Marty's stories in Africa about how the Bay Area drug scene had been changing. Did these folks have only "hippie drugs," or did our house hold something more serious? Maybe I didn't want to know.

The next day, I started hunting for a cheaper, and maybe less risky, place to live. Browsing through the newspaper, I found an ad for a room in an older woman's apartment directly beside campus. It seemed a better fit. With no cooking facilities included, I would be admitting to myself that I was eating almost all of my meals at Peter and John's. But that was fine with them, since I did most of the cooking. They also appreciated the fact that I had scrubbed all the mold out of the bathroom and removed crusted stickiness from the kitchen counters.

A few weeks after I'd officially moved out of the communal Berkeley brownstone, Peter handed me a copy of the *Oakland Tribune*. He raised his eyebrows in a "Wow, do you believe this?" kind of way.

"Largest Drug Bust in Berkeley's History." The headline glared in bold, black letters.

"Keep looking," Peter advised, his tone echoing his eyebrows. There, in the middle of the front page, sat a photo of the very house I'd been living in.

"Close one!"

I vowed to choose my housemates more carefully in the future.

When Peter and I were becoming an item and my living situation was in flux, university classes began for the inner-city teaching program. Walking down Telegraph Avenue the first day, I entered campus through the arch of Sather Gate. I crossed Sproul Plaza, checking beside the student union to see if anyone had put soap in Ludwig's Fountain that morning, but no bubbles were foaming over its sides. At the beginning of that summer, the Board of Regents had officially named it "Ludwig's Fountain," dedicating the popular hangout to the dog who, for four years, spent most of his days playing in the fountain, amusing students and accepting the treats they offered.

Passing imposing, white stone buildings, I found a path through the green belt bisecting campus. Pausing on the footbridge that crossed Strawberry Creek, I let the watery music soothe the butterflies churning through my stomach at the thought of beginning a master's program here.

Arriving at Tolman Hall, other students greeted me, equally nervous about their new careers. The education department, however, proved to be anything but intimidating. A woman wearing blue jeans and a loose, green shirt introduced us to the program. "We have chosen you, because we are certain you will make excellent teachers. Now it's our job to get you there." In just six weeks, we would be paired up to team-teach in our own classrooms in the heart of Oakland. Our instructors would help us create student-centered classrooms, using the same principles to teach us that they wanted us to use with our own students. Oakland needed teachers and Berkeley intended to create them out of the raw material seated in the room that day. An exciting challenge for all sides.

My classroom assignment for observation was Mrs. Brown's fifth grade in a downtown summer-school program. Mrs. Brown—a middle-aged woman with a generous bosom for periodically comforting children—was not brown, although nearly all her students were. With quiet assurance, she kept her classroom in perfect control. Students worked at desks in orderly rows, engaged in the lessons, and were nearly always polite. This, I knew, stemmed from Mrs. Brown's twenty years of teaching experience, and I doubted my classes would ever function with her well-oiled precision. But I watched, took notes, helped students, and eventually taught a few lessons.

As the weeks went by, I got to know individual children. The school wasn't located in Oakland's poorest district, but the students' experiences were narrow. They had been on field trips around Oakland, to the art museum and the zoo, but most had never been outside the city. Many had never seen the waves of the Pacific Ocean, just outside the Golden Gate on the other side of the bay. None had been to the Sierras where Peter and I often camped. The reality of that inequity percolated through my brain for many days.

Toward the end of my classroom observation period (they didn't call it student teaching, because we were still hardly able to handle a class), my parents took their annual, two-week trip up to a cabin in Yosemite. Jean and I were scheduled to join them the following weekend. I suddenly thought of a way I could help at least one student experience more of the world. Running my idea past Mrs. Brown, I initiated a small contest. Several criteria would determine the winner: helping others, doing homework, and turning in their classwork—all things I thought the children could more or less, equally attain. The prize would be joining me for a two-night stay in my parents' cabin in Yosemite.

The Yosemite cabin had no phone. I left a message for my parents with the cabins' manager. My mother loved children, so I didn't think that they would object to an extra sleeping bag and air mattress in their cabin for a weekend. This plan would be wonderful: my parents could meet one of the children I'd been working with and better understand what I sought to do with my life. The winner of the contest would have a new and interesting experience. Win-win.

I introduced my week-long contest to the classroom and the children bought into the idea with varying degrees of enthusiasm, although all began working toward the reward. By Wednesday, I hadn't heard back from my parents, and the winner would be announced the next day. I called Jean and told her the situation. She enthusiastically supported the plan, advising me to leave another message for our folks.

On Thursday, I still hadn't heard back from my parents. I announced to the class that there was a tie; both Maria and Aletha had earned the most points and would come with me for a weekend in the mountains. They could bring overnight bags to school the next day and we'd leave from there, returning Sunday night. Aletha and Maria joined hands and jumped around with glee, while others sighed in disappointment. I felt a pang for not being able to bring everyone.

That night, I finally received a call from my dad.

"Carol," he began in a firm voice. This was odd. "Carol," not "Curly?" He never called me "Carol." I didn't have time to think about that.

"Oh, thank heaven. You called back!"

"I don't think I understand the message you left. You're planning to bring an Oakland student up to the cabin?"

"Well, actually," I cheerfully blundered on, "it's now two students. I ran a contest and two girls tied. So, I'm going to bring them both with me."

"No, you're not. It's not okay for you to assume you can just impose them on us." Stern anger wrapped itself around his words. Icy prickles began circulating through my body at my father's unusual tone of voice.

"But I tried several times to reach you. When I couldn't, I ran it by Jean. We didn't think you'd see it as an imposition. You can meet two of the children I work with. It'll be fun!"

"Two children in the cabin would be too disruptive."

"But they're wonderful girls. They're fifth-graders. They're totally reasonable and responsible and I know they'll be perfectly well-behaved."

"It's not fair to burden your mother with this."

"Burden! They're no burden. Just two extra sleeping bags on the floor. I'll take them away on hikes. They're fun and interesting. Besides, I already told them they're coming. You can be mad at me; I judged wrong, I'm sorry. But please, we can't disappoint them now. They've never even seen the mountains. It's an incredible chance for them. It's only two nights."

"No. I said no. You won't bring those girls here."

The line went dead in my hand. I stared at the phone. I had no memory of my dad ever talking to me that way. Every piece of me rebelled against the statement my parents were making, "You will not bring those *Negro* girls here." Tears of hurt, anger, and disbelief rolled into my lap, darkening the navy denim of my jeans. Who was this man I had loved and respected all my life? A man who voted for Adlai Stevenson over Dwight David Eisenhower because he liked his intelligence and liberal policies? A man who spoke against injustice when we'd taken a trip through the south? Obviously, his actions didn't mesh well with his politics. My parents wanted the world to have more justice for everyone—as long as it didn't inconvenience them.

Nearly frozen with hurt and anger, I called my sister, needing to share the shock of what happened. She agreed that had the girls been white, there would have been no problem. Inner-city Oakland children would not be welcomed by our family.

"When the folks dropped me off at college my freshman year," her pained voice told me through the phone, "Dad left me with only one word of advice: 'take care of yourself, and don't come home with a Negro boyfriend.' I couldn't believe he'd say that. Of all the possible warnings he could have left me with. It still shocks me."

I inhaled, slowly and deliberately, trying to digest Jean's new information. We ended our conversation with an agreement that she still would join our parents in Yosemite, but that I wouldn't be coming up to the cabin. I knew I needed to take the girls elsewhere for the weekend.

Aletha's tight braids bounced, and Maria's long legs skipped happily as we walked to my car Friday afternoon. After handing me permission slips from their parents, along with their small, overnight bags, Maria and Althea climbed into my car and off we went.

Our exact destination didn't matter to them; anything woodsy and not-Oakland would be new and interesting. I fought to ignore the icepick drilling through my heart, not wanting to ruin our time together. Although the Sierra Nevada mountain range ran half the length of California, inside my mind, their entire length was superimposed with images of my parents at Yosemite. I decided to head southwest instead of east, choosing Big Basin, a beautiful park in the Santa Cruz Mountains.

Ancient redwoods towered over our site. We unpacked the car and I instructed the girls in the fine art of putting up tents. The soft duff, spongy under the tent floor, made our air mattresses almost unnecessary, but we puffed away and inflated them anyway. After we'd rolled out our sleeping bags, Maria ran to the nearest tree, climbing the slight rise its roots made up to its base.

"Look at this!" she urged, stretching her arms wide. "Come grab my hand." Althea and I joined her, spreading ourselves against the trunk of the tree. "How many of us would it take to go around it?"

"At least a hundred!" Althea speculated.

"Well," I cautioned, laughing, "maybe not quite that many, but lots and lots."

We made a campfire and found green sticks for roasting hotdogs. Grabbing the wieners with buns warmed on the edge of the grate, we pulled them off, juice sputtering into the coals, and smeared on relish, mustard, and catsup.

"S'mores," they cried after devouring a couple of dogs, "can we make s'mores?"

"Yes," I said, startled. They may not have camped before, but perhaps they'd had cookouts in Tilden Park. Marshmallows got pushed onto roasting sticks as I laid out graham crackers and unwrapped Hershey's chocolate bars, laying a couple of squares on each of the cookies that awaited a squishy, roasted treat.

"Don't let it catch fire!" Aletha cautioned when I joined them, gesturing that I should pull my stick farther back. "Check out this place. Coals are just right!"

Maria and I became her apprentices; Althea proved to be a master marshmallow-roaster. We slowly rolled our sticks, melting the puffs of white into golden messes not deemed ready until seconds before they would have slid off their sticks to become fuel for flames. Moving my stick carefully to the table, I squished my golden gem between chocolate squares and graham crackers, licking melted, marshmallowy chocolate off the edges before taking my first bite. A perfect s'more!

For the next two days, I got to be ten again. We hiked to waterfalls, waded in streams, made pine-needle baskets, read aloud from *Wind in the Willows*, and cooked five-star camp meals. There wasn't a moment when I'd been required to put on my adult hat. If anything, Althea kept us better organized and on task than I ever would have.

When I thought of my parents, which, surprisingly, I seldom did, my only thought was that they had no idea what their attitudes had made them miss. But the rift was real. Our family now had a narrow-but-deep chasm growing between the ground I was choosing to stand on and my parents' racist world.

The fracture of my family mirrored the escalating division of our country. Robert Kennedy's assassination and Lyndon Johnson's announcement that he would not seek reelection resulted in a mostly generational divide within the Democratic Party. At the end of August, we who supported antiwar presidential candidate Eugene McCarthy over the hawkish, "establishment" candidate Hubert Humphrey were appalled to witness live television broadcasts of brutal chaos outside the Democratic Convention in Chicago. Images of police clubbing youthful protestors and dragging them into paddy wagons shocked those of us insulated from any practice of police violence against citizens. Just before the convention started, the Chicago police raided the mostly black neighborhoods of South Chicago, carrying out mass arrests of a black power group, the Blackstone Rangers.

Division and chaos reigned inside the convention hall as Senator Abraham Ribicoff gave the nominating speech for Senator Eugene McCarthy. He added that if McCarthy were president, there would no longer be "Gestapo tactics on the streets of Chicago." Mayor Daley—who was chairing the convention—rose up, screaming over the resulting bedlam. The expletives he swore at the senator included a racial slur on his Jewish heritage, and ended with a demand that Ribicoff "Go home!" The chairman of the Colorado delegation asked if Mayor Daley could be compelled to suspend the "police state terror being perpetrated at this minute on kids in front of the Conrad Hilton?" When a platform passed that would continue the bombing of North Vietnam, the delegation from New York put on black armbands and began to sing "We Shall Overcome." In the end, the Democratic Party nominated Humphrey—although eighty percent of primary voters (in those states holding primaries) elected the antiwar candidate—narrowly defeating the peace plank.

My image of American democracy, one which the country that raised me had instilled in me, quivered like a ballerina before her debut solo. Both the liberalness of the family I belonged to and the legs that I thought my country stood upon had devolved into something questionable. The Tapestry felt like a dusty carpet being beaten on a clothesline.

EIGHTEEN

Twenty-three of us formed a cohort in the first classes of the University of California's inner-city teaching program. The group had become closer as the time approached when we would be paired together and plopped into classrooms of our own. When I learned that Betty Cohen would be my teaching partner, I danced a little happy dance. Betty had already raised two children. She was calm, kind, and unflappable. If I were team-teaching with her, I should be safe from catastrophe.

I also had grown close to a woman who had the locker beside mine in gym class. Sondra was short and bouncy, and often made me laugh. I enjoyed chatting with her while we were changing clothes. We soon began hanging out together in other classes too.

I loved the elementary music class. The young woman teaching us made music theory so easy and visceral that I found myself comprehending basic concepts better than I ever had. She taught us musical intervals by pairing them with the beginnings of songs we all knew. Such a simple way to teach music theory: even elementary school children could learn that. All of us could learn to teach that way.

"New Math" was a bit more challenging. Gone were the long-division problems of my childhood arithmetic books. We were encouraged to think in ones and tens and hundreds and manipulate those differently than the ways we'd once known. There were overlapping Venn diagrams, and problems written for "base 8," along with other strange concepts. Although daunting at first, as I began to grasp the ideas, I started to find new math fun.

I've never been particularly coordinated, but the college expected us to be proficient enough at sports to teach physical education to our classes. Sondra coached me through some of my bumbling athletics and helped me laugh at my lack of skills instead of getting frustrated. Although Sondra was Black, she was raised in a middle-class Oakland family, and I didn't see many cultural differences between us. Sondra was simply a new friend who happened to be Black. Although, coming from the white side of the hills, I had never had a Black friend before.

U.C. Berkeley had a beautiful, Olympic-sized pool in the Hearst Gymnasium. Swimming was included in our classes—a happy situation for me, since I swam way better than I could carry off most other sports. Students weren't allowed to wear our own suits in the pool, but were required to use the suits issued by the university.

One afternoon when our class arrived, the line to get our suits stretched down the rows of metal lockers. Finding ourselves far back in line, Sondra and I chatted to pass the time. Although I didn't consciously think about it, all the women in front of us happened to be white. After reaching the window, each one walked back past us with her neatly folded, black tank suit. When her turn came, a lady in the window handed Sondra a stretched-out and baggy suit, faded to a dull brown. No one else had gotten anything resembling the worn-out suit. No one else had been a person of color. I looked at the woman whose eyes didn't meet my gaze. Mouth agape, I turned to Sondra. It was not a coincidence that the only Black woman in line had gotten the only worn-out suit. I moved toward the window, ready to object to what had just happened.

Sondra put her hand on my arm to stop me as she shook her head, silently requesting that I ignore what I'd just seen. "It happens all the time. Just forget it."

"But..."

"You have to pick your battles; you can't fight everyone."

I accepted the neatly folded black suit handed to me and followed Sondra back to our lockers. We made small talk as we changed clothes. It wasn't my right to cause a scene if Sondra asked me not to. I got it. We had not been raised the same. I had never been denied something or made to feel less-than, simply because I looked different from someone else. *It happens all the time.* As I hung out with her more, I found that to be true. I got waited on first; people in positions of authority spoke to me instead of her; clerks often watched her with suspicion when we shopped together. I was starting to have glimpses of Sondra's world.

John Holt's class on theories of education drew a huge number of students. In 1964, he had written a book, *How Children Fail,* part of a vanguard of change for public-school education. I felt excited to take a class from this dynamic and fascinating man. With my green canvas Berkeley book bag thrown over my shoulder, I made my way toward the stage in a mammoth lecture hall. Hundreds of students were filing in from both sides of the room. Finding a seat, I pulled out the pristine, spiral-bound notebook I'd labelled for this class and pulled the cap off the olive-green fountain pen I'd carried across Africa. John Holt walked across the stage and climbed onto a stool.

"First of all," he spoke, gazing around the lecture hall, "there are way too many people in this class for any meaningful discussions. We're passing around cards on which I'd like you to write down your name and the grade you would like to receive in the class. I'll give you whatever grade you write down. If any of you are willing, please put down a B+ or a B. It makes the administration happier than when I only give out a couple hundred As. The first thing I did when I got tenure was to institute this grading system. They hate it, but now they can't stop me. So, please, all of you who are here only for the grade, don't come back. I only want people here who will discuss the problems of our educational system and want to brainstorm ways to solve them."

I thought back to when I'd lived in Sausalito. The newborn flower children didn't trust college students. Students were considered to be too much a part of "the establishment" and had not, to quote Timothy Leary, "turned on, tuned in, and dropped out." Now I had, once again, become one of those college students. But I was finding that the university culture wasn't quite what the Sausalitoites imagined. Many professors helped organize protests and staged their own mini rebellions. John Holt seemed pretty tuned in.

The next day, over two-thirds of the class was absent. Those of us who remained huddled toward the front, excited to see where this man would take us.

"Our schools were designed to educate nineteenth-century factory workers. They deliberately create groupthink, with standardized texts and standardized tests to make standardized minds. Sit down in your row, be quiet, raise your hand if you want to speak or if you need to use the bathroom. Creativity and originality have little place in the prisons in which we incarcerate our children. The best solution, which, granted, will never happen, would be to close all the public schools for two years and then start again with a whole new model."

Wow, this man definitely qualified as a revolutionary!

By the end of the quarter, my entire view of what a schoolroom should look like and how it should function had changed. John advocated creating learning environments in which children—whose desire to learn is insatiable until our present system closes it down—can find ways to learn anything they wish. Our jobs as teachers were to meet them where they were individually and then supply activities and materials to take them forward.

For our class final, we were encouraged to choose something creative that embodied our principles for education. When I returned from Africa, I had been frustrated by not being able to explain my experience of the Tapestry, what it had felt like to find my consciousness melded into something infinitely larger. I'd made several attempts at painting the experience. If there was anything I hoped to instill in my students, it would be a sense they were connected by love into the Tapestry, as important and integral a part of the universe as anything else. I decided to make one more attempt at depicting my experience.

Choosing acrylics as my medium, I painted a black background of infinite space. Words floated into this universe, written in what looked like thin, shiny, steel pipes. "Fear" slanted across the canvas in large, cold letters. Behind it stood "terror," slightly smaller to give a sense of distance, and slanted in the opposite direction. Behind "terror," smaller still, I painted the word "alone." Finally, written in glowing yellow, rounded letters and small enough that one had to come up close to read it, was the word "together." I wanted the painting to portray my journey through each emotion into my discovery of the unity of everything.

Nerves rattled as I delivered this depiction of my deepest beliefs. John had invited our now-smallish group to meet off-campus to discuss our projects. We were seated on the grass, passing around a few bottles of Chardonnay that John had provided. When my turn came, I unwrapped the large painting and displayed it to the group, explaining how I felt it related to teaching. If I had stepped out of my jeans and pulled off my shirt, I could not have felt more exposed. People set down their paper cups and peered at my creation.

"I get it," one buckskin-clad student offered.

"Wow!" another volunteered, "That's exactly what I found on acid!"

Hadn't Sunjoy told me that same thing about LSD? Didn't she say it dissolved the ego?

"For real?" I asked.

His eyes slid away from my painting, rising to meet my incredulous gaze. "For real!" he responded, holding my eyes as his mouth widened into a large grin.

John Holt stared for a long time. With his gaze locked onto the canvas, he nodded his shaggy head. "You'll be a good teacher."

I exhaled months of frustration. Others understood.

Our teaching assignments came out. Betty and I would have a fourth-grade class at Bella Vista Elementary School. Located southeast of Lake Merritt, Bella Vista was in a racially mixed, "white-flight," neighborhood. The middle-class-ish area had been changing into a primarily Black area, as white families moved to the suburbs. Immigrants from many countries had settled there, offering vast cultural diversity to an anthropologist-turned-teacher. Overcrowded and critically underfunded, no classroom at Bella Vista had less than thirty students. No one in her right mind would choose to babysit thirty children, yet we would be expected to contain them for five hours each day and actually teach them something.

I was excited about our assignment, anxious to get to know such a variety of families, but felt sad when I found out that Sondra had been assigned to a school half a city away. With the responsibilities of our new teaching jobs, it was unlikely that we'd see much of each other once our jobs began.

Thirty-three faces turned toward us on the first day of classes, curious to see who their new teachers would turn out to be. I feared it might be the only time, for a while, that we'd be able to hold the attention of all those eyes.

I leaned against the old, oak desk on my side of the room. Betty stood opposite me, introducing herself in a quiet, steady voice. I'd had such bad indigestion the night before, I thought I'd have to call in sick on our first day. The upset only calmed when I'd given myself permission not to come to school. Once my body thought it was off the hook, my nerves quieted enough to let me function again. As I awaited my turn to talk, I felt like I was made of semi-gelled material, too weak to stand without the support of my desk.

In front of me swarmed a sea of various-sized afros adorning the heads of both girls and boys, a few glossy black heads with hair reaching down the backs of chairs, and one mop of limp, pale hair looking decidedly unbrushed. Baseball caps and stocking caps were perched here and there, and a sweatshirt hood completely obscured one entire head. Nervously scanning the faces below each hairstyle, I focused in on one pair of wide brown eyes sparkling in an eager face. Something inside me relaxed and I smiled. *Yes*, I thought, *this is why I'm here*. Pulling myself erect, I stepped forward and attempted to be worthy of the trust and anticipation radiating from those eyes. Floundering through my introductory speech, I began my new career as an elementary school teacher.

For the next few weeks, when I wasn't at Bella Vista or in evening classes on campus, I continued spending as much time as possible with Peter, often meeting him at his office after work. As a graduate student in Cal's industrial relations department, Peter had a shared office in the white stone building located on Haste Street, just off Telegraph Avenue, a few blocks from the main Cal campus. As I was headed to his office one afternoon, I noticed a group of long-haired people gathered across the street. Some old houses had been torn down nearly a year before, when the university bought the property. With just a few buildings left facing Telegraph, the rest of the lot sat vacant, a square city block of dirt and mud, gathering trash and abandoned cars. Several dozen people were swinging picks and wielding shovels, breaking up the hard-packed ground. Curious, I crossed the street to ask a shirtless young man what was going on.

The well-muscled worker rammed his shovel into baked earth, then left it standing as he turned to me. "Didn't you see what the *Berkeley Barb* wrote yesterday?"

I shook my head.

"It said that we're gonna build a park here," he continued, "and that people should come help. So a bunch of us came. We're makin' a park," he said, grinning.

"The university is making this into a park?" The group didn't look like a crew contracted by the institution.

He took off his beaded headband, wiped sweat from his forehead, and pulled the band back on to restrain his shoulder-length hair. "Nope. It's us, not Cal. This isn't being used for anything, so we thought having a park here would be groovy. We're going to plant some trees, make it green. You know, grow some flowers. We might even put in a vegetable garden and grow food for folks."

I smiled into his eyes when he met my gaze, but declined to take a hit of the joint that had magically appeared, pinched between his thumb and forefingers. A halter-topped woman with blonde braids carried over a flat of pansy-starts.

"You want to help?" she asked me. Wrapping one arm possessively around the man's waist, she took the rolled cigarette he'd offered me, inhaled a deep drag, and held it in.

I shook my head. "Not today. But it's a great idea."

They returned to planting flowers as I continued on to Peter's building, mulling over the boldness of their plan. I liked the idea of making something beautiful and useful out of the year-old eyesore. Even though the university owned the property, why should they object? They were getting free labor for improving their grounds.

I was wrong, however, in predicting the university's official reaction. Chancellor Roger Heyns announced that further work on Peoples' Park would be futile, and that the university would immediately begin developing the land. His announcement was disregarded. It failed to stop progress on the park's construction.

During the next few weeks, we watched from the windows of Peter's office as trees and shrubs were being planted. Some form of music—guitar, flute, singing, or drums—drifted up daily. Huge, red, wooden block letters forming the word "KNOW" appeared, immediately becoming a favorite climbing toy for children. A swing set was put up on the rolled sod lawn. Signs dotted the park, declaring "Flowers are the Root of All Good," "Power to the People," and even "Bugs and Beetles are People too." Vapors of marijuana smoke laced the air around the park. Occasionally, the Hare Krishnas and other groups gave out free food. An ugly lot had been turned into a happy place to hang out. The community of park-users grew.

On May 15, I awoke to hear on the radio that, at 4:45 a.m., one hundred California Highway Patrol officers had surrounded the park, arresting three people sleeping there and dispersing others. One hundred Highway Patrol officers? For our little park?

Needing to get to my classroom in Oakland, I gave the university area a wide berth, taking side roads to the freeway. Those who built and enjoyed People's Park would not be taking the police action lightly. All day, I had a hard time concentrating. Betty and I had difficulty keeping order in our classroom. We wondered what was happening north of us in Berkeley. How were people responding to the government's order?

Returning home at the end of the day, I headed for Peter's apartment on the Oakland side of campus, avoiding anything going on around the park. We turned on the radio and learned that the city was erecting a cyclone fence to enclose the park. Everything within the fence had been removed, and the flower beds bulldozed. Bulldozed! The park had been beautiful!

Leaflets were handed out among students, and by noon, a rally had been organized on campus. Angry at the loss of their park, two thousand people marched from Sproul Plaza down Telegraph Avenue to the park.

North of Peter's apartment, we could hear sirens and see tear gas billowing toward us. Eventually, we could even smell the gas from two miles away. Troops from every branch of law enforcement sped by, lights flashing and sirens blaring.

Choosing to stay away from the fracas, we listened to disjointed news broadcasts on the radio. Reports contradicted each other. Some said people had been shot, but we imagined that to be a gross exaggeration.

I stayed at Peter's, but we had a fitful night, uncertain about what had gone on. In the morning, I called Betty. "I can't believe what's happening! How can we teach today?"

"I can't," she agreed. "Angie was in the demonstration yesterday and she's been arrested. She was beaten and is in Santa Rita. I have to go and try to get her out." Betty's daughter had been active in many protests before, but this was her first arrest, and certainly the first time she'd been beaten by the police.

"Shit! That's awful! I'll call in for us. They'll get a substitute. Do you think they might even cancel school? Well, I hope she's okay. Will you be all right driving down?"

"Yeah, thanks. I'm heading out now."

"Good luck."

While I dialed Bella Vista, Peter jogged to the corner store to grab a newspaper. Hurrying back, he spread it across the kitchen table so that we'd both be able to read it. A banner headline read "Police Seize Park. Shoot 51." Local hospitals had treated fifty-one people for shotgun wounds. James Rector, who had been shot while watching the melee from the roof of Gramma's Book Store, was listed in critical condition. Several friends with him had also been shot. One, blinded, was now in stable condition. Four-hundred-and-eighty-two people had been arrested and taken to Santa Rita Jail. Governor Ronald Reagan was calling in the National Guard.

Peter and I gaped at each other.

"They *shot* the protestors?"

"In *Berkeley*?"

We lived in the center of liberaldom, a place known for welcoming the expression of new ideas. And now the National Guard was here, called in after peaceful protestors building a park had been shot!

"And, look!" My finger punched at a line farther down the page. "*Five-hundred* police from *nine* departments came! That's about one for every four protesters. Where do they think they are, in a war? Nobody's even armed! We're fucking citizens, for Christ's sake!" I babbled in my rage.

We grabbed our bicycles and headed into Berkeley to see for ourselves. The usually heavy traffic along Telegraph Avenue dribbled by at a trickle. Nearing Haste Street, we could see a roadblock ahead: "City of Berkeley, Road Closed." Peter stopped his bike, nodding to the clump of officers behind the sawhorse. As I pulled up alongside them, the men raised their rifles and pointed them at us. I froze in disbelief. Straddling his bike to hold it upright, Peter raised his hands. "Whoa, I work at the Industrial Relations building right over there. I'm just trying to go to my office!"

"What kind of proof do you have of that?"

Peter pulled out his wallet. Driver's License. Student ID card. Nothing proving his claim.

"What about you?" A second officer gestured the barrel of his rifle at me.

"I'm his girlfriend. I'm just going to do homework while he's working." Under his visor, I could see cold disdain reflected in the officer's eyes. Students were his enemies today.

The *whap, whap, whap* of helicopter blades nearly drowned out his response. "We have orders not to let any students go through."

"A curfew is in effect," blasted an announcement from a loudspeaker in the helicopter. "No one is to be out on the streets between 10:00 p.m. and 6:00 a.m." The chopper passed less than fifty feet over our heads. We waited as it passed, hearing the message repeated as the helicopter circled toward campus.

"You aren't going anywhere near the park today. Now back off!" The officer swung his rifle butt at Peter, knocking it into the handlebars of his bike. Peter lunged backwards, stumbled, but managed to right himself and his bike. We turned and peddled back down Telegraph, wondering at the police state in which we'd suddenly found ourselves.

Back in his apartment, Peter and I collapsed together onto the frayed, green couch. "It's like Chicago, only worse! They didn't have helicopters and curfews, did they?" I moaned, recollecting when we'd watched the

Democratic Convention live on TV as Chicago Mayor Daley's "storm troopers" rained brutality onto protestors rallying against the war.

"Nope, just got the shit beat out of 'em."

"But nobody got *shot!*" Disbelief still rattled through my psyche. Could this be the same Berkeley I'd been born in?

"I guess freedom only goes so deep." Peter shook his head. "We're free as long as we don't have any power to really challenge the establishment."

"Have we scared them so much they're willing to kill us?" My voice squeaked on the word "kill."

We spent the rest of the day listening to radio reports and calling friends to find out about their experiences. Stories conflicted. Some said students threw rocks and bricks at the police. Others said some police had not only shotguns, but rifles with spotting scopes. A car was overturned and set on fire. Some businesses had their windows smashed.

Around Berkeley, it was common knowledge that the FBI had people infiltrating the movement. We often laughed at how obvious they were. No one trained as a G-man seemed able to pull off the look or demeanor of a flower child; the clothing was exaggerated and their eyes remained shielded. Now, we speculated that the infiltrators could have easily torched the car and broken store windows, giving the police excuses to use force on the protestors.

None of us knew what to think. Stunned disbelief settled over the city, muffling the sounds of the bravest among us, who continued to carry out their skirmishes. The rest of us gnawed on the bitter bone that had just been thrown at us: our country was willing to kill its young people, and we were those young people.[3]

---

[3] To see images of bayoneted rifles pointed at students, helicopters spraying tear gas, and flowers being woven into chain link fence and razor wire, Google "Images of People's Park Berkeley 1968."

NINETEEN

For days, helicopters circled the city of Berkeley. Scarcely clearing the rooftops, the jarring thrum of their rotors interrupted our sleep and fueled ongoing tensions. Periodic skirmishes occurred near campus. Protesters kept up a cat-and-mouse game with troopers.

I wanted to see what was happening, but I had a class to teach, so I headed south, relieved to be heading away from the turbulence.

At Bella Vista, I met Betty walking toward our portable classroom, halfway across the cracked asphalt playground. Tension squeezed lines into her usually calm face, puckering her lips.

"Hey. All this is just shitty, huh? Is Angie still in jail?" I greeted her without the usual pleasantries.

"No, they let her out." Betty stopped and looked me in the eye. "They beat her!" She spit the words through clenched teeth. "She said they beat almost everyone."

"Fuck! Is she okay?" I asked, putting my hand on her arm.

"Oh, she'll be okay physically, but how does anybody recover? What the hell is happening?"

I'd never heard Betty swear before.

The warning bell rang. Head down, I led the way up four steps into our old, wooden classroom as students poured toward us.

"I'll read King," Betty moved to her desk and picked up the children's autobiography of Dr. Martin Luther King, Jr. "We're on the last chapter."[4]

As Betty picked up the biography of King, I looked around at the clusters of desks filling the classroom. Bethany huddled over Stacey, whispering, prompting Stacey to roll her eyes and laugh. Rondell was sliding his desk back and forth into the side of Joey's. Joey told him to back off. Johnny slid down in his chair, his jacket hunched up to his ears and his stocking cap pulled over his eyes.

"Let's see which group gets quiet first." I turned to the corner of the green slate board where the names the groups had given themselves were written in smeared, yellow chalk: The Flash, The Supremes, Power, Ali's Allies, The Blazers, and The Jackson Six.

"She's giving out checks!" The murmur spread around the room. Checks were a blatant bribe; the group with the most checks each day got some coveted treat, like first dismissal after school. Soon all were quiet. The Blazers got the check.

Betty began to read. Her soft voice was firm and strong until she got to the dream speech. "I have a dream," her eyes began to pool.

I reached over and took the book from her shaking hand. No one spoke. I read on through the excerpt quoted in the book, ". . . when all of God's children, black men and white men . . . will be able to join hands and sing . . ." The words of encouragement seemed to be written for us, right at this day and time. I read on to the end of his speech. "Free at last! Free at last! Thank God, almighty. We are free at last!" I looked around, wondering if one day the children of our class would truly be free. Personally, I had never in my life felt less free.

---

[4] Throughout the state, California classrooms began each day with the Pledge of Allegiance to the mandatory American flag hanging in the front of each room. With our country in turmoil over the Vietnam war, Betty and I felt we could not require our class to pledge allegiance to a flag that used their uncles, dads, and older brothers to kill in Asia. Researching the law, Betty and I had found that California merely required its teachers to have ten minutes of "American Education" each day. After finding out that the pledge was not required by law, we decided to meet the mandatory ten minutes of "American Education" by reading grade-level appropriate biographies of people of color.

For the next few days, Betty and I tried to keep a sense of normalcy in our classroom. Bella Vista was only a few miles south of the occupied zone in Berkeley. One of the tasks we divided between us were the home visits teachers were expected to do with their students. Some had proven difficult to arrange, since not everyone had a phone. Some clearly didn't want their child's teacher in their homes, either from embarrassment at their living situations or out of resentment that any part of "the establishment" might be prying into their lives. But most families were welcoming and grateful when we came.

Leaving immediately after class a few days after "Bloody Thursday," as it was now being called, I headed for my first visit to Belen Newsom's home. These home visits and parent conferences immersed me in Oakland's culture beyond what I could get from my students. Whatever had made me choose to study anthropology also caused me to anticipate home visits with excitement. Belen's mother had already introduced herself. She occasionally volunteered in the classroom. Like her daughter, she was poised and pleasant to be around.

Built in the 1930s and '40s, most homes in Bella Vista School's neighborhood had small yards. They differed considerably in the degree of maintenance they'd received over their thirty-year lives. I drove up to the Newsom's peach-colored, stucco house with its small, neatly trimmed lawn. This house obviously received much loving care.

Mrs. Newsom welcomed me in, gesturing toward a gray-tweed couch in the living room. As I set down my purse and papers on their coffee table, she settled onto the other end of the sofa.

"I love having your daughter in my class, Mrs. Newsom. She is the kind of student who makes a teacher's job easy."

Mrs. Newsom smiled and nodded. This was not new information. She raised her daughter to do well in school and the results were obvious.

"Wait a second. Let me get my husband. Robert should hear this too."

She returned with a handsome man wearing a nicely fitted leather jacket and a Che Guevara black beret. This "uniform" identified him as a Black Panther.

"Good to meet you." He extended a firm hand. His smile was warm and genuine.

I hadn't known Belen's father was a Panther and I felt flustered as I shook the proffered hand. I decided to just get on with my report about their child. Clearing my throat, I plunged in. "As I was telling Mrs. Newsom, Belen is truly a joy to have in the classroom. Her reading skills are excellent and she's such a natural leader that she sets an example for others to follow. I think she's very respected by her classmates." I rattled these words off sincerely, but perhaps too quickly.

Mrs. Newsom smiled and Mr. Newsom nodded, both looking pleased at my praise of their daughter.

"Thank you for that. We like what Belen says you're doing every morning—what do you call it?" Mrs. Newsom leaned forward.

I thought a moment before realizing what she meant. "Oh, you mean American Education? We're trying to give our students information about important Americans who may not be mentioned in the textbooks."

"Well, know you have our support in what you're doing." Mr. Newsom probably understood our underlying motives.

Mrs. Newsom nodded her agreement, then shifted the conversation. "But what's happening in Berkeley? It's hard for us to know what the situation is. The news is frightening."

I saw the concern in both their faces. "It's even hard for us to know! Basically, it's "Occupied Berkeley." Martial law is in effect. Ten p.m. curfew." This wasn't what I was supposed to be here to talk about, but my fury kept the words coming. "Yesterday, I was in my boyfriend's office right across the street from the park. I watched a guy being chased by a policeman run down the alley beside the building. The cop grabbed the guy's camera from around his neck and threw it on the ground, then smashed it with his baton. There hadn't even been a skirmish going on! No protests anywhere near that I could see!"

Mr. Newsom affirmed my thoughts. "You know that Panther saying, 'The Revolution will not be televised'? That's what it means: No photographs. No journalists."

"Exactly! And everybody has a story!" I shot back. "A friend was going home from work downtown when the cops began rounding people up. Again, no protest nearby or anything! Circled around and herded them into a parking lot. My friend was wearing a suit; went up to a cop, saying he was just going home from work. The guy bashed him in the stomach with the butt of his rifle!"

I was getting worked up. I probably shouldn't be sounding so political with the parents of a student, but it felt good to talk with people who understood.

Taking a deep breath, I decided to take advantage of the Newsoms' sympathetic attitude and head the conversation in a different direction. This might be a chance to verify some of the things I'd heard about the Black Panthers. "Is it true Huey and Bobbie [*Newton and Seale*] started a program where Panthers follow police cars around the neighborhoods so they can document police brutality?"

Mr. Newsom didn't move a muscle for a few moments. I imagined my question surprised him, and that he was deciding on how much he could safely share with a white woman. I'd heard that the men who were following the cops were openly armed with shotguns, but I figured I shouldn't mention that. Eventually, he nodded. "If we can manage to intimidate the cops, let them know they're being watched, we hope they won't feel like they have free rein to harass any Black person they see. Maybe they'll think twice before they pull out their batons or guns."

Mrs. Newsom chose to direct the conversation to a less controversial topic. "Have you heard that the Panthers are calling for a boycott of Safeway stores? We've been asking local markets to donate to our Feed the Children program. Most have—day-old bread and stuff like that—but Safeway refuses." I noted that Mrs. Newsom seemed also to identify as a Panther.

Although I felt tense, I wanted to keep this conversation going. There was so much negative press and deliberate misinformation about the group, I wanted to hear from people who knew firsthand. "You've got a clothing program for kids too, right? And I heard that the Panthers are starting free medical clinics."

Mr. Newsom smiled sardonically. "Yes, and J. Edgar [*Hoover*] has called us the biggest threat to America's democracy."

We sat silently for a moment, digesting the irony of that quote.

When doorbell chimes broke our silence, I startled. The front door swung open before the Newsoms could get to it.

"Rupert!" Nervous concern morphed instantly to joy as Mrs. Newsom leapt up to wrap her arms around a nice-looking, fortyish man.

At the sound of her exclamation, Belen and her younger brother flew from their bedrooms, joining in the embraces. My presence slipped from anyone's notice amid the excitement, until Belen turned to me.

"Ms. McMillan, I haven't seen Uncle Rupert since I was a kid! He's my favorite uncle!" She swiveled on one foot and followed him into the dining room.

I smiled at her enthusiasm, wondering what she defined as being "a kid." Thanking the Newsoms, I excused myself, leaving them to their celebration.

Wow, I thought as I backed out of their driveway. The reception the Newsoms gave Uncle Rupert was warmer than I'd seen anyone receive in Orinda. My body felt warmth along with envy.

Driving along the freeway, I realized the Newsom family were a living example of the Tapestry: every member woven into the whole, something larger than each individual, but for which each individual was necessary. I wondered if that was the norm in the rest of the world and if Orinda were the aberration. What if most human cultures had always understood Oneness? Sadness for my own culture blurred the taillights of the car ahead of me.

The next evening, I had classes on campus after work. Knowing there might be activity down by Sather Gate, I drove up toward the hills, and parked on the uphill side of campus, more than a mile from the People's Park. Late afternoon sun glowed through old oaks as I walked across a small, brick-paved square. Enjoying the solitude, I tried to identify various birdsongs. One of my new friends in the program had been training me in the joys of birdwatching. I was an eager student.

I had just identified the lyrical song of a robin when I felt pressure in my ears even before hearing the whir of a helicopter sinking low over the building behind me. I turned to look, angrily wondering what the heck it was doing up here. The helicopter sped directly over me. I stared in disbelief as a streaming, white cloud poured out, floating down onto me. I closed my eyes, and tried to keep the gas out of my nostrils. But acid tears formed under my lids, and flames seemed to erupt in my throat. Coughing uncontrollably, I gasped for air, inhaling more of the stinging, burning cloud. I stumbled ahead, making my way blindly toward the nearest building. When I reached the door, arms dragged me inside, pulling me along to a water fountain where many hands splashed cold liquid over my face.

"What the hell?" I croaked when I could open my eyes again.

"It's CS gas. They admitted they were going to spray any gathering today."

"I wasn't gathering," I whispered, trying to minimize the pain when I spoke. "I was alone."

"We saw. We looked out when we heard the chopper. It's not even *legal* in this country to spray your own citizens."

"Thanks for your help. I don't know what I'd have done." I could barely mumble the words.

"Man, if I'd had a rifle, I'd have shot that pig down!"

A woman beside me had a blue-denim work shirt over her T-shirt. She took it off as another peeled my own top up over my head.

"Here, wear this. The gas is in your clothes too, you don't want to keep wearing that."

I nodded, deferring to their control of the situation. Modesty was not a consideration.

"It'll get better. But it'll take time." They all seemed to be veterans. Probably everyone there had been involved in at least one of the protests.

The agony slowly subsided. As I began breathing normally, the crowd around me dispersed, but each one touched me and left encouraging words: it was miserable, but I'd be better after a while. Salty tears of gratitude left my eyes stinging again.

I'd read about Che Guevara's idealism in the Cuban Revolution. Were we trying to create the same kind of selfless society here that he had worked to manifest? The same government that appeared to be trying to kill us, or at least kill our spirit and our causes, had helped to kill him. He had been willing to take up arms to fight the selfishness of capitalism and imperialism. Would I? Did my understanding of the Tapestry require me to fight my own government? Or did it forbid violent action? My government had betrayed my trust and my wounds were more than just physical. The group of people who had spontaneously come to my aid seemed to have wrestled with these questions more than I had. What conclusions had they reached? Since speech wasn't an option for me now, I couldn't ask.

Since I knew whatever I did next would feel terrible, I decided to go on to class. One of my rescuers came with me as I made my way down to Tolman Hall. I must have looked pretty awful, since my appearance caused quite a stir. I was grateful that I had someone to explain for me. My raw throat bled when I tried to speak.

I went to the medical center the next day, along with many who had been on the other side of campus. Nothing was to be done. We'd have to simply let the effects of the gas heal on their own. For the next two weeks, I tried to teach thirty-three students in a fourth-grade class while occasionally spitting out blood with my saliva. The country was at war. It was not a metaphor. I'd become a casualty.

During those weeks, Berkeley remained a military encampment. James Rector died from his wounds. The helicopters never stopped. Police targeted journalists, so there was virtually no coverage in newspapers or on TV. But even without the cell phones and social media of today, photos began leaking out to the press. One iconic picture showed a young woman placing a flower into the mouth of the rifle pointed at her chest. Sometimes people lined the streets with bouquets of flowers, handing them to the troops who endlessly patrolled the city. On rare occasions, the gifts were accepted. The chain-link fence built around People's Park and the barbed wire coiled above it became festooned with flowers, replaced daily. The troops lolled and slept on the gutted grounds inside those barriers, apparently safe from the dangers of petalled projectiles. Slogans like "Make Love, Not War" and "Power to the People" covered store windows, sometimes written by the owners of the business, and sometimes sprayed on by the protesters.

On the weekend, I ventured downtown to buy books I needed for a class. While waiting to cross Telegraph Avenue, my skin began to prickle at the hateful sound of an approaching chopper. Air forced downward by the blades met resistance in hitting whatever was below it, keeping the copter aloft. I was below. I felt the force as it passed over. My body was being used to hold up that damn machine! The chopper flew so low over our heads that I could clearly see the young man in the pilot seat. *Shoot it down*, I thought. *Would someone please shoot it down!* I imagined a rifle in my hands. I could have shot him through the glass. *He's undoubtedly National Guard. He probably has kids at home. He has a wife he loves.* After giving myself those reasons to back off from contemplating murder, I checked back in with my emotional self. Still there: I wanted to shoot that machine out of the sky. The pilot would be collateral damage. I didn't hate him; I hated the helicopter he flew. Too bad if he died.

How fleeting my pacifism was proving to be! Where was my connection to the great and glorious Oneness? Had I instantly lost all comprehension of the Tapestry? One act of violence against me, one bleeding throat, and I felt ready to kill. Interesting. I began to viscerally understand how attacks breed counterattacks. Within my body, a genetic wiring for revenge lurked, instantly ready to leave my metaphysical ponderings in the dust. I recalled that Gandhi, as he was dying, requested that everyone have mercy for his assassin. Impressive as hell! Some people could hold to their knowledge of our connectedness despite their blood-and-bones response. Clearly, I wasn't one of them. But what about Che and the Cuban revolution? Was there ever a justification for violence?

Since I had no rifle, I stepped off the curb as the helicopter and its pilot continued on to live another day.

For two interminable weeks, the helicopters continued their ceaseless rounds. Nerves frayed. Everyone in Berkeley stumbled through sleep-deprived days. The government was winning. Skirmishes tapered off. We had learned that Ronald Reagan, governor of California, was willing to kill us should we provoke him past whatever line we had obviously already crossed. He had the full support of President Richard Milhous Nixon.

Protests no longer beckoned as a chance to join friends in a platform for messages of worthy causes. Masked and vested officers carrying bayonet-tipped rifles armed with live ammunition could set upon peaceful demonstrations. Gathering in groups in public, for whatever reason, meant risking our lives. My courage faltered. I was no longer eager to join any protests. After nineteen days, and at the same time our school year was ending in Oakland, martial law was finally lifted in Berkeley and the helicopters beat their way home to whatever bases they had come from, waiting for the next time citizens needed to be shown the reality of our so-called democracy.

It might have been a blessing that the lack of media coverage of "occupied Berkeley" left the rest of the country less intimidated than most of us. In New York City, protestors rose up in anger when police raided the Stonewall Inn, a gay bar in Greenwich Village. Local residents, as well as gay and lesbian patrons, were dragged out of the bar on the grounds that any display of homosexual affection in public was illegal. Riots began in protest and continued for six days. Angry citizens threw bricks, stones, and even Molotov cocktails at police. The protestors were far more violent than any had been in Berkeley, but no one in New York was killed by police. There was no National Guard called in. I wondered if New York's liberal mayor John Lindsay helped keep police action under some degree of control. Maybe the government didn't think a gay-and-lesbian cause could be large enough to gain momentum. But I felt the protesters were part of us.

I hadn't thought a lot about homosexuality before the riots. I knew that my mother's sister was lesbian. She'd been living in Michigan with her partner, Phyl (Phyllis) for most of my life. Although my family liked Margaret and welcomed her periodic visits, they never invited Phyl, and scrupulously avoided any mention of Margaret's sexual orientation. I wondered if the Stonewall Riots would cause my family to rethink their attitudes toward homosexuality, although I figured that was unlikely.

Bella Vista's school year had ended before my throat fully healed. Betty and I survived our first year and were the wiser for it. A new crop of students would be coming next September, when we each would have our own classroom. I would miss relying on Betty, and I'd definitely miss individual students, some more than others. I felt sorry for students we hadn't been able to help as much as we should or could have: Rashad, diagnosed with attention deficit, took Ritalin every day, but still had a hard time being still for more than a few minutes at a time; Lawrence was extremely bright but disengaged, so we'd suggested moving him up a grade (neither his parents nor the school took our suggestion); and Harriet, a diminutive white child who seldom spoke, got through the entire year without either of us realizing that she could scarcely read (squeaky wheels get the grease, and conversely, silent ones can go unnoticed). With thirty-three students and two novice teachers, every day had passed in a state of triage. I was ready to move on to new challenges. Meanwhile, we had the summer before us, having only to attend classes at the university and recover from what, on so many levels, had been a hard year for all of us.

TWENTY

Now that school was out, I called Sondra. We'd only had intermittent contact during the past few months, and I wanted to know how her class had gone.

"Hey, what's up, girl?" Her greeting had more of the vernacular and cadence of Black culture than I'd remembered.

"Want to meet somewhere, now that we both have more time? Drown our sorrows and celebrate our successes with a beer or two?"

"Sure, girl!" Sondra named a bar in downtown Oakland, giving me the address. We agreed to meet the coming Friday.

At the appointed time, I entered a bar in an unfamiliar section of town. Vertical windows framed the doorway of the plain-looking building that shared walls with neighboring storefronts. As I entered, Sondra's elegant hand waved to me from a curved booth across the room. Three others about our age sat with her. By now, I was used to hanging out in mostly Black areas, but here I felt like my face glowed neon-white.

"Scoot over, y'all. Give this sister some space to get in."

Several empty beer bottles were already clustered in the center of the table. Sweat beaded on their replacements, dripping water into pools on the polished wood.

Sondra listed off the names of her friends, introducing me as a fellow new teacher, then waved down a waitress to bring me a beer.

A man seated at the bar threw a comment at the woman sitting beside Sondra as I slid into the green-leather booth.

"Mama, you got room in your saddle fo' one more rider?"

Sondra's friend looked back at him with mock disdain. Not missing a beat, her rejoinder sailed back as she lifted a menu. "My saddle done be full up. Go fine yo'self anotha haws to ride."

"Honey, my stable be plum em'ty and I'm lookin' at somepin' prob'ly gonna fit me jes' fine!" He drawled out the last two words.

"Nuttin' gonna fit you 'cept for the teeniest mouse. You betta' go fine yo'self a tiny little mouse to ride."

The group at our table burst out laughing and the man turned away, smiling in acknowledgement of his defeat. The victor leaned across the table toward me.

"Honey, tha's the way you play da dozens. You come here much, you gonna haf to learn." She sat back, satisfied with her verbal victory.

The game continued as others chimed in. Thinly veiled sexual banter flew around me faster than bees could swarm. Topics could shift, but the double meanings always slid right into the new form. Quite literally, the whole scene was breathtaking.

Sondra participated with alacrity, giving back as fast and sharp as she received. I sat laughing but mute, half-terrified that someone would expect me to join in. There was no chance I'd be mentally quick enough to quip back some sexual metaphor in response to one thrown at me. Thankfully, they had mercy on me, their language-deficient, white friend, and allowed me to merely enjoy their clinic for nuanced, lightening retorts. I was spared the embarrassment of certain failure.

Sondra had been raised in a suburban home like I had, but she fit into Oakland culture in a way I could not. There was a camaraderie in Black experiences that I would never share. I hadn't had a life of being handed stretched-out bathing suits or being waited on last by white waitresses. The unity may have been birthed in hardship, but something warm and connected had grown from that. I felt privileged to be trusted enough to sit there and enjoy the fun.

With the summer before us, Peter and I turned our (slightly cowardly) backs on protests and chose a summer of play. We shamelessly took advantage of our ability to escape, something the privilege of our white skin allowed us to do. Hiller Highlands, the community where Peter's parents lived in the Oakland Hills, had tennis courts and a pool that we frequented often. My brother-in-law, Bob, had returned from Vietnam, so Jean was once again living with her husband in a sweet little home in the Berkeley Hills. My folks and I functioned on a polite, don't-ask-don't-tell basis. They had been back in Yosemite again during the time of the riots, so I never even told them about being sprayed with CS gas. Any mention of the People's Park, Vietnam, Muhammed Ali's protest of the war, or the Black Panthers was scrupulously avoided by both sides. Mostly, they stayed on their side of the hills and Peter and I stayed on ours.

On weekends, Peter and I would pack up a cooler, sleeping bags, and a tent, and head to the mountains. A favorite activity was floating around on air mattresses in some icy Sierra lake, playing "armada" and attempting to unseat the other. Laughter and great sex helped heal the trauma of the past few months. "Occupied Berkeley" became surreal when surrounded by granite cliffs and vanilla-scented Ponderosa pines. We discussed heading to New York for a gathering that would happen in August, something called "Woodstock." Summer sessions at the university would be over, so we'd have the time to drive across the country. Peter, always anxious to dance at a concert, had more enthusiasm for the venture than I did; it seemed like a very long drive. Ultimately, we decided to use the time instead to find an apartment and finally move in together, something still disapproved of in mainstream America. My parents wouldn't like it, but I imagined the don't-ask-don't-tell policy we were living by would probably apply. Besides, trying to please my parents no longer rated high on my list of motivations.

An old house on the corner of Grove and Hearst backed up to a long, open space where powerlines ran through weedy grass for several blocks. We rented the upper, back quarter of the house, with a view across the fields to a very distant bay. Rickety steps led up steeply from the fenced parking space behind the house. I excitedly planted snow peas and flowers in the foot-wide dirt border between asphalt and the fence. Both of us bought ten-speed bicycles, a wonderful invention we could now afford, with derailleurs that offered different combinations using two sets of gears, a vast improvement from our old Schwinn three-speeds. With our new bikes, we roamed the streets of Berkeley, once making it all the way up Marin, a street that led straight up the face of the hills. We felt intrepid.

One of the reasons that "Occupied Berkeley" remained unreported that summer was that Apollo 10 and 11 space missions were filling the news. Headlines all over the world announced that the United States was preparing to send astronauts to the moon! Just three days after "Bloody Thursday," Apollo 10 launched, carrying three men in a test flight that paved the way for the landing itself.

Less than two months later, the stage was set for the real landing. No one had ever before left our planet to set foot elsewhere. The odds against success seemed astronomical. I was still on a shaky footing with my family, but they invited me out to watch the landing itself on their television. We'd declared an implicit truce. We simply never spoke of Yosemite, Peter's and my living situation, or anything remotely political. Our relationship consisted of an occasional dinner in Orinda or meeting at a restaurant on the east side of the hills. But on July 20, 1969, I arrived at their house full of excitement over watching an event unparalleled in human history.

Mom and I sat on the couch in their den, the small room dedicated to TV-watching. Dad pulled up an extra chair. Bob and Jean were at their home in the Berkeley Hills. Peter was watching with his parents in their condominium. The moon landing seemed to be clumping folks together in their nuclear families. Here at my folks' house, Mom had put frozen TV dinners into the oven to heat. In an unprecedented broadcast, CBS coverage with Walter Cronkite had been going on for four days, ever since the Apollo 11 had been launched.

"In just fifty minutes from now, well within the hour," came Walter's familiar gravelly voice from the square wooden console, "the moon is due to have visitors from another planet."

Mom scurried to bring out the dinners. I grabbed folding TV trays from the side of the room and set one up on crisscrossed table legs in front of each seat. I peeled back the foil covering the three compartments of the aluminum dish Mom set before me. My favorite Swanson TV dinner: Three slices of turkey rested on a bed of squashed stuffing, covered with a drizzle of gravy coagulating into a brown coating against the wrinkly sides of the container, pale peas filled another section, while a flattened mound of mashed potatoes matched the shape of the third. But I scarcely tasted it, pausing between bites to listen to the conversations coming to us through 238,000 miles of space. Houston to Columbia, Columbia to Eagle; the lunar landing module had already separated from the control vehicle.

We were joining nearly every other American family in living rooms across the country, about to watch humans reach another celestial body. We held our breath through many tense moments of silence when the spacecraft crossed the far side of the moon and communication was lost. Precise engine burns had to be made without the assistance from Mission Control on Earth in order to get the module into alignment for the landing. We didn't exhale until the voices of Mike Collins, Neil Armstrong, and Buzz Aldrin returned, letting us know all had gone perfectly.

"Go," "Go," "Go," "Go," "Go," came from each of the lightning-quick reports from each separate system in Houston. Our eyes were glued to the black-and-white image as lunar craters grew to fill the screen. No one knew for certain what footing the spindly legs of the lunar module would find as it touched down. Some predicted that the moon dust might be so deep it could simply swallow up the lander, or the dust might clog the engines so that it would not be able to lift back off. Craters grew bigger on the television set, until the image froze with the words, "Houston, the Eagle has landed."

"Roger, Tranquility, we copy you on the ground."

"Whew, boy," Walter Cronkite said for all of us, removing his glasses and rubbing his hands together. Speaking to astronaut Wally Schirra, a veteran of former spaceflights, who was sitting beside him at his desk,

Cronkite enjoined, "Wally, say something. I'm speechless." This from the man who had been talking to us in our living rooms every evening for over seven years. Schirra obliged as Cronkite wiped a tear from his eye.

Conversations continued between astronauts and control until the hatch opened. From a camera attached to one of the Eagle's splayed legs, we could just make out the fuzzy image of an oversized white boot stepping off the bottom rung of the United States' lunar landing module. Armstrong's voice announced, "It's one small step for a man, but one giant leap for mankind."

Buzz Aldrin followed, becoming the second man on the moon, while Collins talked to everyone from the orbiting craft above. The men bounced around in the moon's low gravity and planted an American flag, wired to make it appear to be waving on the atmosphere-less moon. Despite everything else, those guys were having fun!

Mom opened the door and led us outside. A spectral, full moon showed above the Orinda hills. "He's standing there," she said. "Neil Armstrong is standing right there."

I took it in, trying to imagine I could see the dots of two humans whose footsteps, for the first time ever, were marking the moon's familiar face.

"Can you imagine that, in my lifetime, we have gone from not being able to fly at all to sending someone to the moon," Mom continued. "They're really there!"

The dust that puffed around that first step shrouded all of our disagreements. For one moment, a country at war with itself stood united in awe: one of our own was standing on the moon. I closed my eyes, trying to take in the human kinship, trying to feel the woven Tapestry of Planet Earth. And I remembered that the Tapestry included the moon, included the Milky Way, included every aspect of the Universe. For just an instant, I imagined I could feel the connection again.

After I drove back to my apartment, the world divided itself once more. But maybe not as strongly as it had been divided the day before.

TWENTY-ONE

As the summer wound down, I prepared to venture into my first solo flight as a fourth-grade teacher. Betty and I had floundered through the previous year, making many mistakes but always leaning on each other and the university staff for consolation and guidance. Now I'd find out if I could meet Cal's gold standard of student-centered learning on my own. Could I find students' individual strengths and build on those strengths, help students gain a positive self-image and a belief that they could learn, then create an environment where they'd be excited and able to do so? The university's mantra had soaked into me until it felt integral to my being; I was a born-again teacher going to work in a rotting portable classroom filled with thirty-three restless children. A tall order, but I was eager for the challenge.

My desire to become a teacher had resulted from my experience in Africa. I wanted to help equalize the playing field for everyone in our country, and I hoped to somehow be able to show the Tapestry to my students. I wanted each one to know she or he was an equal and integral part of a Whole.

I gathered materials, made lesson plans, and decorated my classroom. Looking out the wall of dusty windows facing a chain-link fence bordering the street beyond, I watched a few cars pass. It was a view that left much to be desired. Since I wanted to show films and to occasionally block out that street view, I bought green vinyl shades and painted huge flowers on them. Teachers in Oakland had no discretionary budgets, so I paid for the shades myself, as well as an SRA (Science Research Associate) kit for individualized reading and Cuisenaire Rods for teaching basic math concepts. Those were large-ticket items coming out of my nine-thousand-dollars-a-year salary, but I needed to make the classroom fit the style of teaching for which Cal had been training us. Carolyn Middleton, my team leader from the university, took me to Oakland's warehouse for discarded materials, where teachers could pick out anything they wanted for their classrooms. I chose boxes and boxes of discontinued reading texts so students could be free to find their own reading level, without the stigma of being in a high or low reading group.

Carol in a fourth-grade classroom.

Taking time out from painting flowers and stapling colored paper onto bulletin boards, I headed up to the main building one morning to ask our white-haired principal, Miss Tobin, about my plans for the room. I knocked on the wooden door with its opaque glass window. Below it was the word "PRINCIPAL" stamped in gold lettering.

"Come in," her voice had a singsong quality. Small, gray eyes crinkled into her cheeks as I stepped into the old-fashioned office.

"Good morning, Miss Tobin."

"Oh, Miss McMillan. It's so good to have both you and Betty back this year. Are you finding everything you need to set up your classroom? You know you must do a bulletin board out in the hall, don't you?" She didn't gesture for me to sit down.

"Yes. I know which one is mine. I'm going to put up a display about fall leaves tomorrow afternoon. But I have a question for you."

"Oh, leaves, that's a nice idea. A question?" Her sweet, little-old-lady expression remained frozen in place beneath her tightly permed hair.

"I plan to arrange the desks so that students won't be sitting in rows, and I'd like to create a quiet corner where students can sit and read or study on their own."

"Oh, but that's not how we've always done it. Desks have always been in rows." Her eyes were still crinkled and the smile was still there. "What do you mean by a quiet corner?" she queried.

"Well, I wanted to put a carpet in part of the room and a couch. I'd like to make it look a little homier and more friendly. My parents are getting a new carpet and couch for their living room; they've offered to donate their old ones to my classroom."

"Oh, my, no. We've never had a couch in a classroom. You're out there on the playground outside the building. Who knows what students might break in and do on a couch at night!" When she shook her head, the curls remained immobile.

What went through this woman's mind? I couldn't have a quiet place for students to read because kids might break into my portable to have sex on the couch? I turned to leave, seeking to cut my losses before I stumbled onto other fiats that "we have always done" or "we have never done."

"Have a good day, Miss Tobin. I'll be certain my bulletin board is finished by tomorrow afternoon."

"That will be nice. I'm sure it will be lovely. You can close the door when you go out. Thank you, dear."

Never once last year had Miss Tobin tottered down the steps on her black, sensible-heeled pumps and visited Betty's and my classroom. Odds were good she wouldn't this year, either. Later that day, I called my parents and accepted their offer. Peter arranged to borrow a friend's truck, and by the next day, my overcrowded classroom had a quiet corner. The desks arced in semicircles; later, I'd let students move them into groups like Betty and I had done the previous year. Apparently, we'd unwittingly instituted a small rebellion that slipped under Miss Tobin's radar.

On the first day of school, my portable classroom smelled of white glue, wood rot, and damp clothing. As children walked through the door, my anthropologist's heart swelled at the mixture of cultures they brought to the class. Cathy was Navajo, and until that month, had lived with her grandmother in a hogan on the Window Rock reservation in Arizona. Her grandmother spoke no English, and Cathy's first language was Diné. Although Larry had recently arrived from China, his English was fluent. He excelled at every subject and went to Chinese school for two hours after

Class photo.

public school every day. Anthony had just come from the Philippines; his warm, brown eyes won my heart immediately. Tagalog was his first language. Mark was Japanese-Brazilian. I soon discovered that his mother cooked the best noodle dishes I'd ever tasted, a cuisine unique to their mixed culture. Mark spoke Japanese and Portuguese, as well as English. Maria, from Mexico, spoke Spanish, dressed very nicely, and constantly sought to be teacher's pet, a quality that irritated me but that I tried to look beyond.

The rest of my children were from Oakland. Princess' light-brown skin spoke of her mixed parentage. Other students called her "high yalla," which I gathered they did not intend as a compliment. She had a bit of an attitude problem that I struggled to treat with compassion. Lisa and her diminutive cousin, CC, were obsessed with the Supremes. Every recess they'd put on a tape of their music and perfect new dance routines. With hands thrust forward, they did a great rendition of "Stop, in the Name of Love." Annie liked to keep her desk back against an open window. When someone or something upset her too much, she'd simply climb out and disappear until her temper cooled.

I did not find "troubled" children in my classroom. I found creative individuals and developed unique ways of dealing with a variety of situations. In the cultures of inner-city Oakland, I was a student as well as a teacher.

My greatest challenge was Willie Harrison. Willie was twelve, too old for the fourth grade, and already had been thrown out of three schools. In kindergarten, he had developed a rather ingenious method of stealing from his teacher's purse, carefully extracting just one bill, then refolding the rest and returning everything as it had been. Apparently, it had gone on for several months before he was discovered and promptly expelled. Willie was a clever kid. I was told that his most recent expulsion resulted from threatening to hit his third-grade teacher over the head with a chair. I never learned why he'd done it, or what his offense at his other school had been. During class time, Willie seldom stayed put. He liked to bug other children, especially the girls, but he was seldom angry and never cruel. Willie had mischievous eyes and a unique sense of humor that endeared him to many of the girls. I couldn't help liking Willie a lot, despite some of his actions.

Sharett broke all of the stereotypes I held concerning traumatized children. Raised in Los Angeles, she had witnessed her uncle shoot her mother. During the Watts riots of 1968, her father had also been killed. His financially successful sister lived in the hills above Oakland. Sharett's aunt swept down to Watts to do her social duty and "bring the child home." During several conferences, I could detect little interest in Sharett from her fur-clad aunt. The aunt housed, fed, and dressed Sharett well, but obviously expected minimal disruption from her new boarder.

Sharett responded to the events in her life not with anger, but by developing a compassionate ability to see inside people. One day, a lesson I taught had gone particularly poorly. I barely managed to contain the chaos as we limped along until recess, when we all could let off steam and return as our better selves. Assuming that the escaping students' rush outdoors had included everyone, I laid my head on my scarred wooden desk and closed my eyes. Gently, a small hand was laid on my shoulder. A voice whispered, "They'll be better after recess, Miz McMillan." With one last, knowing pat, Sharett quietly left the room. Who was teaching whom about Oneness and compassion here?

One of my favorite lessons from a student happened when I was outside on playground duty. A fight broke out between two sixth-grade boys. Both were strong, angry, and bigger than I was. A ring of children quickly surrounded them, shouting and egging them on. I had no idea what to do. I stood with the ring of children, ineffectually shouting at the two boys to "break it up." Luckily, a large male teacher arrived and ended the brawl. I turned to see CC, all three-foot-eight of her, watching me with interest. As the crowd dispersed, she came up to me.

"Miz McMillan, you 'fraid a fightin', ain't you?"

"Well, CC, I didn't grow up with it. I didn't have any brothers."

"You 'fraid a gettin' hurt?"

"I'm not sure. Maybe I am."

"Miz McMillan, I gonna tell you what my brother tol' me. He say, CC, 'cause you so small, you never gonna win a fight. But you don' hafta win. Somebody pick on you, you just make sure you hurt 'em. You hurt 'em bad enough they never gonna pick on you again."

I thanked her seriously. Several times in my life I've found that advice useful, verbally if not physically.

The master's degree I was working on at Cal was in elementary mathematics education. For my thesis, I was attempting to improve students' attitudes toward math by using the Nuffield Mathematics program from England, teaching it after school to any student who wanted to stay. It was an environmental, hands-on approach. We did things like learning about circumferences by taking long strips of paper, wrapping them around anything slightly spherical or cylindrical the students could find, cutting and labeling the strips, then laying them out on a huge sheet of one-inch-square graph paper, creating a bar graph that compared. I called these afternoon sessions "Explorers' Club," never mentioning the words "math" or "arithmetic." When I began, only two students joined me after school, but months later, thirteen regular attendees complained in unison when I told them we were going to be doing "math" in Explorers' Club. It was fun letting them know that's what we'd been doing the whole time.

During regular class time, I needed to teach the more traditional aspects of arithmetic. No affordable hand calculators existed in 1969, and students were required to memorize the multiplication tables. I remembered hating the way we'd been taught the "times tables" when I was a kid, so I gave no tests and never drilled my students. I filled the room with various games they could learn from and offered praise and prizes for anyone who conquered one set of numbers. The easy numbers got pencils and buttons, but the sevens and nines earned an address book or a journal.

One afternoon, thirty-three faces looked at the prize Jimmy Bradford was about to receive for reciting his sevens' times tables. The attention of all thirty-three students at the same moment erased most of my guilt over resulting to bribery. By demonstrating his mastery of the sevens' tables, Jimmy had just earned respect and envy from his classmates. No one from U.C. Berkeley's elementary education program advocated bribery in the classroom, but I wasn't looking any gift horses in the mouth. It worked. Even the most mathematically challenged students could master the ones' or twos' tables, guaranteeing success. I handed Jimmy his red, spiral address book, complete with a small, attached pencil. I had no idea whether or not he'd ever fill it with telephone numbers of his friends and family, but his smile showed he enjoyed getting the reward for his accomplishment. Danny Richards had just done his eights and seemed equally pleased with his Oakland Raiders' keychain.

Carolyn Middleton, my team leader, arrived after school for her weekly rescue mission. Carolyn folded her long legs under a fourth-grade-student chair and asked about my current successes and fiascos. Pushing a now nearly waist-length braid behind my shoulder and attempting to corral the loose papers covering my desk, I told her about the students' engagement in my new reading activities, but failed to mention my less orthodox methods (bribery with small items) for encouraging arithmetic memorization. She didn't dispense key chains or notebooks, but she did reward me with praise and congratulations for my successes.

I tried to hold my emotions in check as we started into the second part of her visit. This part, the recitation of my problems, was always the larger one: breakdowns in classroom control, failures to engage students in what I thought would be a fabulous lesson, and the incident when Annie Samuels climbed out the window because Almira threw her science paper on the floor. Mark, a cheerful student on high doses of Ritalin, had seemed unable to focus on a single lesson that day, preferring to open and shut his desk continually between strolls around the classroom.

Carolyn handed me tissues and waited patiently for my quiet tears to cease. She offered a suggestion for handling Annie and handed me a new book on classroom control. After asking what I'd learned from the failed lesson, she reflected back on what she'd heard me say. When my paraphrased words came out of Carolyn's mouth, the situations didn't sound as hopeless as I'd felt they were. Patched and emotionally mended, I regrouped my forces for another day.

Everyone who taught in Oakland did not share the same motivations. I would guess that our faculty was divided about fifty-fifty: half of us were there with a passion to help the children, the other half taught in inner-city Oakland, because they couldn't get hired anywhere else. Oakland was considered a difficult district and did not have a flood of applicants for their teaching positions. Occasionally, the reality of what students faced from the second group of teachers heated my face with anger.

When I began teaching, the California education code required all women faculty to wear dresses or skirts and nylon "hose," incredibly impractical for the classroom. Soon after, however, someone managed to get the rules changed to allow pantsuits: slacks with matching jackets. A conversation I overheard about the pantsuit rule revealed just how devastating some teachers' attitudes might be for their students.

While sipping coffee in the teachers' room, I heard two (white) kindergarten teachers discussing the new pantsuit ruling.

"Do you have a pantsuit yet?"

"Yes, I've bought two. How 'bout you?"

"Oh, I have one all right, but I'm certainly not going to waste it on *these* children!"

I could feel my coffee curdling in my mouth. A kindergarten teacher! Thirty children sentenced to spend their first year in the educational system incarcerated with someone who saw them as substandard humans. I would forever hear her tone of disdain. Could a child's self-image ever recover from that? I feared it might be impossible.

Undoubtedly, that woman also shamed her students for their language. African slaves who survived the voyage across the Atlantic, eating rotten food and being nibbled on by rats, gave birth to children who then faced lives as slaves for many generations. The language that evolved among them differed from the American language spoken by whites, just as standard American language evolved to differ from British English. The language spoken in inner cities had rules of grammar equally as complex as those of any other language. It was not merely poorly spoken American English. No one had yet named the language "Ebonics," or African American Vernacular English (AAVE). The fact that this language had been evolving for several hundred years wasn't yet acknowledged in the educational community.

Bella Vista contained many students reading "below grade level." I was trying to teach reading from books written in Standard American English, a dialect most of my class didn't speak. The textbooks showed white children with two suburban parents, happily playing with a dog and a cat. Little white boys did interesting things. Little white girls watched in awe or played with dolls. Mothers wore high heels and aprons; dads came home in shiny cars, wearing brown suits, hats, and ties, and holding folded newspapers. Nothing in the texts portrayed the daily lives of my students. No Brown, Black, Native American, or Asian faces. No tenements. No stickball in the street. And our government wondered why Oakland had so many "slow readers."

Abandoning reading lessons that resembled the ways I'd been taught, I began experimenting with all things written and read. I felt confident about teaching math, but I had no idea how to teach reading. Cal had taught us that the best way to help a student learn to read was to help them *want* to read. I took that to heart by reading aloud to them daily from books that interested them.

Maintaining the "American Education" program Betty and I had started the previous year, I continued collecting biographies of famous Americans of color and reading them aloud to the class first thing each morning. These tended to hold their interest and show them positive role models. To quiet them after lunch, I also read aloud. I chose books holding great stories; the students always begged for one more chapter whenever I stopped. If Harry Potter had existed then, he, Hermione, and Ron would have been part of our classroom.

I instituted a quiet time. They were allowed to read whatever they wanted, including comic books (approved by me for content), anywhere they wanted. Some lay on the couch, others sat backward in their chairs, and many liked to sprawl across the floor in various positions. In the beginning, students often chose difficult books from the discarded readers that lined the shelves, pretending to read what they could not. I never interfered. Eventually, they got bored and found other material they could make their way through. Sometimes they read in pairs, helping each other decipher the words.

I was on a constant quest to find books at various levels that showed a diversity of people doing interesting things. Animal books were also favorites. During the fifteen-minute "quiet" period every day, I sat at my desk and read too, choosing some good novel that absorbed me completely, modeling for them my enjoyment of reading. I had a box of suggested exercises they could do about what they'd read, from making a diorama of a scene in a book to simply writing a book report. Those exercises were things they could record in the weekly contracts they'd made about work they planned to accomplish.

Once the students understood the value books could have for them, they did a pretty good job of teaching themselves to read. I have no idea how they managed this, but although I hate standardized tests, at the end of the school year—according to the mandatory tests of the time—I was astounded to hear that their reading levels went up an average of two-and-a-half grade levels.

Some unexpected problems arose from this laid-back approach. Learning stations for various subjects occupied much of the sparse classroom space. When each student filled out a weekly contract stating what they planned to accomplish, I reviewed the contracts with the students, sometimes suggesting alternatives. One afternoon, Larry Tam quietly took a seat by my desk. His crisp, clean contract slid toward me, filled out in his perfect, penciled lettering.

"Larry, I can see you've put a lot of thought into what you want to accomplish this week. You have very high expectations for yourself. Do you think it might be too much to get done in a week?"

The goals he had written seemed absurd. He would have no time for anything else in life, especially since, as I had recently learned, most of Oakland's Chinese parents sent their children to two hours of "Chinese school" after class each afternoon.

I tried to look into the eyes under his close-cropped bangs, but Larry's gaze was fixed on his black-and-white sneakers.

"That's what I want." His reply left little wiggle room for my negotiations.

"Well, how about, for math, just doing the workbook pages for one chapter? I think that would be enough."

"No, I want to do two." His eyes were still unavailable.

"Okay, but let's talk about this at the end of the week and see how you felt doing this much. It seems like an awful lot of work to me."

"Okay." Still, no eyes.

Larry got up and went back to his group. This conversation paralleled ones we'd been having for several weeks. I chewed my lip, frustrated at my inability to tone down Larry's nearly unreachable goals. I did many home visits with my students, but had never managed to arrange one with Larry's family. I had no barometer for expectations there, but visualized an overly strict environment where he feared failure.

Two weeks later, the last student had disappeared following the three-fifteen bell. I'd been straightening desks and picking up stray papers for barely five minutes before a brusque knocking against the open doorframe interrupted my housekeeping. A beautiful, young Asian woman stood scowling at me. Her forehead formed a set of concentric "Ws" and her lips held a tight pucker. I gestured for her to come inside and wondered what this could be about. She settled herself into a chair, neatly sliding her hand down the backside of a powder-blue summer coat to prevent wrinkling as she sat.

"I'm Larry Tam's sister, and I'm very unhappy with what you're doing." Her firm, angry posture came face-to-face with my confusion.

"I'm happy to meet you. I'm sorry we haven't had a chance to meet before. What is it that's upsetting you?" I hoped to defuse her apparent fury with a genuine dose of friendliness.

"You push him too hard. You make him sign these impossible contracts. He can't even sleep at night." Her words flew at me like carefully aimed darts.

"I argue with him every week, trying to make him write more reasonable goals. I can seldom convince him." I tried not to sound defensive, even though I felt intimidated by her anger. I wondered what the home situation looked like, guessing she had been chosen to confront me because the parents didn't speak sufficient English. "Do you think someone else at home is pressuring him?"

"No, no," she said dismissively. "Our mother sent me to reason with you. We are very worried about him."

I don't remember how I led her to an understanding of the classroom structure. I do know that I felt panic she wouldn't believe me if I began by trying to blame it all on Larry. Eventually, she softened a bit.

"Maybe you could talk with him about both of our worries. Tell him he can get excellent grades doing far less," I suggested.

She slowly nodded her head. I hoped she was beginning to believe we were on the same side. Working together, perhaps, we could calm him down and help him set reasonable goals. We agreed to meet again in two weeks.

Most of my students weren't especially grade-oriented, a fact I appreciated. Larry's problem helped me understand that my teaching style could be disconcerting for someone who had always gotten "As" in other classes and might not know what would guarantee them "As" in mine.

Whatever his sister told him after our conference did help Larry relax. His expectations became more reasonable and he began behaving more like an exuberant ten-year-old boy. I admit to appreciating and probably advocating a spark of rebellion here and there.

The situation with another Chinese student underscored the pitiful lack of resources in our system. Gordon Chan's exceptional intelligence became obvious within the first week he joined my class. Arriving midyear, the administration chose to put this thirteen-year-old into the fourth grade simply because he spoke no English. Mature and always polite, Gordon quickly won my respect. Brilliant at math, which had little language requirement, he could do any long division problem in his head. I never comprehended how that was possible.

As the school year progressed, so did Gordon Chan's English. Gordon developed a bit of a crush on me—as students sometimes do for their teachers—and often hung around with several other students after school let out, helping me straighten up while we chatted as a group about a variety of things.

"I go to home now." The room looked acceptably tidy.

"Gordon, you're doing amazing at learning English. I speak some pitiful Spanish, even after I studied it for years in school. Really, I only can speak one language."

"Then I teach you Chinese!"

"Gordon, I'd love that!"

"Tomorrow, we start."

And "tomorrow," we did. Gordon turned out to be an excellent and patient teacher. Other students began joining us.

"Gordon, why don't you teach Chinese to the whole class?"

"I do that, Miss McMillan."

Gordon began teaching an hour of Chinese language every Friday during regular class time. To the students' joy and my embarrassment, virtually everyone did better than I did. Their younger brains sponged up the language with ease. Even at twenty-five, my brain proved less adaptable to language acquisition than any nine-to-thirteen-year-old's. Humbling.

When the Chinese New Year drew near, I wanted Gordon to teach us how to celebrate. I'd seen the lion and dragon dances in parades, and I'd read about the red money envelopes adults gave children, but knew little else about the traditions. I asked Gordon.

"What you say, I teach you." Gordon bowed. "Gong hay fat choy."

"Oh, is that what you say when you give an envelope?"

"No, when you get. You learn."

The other students and I smiled in agreement. They certainly would try anything that might get them an envelope full of coins. We all put our hands together and faced Gordon. Bowing, each one of us tried a uniquely butchered version of what he had said.

By the time the Year of the Rooster drew near, all of us could bow to each other, saying an acceptable approximation of "Gong hay fat choy." Searching Oakland that weekend, I had little trouble finding the appropriate shiny-red envelopes. We all worked to create a display about Chinese

New Year for the bulletin board in the main hall. When the day came, we made dragons and loud noises and each student bowed and got a coin-filled envelope.

I have no doubt that our Chinese lessons enhanced the self-esteem of all the students: they were genuinely better at learning than their teacher who was getting her master's degree at the University of California. Hopefully, that fact expanded their perspective on life's possibilities. The whole experience encouraged my belief in collaboration. Even fourth-grade classes could function with a sense of equality.

Parent conferences came in many forms. Most were informative for both parties. Some conferences turned out to be more mundane than others. I never knew beforehand what they would be like. I could only recall one parent meeting that left me terrified. As a teacher, you are warned of many things to expect, but what happened with Jimmy Bradford wasn't in the rule book. Jimmy was an excellent student who exhibited a lot of maturity. The other students liked him and he often could be counted on to defuse tense situations with his relaxed style. Tall for his age, Jimmy had smiling eyes under an always-perfect afro.

I woke up one morning having had a disquieting dream. In it, I was ten years old, sitting at an ancient, wooden school desk that had an inkwell in one corner. I was sitting in a straight chair with an adult-sized seat. Jimmy Bradford came and nudged me over, sitting down to share my chair and desk. Smiling, he threw his notebook onto my desk and opened it for the lesson. I felt all the emotions that a ten-year-old feels when she realizes that a boy in school likes her.

Waking up, my emotions entwined into a braid of humor, bemusement, and horror, equally proportioned. I had a ten-year-old's crush on Jimmy Bradford! Had I been an adult in my dream, I might have feared some pedophilic tendencies. But it was just a delightful child dream. I wanted to be in Jimmy's class and have him like me. The terror part came as soon as I realized I had scheduled a parent conference with his mother that day.

Hello, Mrs. Bradford. It's so good to meet you. Oh yes, and your son is so cute that I have a crush on him. Nooooo! I didn't think that would do.

People had often pointed out that they knew what I was feeling just by looking at me. I didn't lie, because I couldn't lie. My body performed in a lovely concert portraying whatever emotion it currently possessed. Border patrol should have used me as a model of what to look for when someone attempted fraud. So how was I going to muddle my way through a conference with Jimmy Bradford's mother!

I spent the entire day in class trying not to think about the parent conference and trying not to look at Jimmy Bradford. Part of me wanted to giggle at how funny it all was. Part of me wanted to visit Australia. The actual event ended up being anticlimactic. Mrs. Bradford chatted with me pleasantly. No matter how transparent I might have considered my face to be, I'm certain that she never once thought, *Oh, did you just have an inappropriate dream about my son? Is that what you're hiding?* Not likely. I got a grip after our standard parent-teacher conference and was able to see the dream as humorous and sweet. I accepted my age, and life went back to normal between Jimmy Bradford and me.

All Barbara Wilson's students were in love with her. Spectacularly beautiful and beautifully confident, she wowed us for a while by dating a member of the Oakland Raiders football team. This was during the golden years for the Raiders, when they were first coming into prominence: Daryle Lamonica, Fred Biletnikoff, George Blanda, all coached by John Madden. We loved the Raiders. I think Barbara purposely gave the whole school a thrill by sometimes having her pro-football-player boyfriend pick her up from work. I remember he drove a red convertible and we all tried to sneak peeks at the two of them as she lifted a shapely leg to climb in. I'll bet she winked at us, though I was always too far away to tell.

Through Barbara, I found out that Carlton Oats, another Oakland Raider, had his name on the district's substitute list. One day in class, I could tell I was coming down with the flu and knew I'd probably be out for a week. Thinking, *why not give it a try?* I called the district and requested

Mr. Oats as my substitute. They checked it out and said he would be available. Returning to class, even though I felt like shit, I couldn't wait to share the news.

"You can all tell that I'm getting sick. It feels like the flu, so I'm afraid I'll be out for a while." My ego got stroked by some responding moans and sad faces.

"I've called the administration and requested a special substitute for you. You're going to have Carlton Oats as your teacher for a week."

Everyone knew who Carlton Oats was.

Young faces stared back at me in disbelief.

"You shittin' us, Miz McMillan?"

"Nope. For real."

Shaking their stunned heads in silence, I don't think they believed this was going to happen.

I had my miserable week away, wheezing and hacking, and returned to find my desk covered with stacks of papers. In sets of thirty-three, each separate assignment carefully clipped together and laid out by subject matter, the work of each and every student had been turned in for each and every lesson for an entire week. Never had anything close to this happened before. The class sat in silence while I sifted through the mountains of paper for a moment, reeling.

Carleton Oats played the position of defensive end on the football field. I never got to meet him, but I'm sure he cast a very, very, very large shadow, especially in my little Bella Vista portable.

One voice piped up as I pondered the papers on my desk. "Miz McMillan. Please don't aks for him if you goin' be out again." The rest of the class nodded their agreement. Visualizing what the week must have been like, my giggle had to stay stuffed somewhere down my throat.

Our classroom was literally a rotting, wooden, portable box plopped onto a section of asphalt playground: baking in summer and chilly in winter. Once, when bending over to help a student, the back of my leg pushed against a built-in bookshelf. A splinter broke off, so large and rotten that a doctor gave up trying to remove it, giving me antibiotics and telling me I'd be living with it like soldiers did with shrapnel. (For many years, I could wiggle it under my skin.)

Jerry Polk also taught in an old and rotting "portable" classroom. It sat back-to-back with mine behind Bella Vista's main building. While I was the unconventional flower child on staff, Jerry was the arch conservative. His dark, imposing body came dressed in neat suits every day, while my usual garb varied from flowered prints to an (inappropriate?) African dashiki. Jerry took my class for P.E., and I took his for music. His lessons tended to be "by the book," while mine arose from the unpredictable depths of my imagination. I usually tried to stand up straight and never to say "shit" in front of Jerry. But Jerry gave me one of those inner-city lessons that still makes me laugh. One Friday afternoon in the teachers' lounge, he sat talking with another African American male teacher. They discussed plans for the coming weekend. Sitting nearby, I couldn't help but overhear their conversation. "You two are going to Reno?" I asked.

"Yeah, we like to let off a little steam, occasionally." Racial tensions had reached a peak that year, and Black people faced slights and hostility everywhere.

"We gamble a little, then we put on our black leather jackets and walk down the sidewalk swinging chains. Gotta scare the whities a little sometimes." They both grinned conspiratorially. They meant it. I couldn't stop laughing. No one was gentler than Jerry. I loved it! Just use white folks' own racial stereotypes to get back at them.

A visit to one of my student's homes offered another lesson in cultural differences from my white, suburban upbringing. In sociology classes, we learned about the many "broken homes" in inner cities. Children were thought to have extra problems due to the many fathers missing from their homes. My anthropological training, however, had already allowed me to recognize a flaw in this reasoning. Many cultures in the world are matrilineal. In matrilineal societies, the biological father does not play the social role of father. Childcare and training are supplied by the mother's brother.

A man's role is to assist in the upbringing of his sister's children. The system meets everyone's needs; it's simply different from the American ideal. The mothers of many of my students seemed to be strong heads-of-household. Uncles often played important roles in their children's lives. I recognized that some families had carried on the matrilineal traditions. These were not broken homes.

The sense of security I discovered while visiting one of my student's homes differed from my own childhood experiences. My sister and I had been well-praised for our accomplishments: we were expected to be polite, get good grades, do our best at whatever we attempted, be independent, not whine . . . the list went on. We had done these things acceptably and had earned the love of our parents.

Rondell's family showed itself to have different requirements. The living room at his house felt warmed by the many family members present for my visit. The relationships of those present weren't clear to me, but obviously I was being introduced to a large extended family. Conversation flowed easily; everyone contributed; adults and children listened to each other enthusiastically. In the midst of my visit, the door swung open, admitting a gaunt young man in his early twenties. The room erupted.

"Jordan!" Shouts from everyone. Just like with Uncle Rupert at the Newsoms', arms were thrown around Jordan's body. Short humans wrapped themselves around his legs, while larger ones engulfed his head and shoulders, blocking my view. Eventually, when their surprise and joy ebbed long enough for him to settle into an overstuffed chair, Rondell's mom introduced us.

"Jordan, this is Rondell's teacher, Ms. McMillan. Jordan, here, is my oldest son. He's been in prison for two years and we didn't expect him home for another several months. This is a great surprise for us!"

Shift the mental picture to my parents' living room in Orinda. Fill the room with family and friends. Imagine myself, having been in prison for two years, surprising the group with my sudden appearance. Imagine silence. Imagine awkward. Imagine false laughter. Most of all, imagine strained discomfort. In the culture where I'd been raised, returning from prison could not possibly engender such uninhibited displays of love and welcome.

I visualized Jordan's family holding a wide, unbreakable net; any of them could safely fall. They would land and be held in that net of love. Love here was not conditional. As with the Newsoms, family was family, and love in the family existed unconditionally. An action might be totally unacceptable, but it wouldn't make the *person* unacceptable.

Disapproval had been the strongest weapon my parents held over me. I never believed that I would always be held safe in the love of my family regardless of my actions. Actions held consequences, one of which, I believed, could be the loss of their love. Love had to be earned in my family. Be polite, act nice, get good grades, don't upset people. The illusion of the perfect family had to be supported at all times, but not necessarily support the people within it. I tried vainly to imagine what truly unconditional love might have given me. Perhaps my parents had loved me unconditionally, but that was not the message they'd conveyed.

No, these Oakland homes were not broken. Perhaps my own exemplary childhood had been more broken.

TWENTY-TWO

Toward the end of 1969, an increasingly heavy weight loomed over Peter's head. Although President Nixon had declared he would begin the "Vietnamization" of the war, bringing increasing numbers of soldiers home, the media continued to blast out daily body counts. Whichever side reported the most casualties determined the success or failure of each twenty-four hours of fighting. Vietnamese civilians got counted, along with the deaths of Viet Cong, enhancing the U.S. kill-ratio in comparison with the body counts of young American men, a number that continued to grow.

The United States government had announced that they would initiate a lottery system to call up young men for the draft. Numbers would be drawn randomly, like in a bingo game, each one with a date written on it. The first date drawn would be number one, people with that birthday would be the first draftees sent to Vietnam. Several men I knew, including my brother-in-law, had enlisted solely to choose the nature of their service. Bob had served in the signal corps and had been stationed in Saigon, a relatively safe location compared to the others. Bob survived with minimal physical and emotional scars. Draftees had no choice of where to serve, and were often sent to the infantry, becoming "cannon fodder" on the front lines. No one I knew wanted to fight in this war we had been protesting for years. My friends certainly didn't want to kill people or die themselves. Draft deferments were given to men attending their first four years of college, but deferments were not guaranteed for graduate students. Peter's birthday fell within the first group of dates to be drawn, 1944 to 1950.

On December first, we made our way to the "Med"—the Café Mediterranean—a gathering place for the radical left. There, we could watch the lottery drawing with others as nervous as ourselves. We ordered Italian coffees with plenty of milk and found two cane-backed chairs to sit in. Setting my cup on the stained table, I put my hand over Peter's. If I was this nervous, I couldn't imagine what he must be feeling. Peter's birthday was March 12; we desperately hoped it wouldn't come up until the end of the draw. Moisture beaded on Peter's forehead as the program came onto the large TV screen.

"Because of the CBS special report which follows, Mayberry RFD will not be shown tonight." *The Draft Lottery* filled the screen in bold letters. Correspondent Roger Mudd began talking softly to the camera from Selective Service Headquarters in Washington, D.C. The TV screen showed young men from the Youth Advisory Council picking from a bin of three-hundred-and-sixty-six little blue plastic capsules, each one holding a single date, including February 29 in order to cover leap years. A chart on the wall was being filled in with the draft number and each matching birthday as it was drawn. Roger's voice on the TV informed us that they hadn't started broadcasting at the beginning; the drawing was now more than halfway completed. Roger went on to let us know what numbers had already been picked.

"The famous first pick tonight is September fourteenth, the first birthday designated double zero one."

Local draft boards would first induct men with birthdays falling on that day. Relieved sighs. No one in the crowd must have had that birthday.

Roger began reading us the picks in ascending order. "April twenty-fourth, double zero two." Two cries of pain. Two number twos in the room.

"December thirtieth, double zero three." One groan.

Peter and I looked at each other. We wanted this to last forever because we wanted his number to come at the very end. Each number called was a shot being fired into some luckless men. Cries of agony involuntarily flew from each one, acknowledging the imagined bullet being fired at them. It might take six months to find their chests, but the rifles were aimed and the triggers had been pulled.

"What are my options?" Peter turned, sipping his coffee.

"You won't be called. You'll get a deferment. Your number will be high."

"October eighteenth, double zero five," from the TV voice.

"I could go to Canada. Lots of men are doing that."

"It's going to be okay. Don't worry yet."

"I'll go to jail before I'll go over there and kill people."

"You aren't going to have to go to jail. It's going to be all right." I was running out of platitudes to feed to Peter. Of course, he knew my statements were nonsense; I couldn't predict his future. Still, I continued babbling responses in an effort to calm us both.

Roger Mudd informed his TV audience that four or five members of the Youth Advisory Council had declined to participate; they wouldn't be the ones to draw out capsules that determined other men's futures. They refused to be pawns of the Nixon administration. Peter and I raised our eyebrows at each other. Younger people than the two of us were also protesting.

We agonized through the list as it was read, feeling the pain of others as their birthdays were drawn. Peter finished his coffee and I went to buy him another. More numbers were read.

Roger Mudd now told us that the lowest third was finished, the numbers one to one hundred and nineteen had determined the men whose birthdays sentenced them for immediate draft. Peter's birthdate hadn't been in that group. The next third, numbers one hundred and twenty to two hundred and forty, would have a fifty-fifty chance of being drafted. The birthdates kept ringing out across the room.

"March eleventh, number one thirty-six." One day off Peter's birthday.

"Should we be doing this? Maybe I'll just read them in the morning?"

"Peter, you know we can't leave. The longer this goes, the better it is."

The odor of marijuana smoke drifted through the café. No one was worrying about its illegality.

"March twenty-sixth, one seven zero."

We both startled; that sounded too similar to March twelfth. But it wasn't Peter's number . . . yet.

Eventually they had drawn two hundred and forty-one birthdates. No one else would be drafted in 1970. Tears filled both our eyes; Peter swiped at his with the back of his hand and kept looking down at the dark stains in his empty white cup. I took several deep breaths.

"Maybe they'll end this damn war before we have to go through this all over again," Peter grumbled.

Many people left as we continued waiting for the announcements for the final third. I watched folks filing out. Ponytails and crew cuts, bearded, mustached, or clean-shaven, jeans or leather pants . . . where were their numbers? Who was safe and who would hold a rifle in his hands come January? Over and over again, one small plastic capsule rolled against another, one young man had moved his fingers around inside a large glass bowl. Each person's fate depended on those tiny random happenings. Which ones would be dead this time next year just because someone's finger twitched a bit at the moment he picked out a little blue capsule? Peter was safe for now, but a third of these guys hadn't been as lucky.

"March twelfth, three hundred."

We reached for each other's hands. Our wooden chairs made a screechy sound as we pushed back from the table.

"I didn't catch Tim's number; I'd better give him a call." Peter's brother was two years younger; he would be in the pool too.

I hadn't been aware that I'd also been listening for December second. Steve's birthday hadn't been called yet. He too was safe for now.

We paused outside the front door of Café Med. I tried to read the faces of people up and down Telegraph Avenue. Some looked dazed, some relieved, but no one had been untouched by what just happened. I glanced up at Peter. He was lucky. We were lucky. I squeezed his hand and he squeezed back. Both our eyes were moist as we headed home.

Facing my students the next morning, I felt as if my chest were filled with molten lead. Almost everyone there had a close relative who had just experienced the lottery drawing exactly as Peter and I had. Some would be going to 'Nam and some would never return. Tyrone was the first to speak.

"My brother got two hundred thirty-one. He's not going."

"My uncle's number sixteen. Says he proud to get called."

"Then yo' uncle's dumber than pig snot. He jus' gonna die there!"

I waved my hand, gesturing around the room. "Almira, that's enough. We don't know what's going to happen to Tommy's uncle. Yesterday was hard for all of us, and people have different feelings about what happened. We need to respect that. Now what chapter were we on in *Harriet Tubman*?" I picked up the book and began reading. My rule was that they could draw or color while I read. They'd come to love being read to. It soothed all our nerves and calmed us down.

We'd left most of our feelings about the draft behind by the time we began a social studies lesson. With our focuses once more in the classroom, it began to feel like a regular school day. At the end of an hour, Willie came up to my desk. "See what I wrote in my book, Miz McMillan?"

After trying countless methods of classroom control for Willie, and having failed nearly every time, I finally had come up with a method that seemed to be working. I'd asked Willie to decorate a notebook I'd bought him, and to title it "Willie's Book." At the end of each hour, he'd come to my desk and write what he'd done that hour. Then I would ask him what he might have done instead. I made no judgements about his answers, but merely initialed his entry in the book, agreeing with what he'd written. A common entry in the beginning was something like "I took Rondell's pencil and put it on Almira's desk. I could have done the work in the social studies book." The point was to show him that he was in control of his own behavior and was making choices.

I reached out for his book. "What does it say, Willie?"

"I did two pages in my math workbook."

I nodded. He knew there was no need for him to write what he might have done instead. He'd done his assignment. I smiled, signing my initials at the end of his uneven printing.

"You've done a lot of good work recently, Willie. I'm glad you've written it all in here."

Willie took his book back from my desk, looking down at it and rubbing his thumb along the binding. He peeked up at me shyly. "Can I take this home and show my mama?" It was the first time the now-fourteen-year-old had shown any vulnerability.

"Of course you can, Willie; I know she'll be proud of you."

It was a positive incident in what had started as a difficult day.

With Peter not being drafted, our lives settled into a rhythm. His work continued on his PhD, and I became more confident, finding my own style as a fourth-grade teacher. When the school year was drawing to a close, Miss Tobin called me into her office. Mr. Simpson, our lanky, easygoing vice-principal, was already seated in a heavy oak chair just inside the door. Miss Tobin gestured toward another chair. I sat down, uncertain what to expect. Had Mr. Simpson, who often visited my classroom, snitched on me about the couch? I liked him a lot, and I doubted that was it, but my heart was pounding anyway.

"I want to compliment you, Miss McMillan, on how well you've been doing with Willie Harrison. You two seem to get along well. We haven't had to deal with him as a discipline problem out on the playground in several months."

Surprised, I let my shoulders relax. "Yes, I'm very proud of Willie. He's taking an interest in schoolwork and has come a long way with his reading."

"Mr. Simpson and I have decided that you've been doing so well with him, we're going to keep Willie with you for another year."

"But I don't teach fifth-grade."

"No, he'll be repeating fourth."

Had I heard that right? I was incredulous. "You're going to flunk Willie because he's doing well?"

"We're not flunking him, we're retaining him because of your special relationship."

"No. NO! You can't do that. It makes no sense at all! It will destroy all the progress we've made." This was totally crazy. I was furious.

"The decision has been made. You'll see; it will be fine."

I continued shaking my head in disbelief as Miss Tobin went on.

"We think you must be the one to tell him, because he'll take it best from you. I know you'll find a way. Further argument is futile."

"This is just *not* okay."

Miss Tobin never backed down. "But it's what's been decided. Now go find Willie and tell him."

I squeezed my lips tightly over my teeth and rose stiffly. Mr. Simpson didn't meet my gaze as I turned and left the office. It took a conscious effort not to slam the door behind me.

As circumstance would have it, I ran into Willie on the steps of the building. I swallowed hard. This was just plain shit! "Willie, I have some important news. I just came from Miss Tobin's office. She and Mr. Simpson decided that, since you've been doing so well in my class, they're going to keep us together again next year."

"What?" Willie's head jerked back. "You tellin' me I flunked fourth grade?" Willie was not going to be duped.

Tears welled in my eyes. "They said they're retaining you."

"They flunkin' me."

Willie's shoulders sagged slowly as I watched his pride and motivation drain away. He moved toward me and I hugged him to me.

"Miz McMillan, this ain' right."

"I know, Willie. I know. I argued with them."

We stood for a long moment. When I loosened the embrace, Willie still held on. His bent head was buried against my breasts. I tried to move back and he still held on.

Shit, although hurt and discouraged, a piece of Willie's sharp mind was finding some advantage in this situation; Willie was copping a feel!

Ah, Willie! I pushed his shoulders a bit more firmly and we stepped apart.

The bottom line remained: the effort I had put into building trust with Willie and the year it had taken to produce his tentative acceptance of the educational system had just been thrown back into both of our faces. Any chance I'd had of helping rescue this boy from a difficult life path had just slipped through my fingers through decisions from people who scarcely knew him. They saw him as little more than a troublesome problem to be solved. I felt defeated and deflated.

Willie skipped a lot of classes in the final two weeks of school. I didn't blame him, but I worried what he might be doing instead. The horrifying injustice of "the system" had imprinted itself indelibly on my soul.

On the last day of school, Gordon Chan joined me during recess, both of us leaning against the schoolyard's chain-link fence. By that time, his English had become nearly fluent. We stood silent for a moment. Then, eventually, he spoke.

"Miss McMillan, I would like to give you something."

I turned to look at his serious face. "What is that, Gordon?"

"I'd like to give you a name."

I waited quietly. I could tell from his voice that whatever this was it meant a great deal to him.

"It's *Lei Su Lan*."

"*Lei Su Lan*? That's very beautiful."

"It means, 'White lotus blossom opening'."

Tears sprang to my eyes. What a gift? What did he see in me? Had the seeds planted by the airplane flight to Africa finally grown into a plant beginning to bloom? Was my white upbringing opening to a more encompassing worldview?

"Oh, Gordon. Thank you." White Lotus Blossom Opening. Yes, that was what I was working to become. That was what I hoped I could be. "Gordon, I promise to try to live up to that name."

We smiled at each other, silently acknowledging the gifts each had given and received from the other during the past months. My mind would often replay the sound of Gordon's voice pronouncing the name, *Lei Su Lan*.

TWENTY-THREE

The death of James Rector and the brutal beatings at People's Park had sorted the protestors. We differed in our levels of courage and our opinions about what to do. Many young people backed off, digesting the reality of their government's willingness to silence them. Others, like the Weathermen and the Students for a Democratic Society went underground, contemplating more violent means of changing our country. Native Americans had occupied Alcatraz Island in 1969, and a group continued living there.

The drug scene also shifted. Marty's prophecy manifested in the changing images of Haight-Ashbury and Telegraph Avenue. Flower-adorned young people playing music on the street corners were slowly being replaced by strung-out panhandlers begging passersby for a few dollars for food (or so the line went). No one knew how much the government had colluded with the Mafia to undermine the peace movement of the Flower Children. Whatever the truth, the effect was obvious to all of us.

I began singing again, joining the San Francisco Civic Chorale, and was part of a small group who sang with Arthur Fiedler when he came to conduct the symphony that summer. I began attending Glide Memorial Church, where Reverend Cecil B. Williams somehow managed to get fur-clad Orinda matrons singing together with unwashed street people, arms around each other's shoulders. Reverend Williams kept us apprised of the situation with Angela Davis, the Black activist who had been on the FBI's most-wanted list. He visited often during her incarceration—on charges for which she was later acquitted—and he relayed to us ways in which we could be supportive.

After we moved in together, Peter's and my relationship deepened. I worked all summer writing my thesis on the Elementary Math Curriculum, and received my master's degree. Peter traveled often, doing his final research for his PhD.

In the fall, I settled into a comfortable routine teaching my third class in Oakland. The techniques Cal had instilled in us served me well, and at the end of the year, Oakland offered me a position teaching in their demonstration school.

I met Peter at his office to share the news. He had accepted a two-year teaching position at the University of Oregon, replacing a faculty member going on sabbatical. We walked out of the Industrial Relations building and plopped down on its front steps, looking across at the chain-link fence that still guarded the empty wreckage of the former People's Park. The late afternoon sun warmed us as Peter and I leaned our shoulders into each other.

"I've been offered a new position next year. Team-teaching with another woman at Oakland's demonstration school."

"Congratulations. I guess that's an honor."

"Yep. Caroline Middleton just told me. She came to my class after school."

"What did you tell her?"

"Not much. I guess I thanked her."

"Are you going to take it?"

"I don't know. We need to talk about us."

"I hoped you'd come to Eugene with me."

"I know. I could tell you kind of assumed I would." I propped my elbows on my knees, resting my chin in my palms. Uncertainty wove around our bodies like an anxious cat.

"Well, do you want to come?"

"Yeah, I do. I'll be sorry to turn down that job, but I've figured I'd be going with you." I turned sideways to look at him. "Do you think we should get married?"

"Sure. Let's." Leaning in, he kissed me.

"Okay."

Our engagement sounded a bit more like a business negotiation than a romantic proposal, but it felt like the right decision.

As the school year wound down, I paid more attention to wedding plans than to some of the issues around me. The school year had gone well. I knew I'd miss Bella Vista and many of the students and faculty who had become close. Gordon Chan occasionally dropped by to visit me after school, challenging me to remember the Chinese he'd taught the year before. Belen Newsom, Lisa, and CC were all doing great in Damen Cropsey's fifth-grade class, as I knew they would. Willie and I continued to do well together, although he had no enthusiasm for the curriculum he was repeating. He'd resigned himself to surviving another year in the fourth grade as he passed his fifteenth birthday.

During the last week of school, Mr. Simpson sauntered into my portable after all the children had gone. He sat down on the edge of my desk, propping himself up with his long legs.

"What you gonna do about Willie, Carol? What he's doing behind the portable after school?"

I had no idea what he was talking about. "What's Willie doing behind the portable after school, Mr. Simpson?" My response was rather flippant.

"You haven't noticed all those high school girls coming down?"

Girls liked Willie, though seemingly not in a romantic way. He had far more girls as friends than boys.

"No, I haven't noticed. Willie likes girls and they like him. What is it that you think he's doing with those girls?"

"He's putting together a stable."

"A stable?" I asked, having no clue what that meant.

"He's a pimp, Carol. Willie's becoming a pimp." Exasperation in his voice.

My heart lurched for Willie before I barked out a sardonic laugh. "Shit, Mr. Simpson! The whole system dumped on Willie's head. What do you think he's going to be now, an airline pilot?" I was still angry about it. I was sure that keeping Willie in my class this year had been Miss Tobin's idea, not Mr. Simpson's, but he'd been complicit. "Willie knows what options he's got."

Mr. Simpson didn't respond. He was looking at his shoes.

"Oakland has pimps," I went on. "Some are mean and some aren't. It's a business. Willie'll treat his women right." I couldn't believe I was defending Willie's choice of profession, but the hypocrisy of the school's administration position infuriated me. They'd forced him into an alternative life and they should own up to that. Whatever. It was their problem if they wanted to do anything about it, not mine. I wasn't judging Willie.

I'm certain my response wasn't what Mr. Simpson expected. He slowly stood up, shaking his head from side to side as he ambled out my door. "You're sure no little Orinda girl anymore, Carol."

"Thank you, Mr. Simpson."

I watched him smoothly descend the steps of my portable. Although he was also raised in Oakland, the road of Mr. Simpson's life had led him to a university. The road of Willie's life had been lined with concrete walls. He was left with very different choices.

I turned to finish straightening the classroom. This was part of the Tapestry too. My eyes welled in frustration. Miss Tobin and Mr. Simpson had created this mess. I wished them luck if they were going to try to fix it.

Live oak trees formed a canopy over friends and family gathered for our wedding. Peter and I held hands as we climbed the steps of the natural amphitheater in John Hinkel Park. The scent of eucalyptus filled the breeze, rustling the veil that Peter had lifted just moments ago when the Unitarian minister suggested he might "kiss the bride." I gathered up the skirt of my white organza wedding gown, trying not to trip on the uneven stones. The intricate beading of my bodice couldn't contain the happiness that swelled inside. Glancing up, I was proud that my brand-new husband looked so dashing. Peter's blue eyes matched the velvet Edwardian jacket I'd sewn for him. As our guests fell in behind us, I could pick out different dialects and even different languages in the chatter that filled the park. The Chinese came from Larry Tam's family, Spanish from Peter's brother's wife; I wasn't sure who was speaking in a broad Southern dialect.

Aromas greeted us when we entered the park's brown wooden hall. They wafted from a long table covered with dishes as varied as the people who had contributed them to our potluck wedding feast. We had invited my students and their families, Peter's colleagues from the industrial relations department at Cal, and Bella Vista teachers, all of whom began mingling with our families and their friends. There were a few gaps, people who left a hole in the gathering. Steve and Libby had moved back east with their daughter, and Sondra was on vacation in the southwest. I'd lost contact with Marty and Alan, and had not invited Ed Ross.

Belen Newsom came up to me shyly, reaching out to touch my dress. "Miz McMillan, you look so priii-ty," she said, drawing out the word as her family walked over to join us. Mr. Newsom wasn't wearing his Black Panther leather jacket, but I was happy to see him wearing a black beret above his white turtleneck. I wondered how the Orinda contingent was reacting. I glanced around, but saw no one giving him long looks.

"But I thought your skirt would be bigger. Like Cinderella's," Belen continued.

Her mom shushed her as I laughed. The white dress had been a nod to the indelibility of my childhood brainwashing.

Fran McMillan with CC, Lisa, and their aunt.

"You can have a Cinderella dress if you get married, Belen. Or, maybe, just buy one for fun sometime and wear it to a party when you're in college." I had to get in a final teacherly comment, but was careful not to feed her the same script I'd grown up with. I wanted to help my students be free to explore whomever they wished to become. I did not intend to make any more scripted, middle-class individuals who happened to have more melanin in their skin.

After the Yosemite incident a few summers ago, I was startled and gratified to see my mother standing with a smile across her face, arms embracing Lisa and CC, who looked adorable in their matching pink dresses. Scanning the room to find my dad, however, I saw him off in a corner, deep in conversation with Tom Mika, while Paul Williams stood nearby. They were an isolated enclave of white men. Coincidence or choice?

Too excited to eat anything, I flowed around the room, chatting with people I hadn't seen for years, as well as others with whom I'd worked daily. Hippie friends sat cross-legged on the floor, plates of food balanced on their laps. Barbara Wilson looked spectacular in spike heels and a flattering dress, but she hadn't brought her Oakland Raider boyfriend. Mr. Simpson towered above most of the crowd, looking relaxed in a pale rose sports jacket, a collarless rose shirt, and maroon, bell-bottom slacks. My brother-in-law, now a Vietnam veteran, held Jenny, their newly adopted baby girl. They were introducing her to the one-year-old son of Jean's best friend from high school. Smiles and happy chatter filled the old log building.

Peter and I found each other again when it was time to cut the elegant Larsen's Bakery cake, a gift from my parents who had valiantly tolerated the notion of a potluck wedding. As plates were passed, I looked around the gathering. We were human threads of the Tapestry, diverse in our cultures, colors, worldviews, and experiences. Africa had taught me the truth of our connection. Perhaps, in my own small way, I was spreading that knowledge. The life script I was writing for myself seemed pretty okay. I smiled, thinking of Gordon Chan and wishing he had been able to come to the wedding. In my white gown, surrounded by those who nurtured me, perhaps, for this moment, I could live up to the name he'd given me. *Lei Su Lan*. White Lotus Blossom Opening.

Conversations drew threads from the core of each person, intertwining with those of others. I could almost see the ethereal Tapestry being created, a weaving I might not be able to hang on the wall, but one that I would certainly hold in my heart.

ACKNOWLEDGMENTS

My deepest gratitude goes to Laura Kalpakian and the excellent authors of her writing group, without whose fierce and loving critiques this book would never have emerged. The close ties that developed among us form a net of love and trust that allows the sharing of honest feedback while our—sometimes fragile—writers' egos can remain undamaged.

Love and thanks to Andrea Gabriel, Frances Howard-Snyder, Jolene Hanson, Jessica Stone, Pam Helberg, Mary Ann Boyle, Brenda Wilbee, Laura Rink, Tele Aadsen, Victoria Doerper, Connie Feutz, and Cindy Sherwin. I extend these thanks to the entire close-knit community of Bellingham writers, including Kim Harris, who gave my book clearance through the lens of cultural sensitivity. I am also indebted to my new writer friends in the Hawai'i Writers' Alliance, especially Johnson Kahili, who offered feedback from a younger and male demographic. I hope all my friends—especially Stephanie Stika—who listened to my whining during times of frustration and helped celebrate my joy when the words flowed smoothly, can feel the tremendous hugs of appreciation I am sending.

And finally, many thanks to Lisa Dailey and Sidekick Press for helping me put this all together.

ABOUT THE AUTHOR

Carol McMillan is an award-winning writer whose work has been published in several anthologies and scientific journals. She is the author of *White Water, Red Walls*, a memoir in poems, paintings, and photos of her rafting trip through the Grand Canyon. She lives on Moku O Keawe, the Big Island of Hawai'i, where she has served as president of the Hawai'i Writers' Guild. Her two cats' combined names are *Ho'opalekana*, meaning "to rescue" in the Hawaiian language. During the pandemic isolation she rescued the kittens and they rescued her.

Carol is working on her next book that will share her experiences living with free-ranging rhesus monkeys on Cayo Santiago, a tiny island off the coast of Puerto Rico.

PRAISE FOR
WHITE WATER, RED WALLS

Everyone needs to read this!! Such a lovely book; you float through it like you are on a river. A terrific read!!
—Eve London

Worthy of Five Stars . . . If you are thinking of taking on the mighty river that flows through the Grand Canyon, this one's for you. It will fit neatly into your backpack and should be tucked away in a plastic bag to keep it dry. There's a lot here to encourage thoughts about nature and the way we confront it . . . a damn fine effort by a writer we need to see more from.
—Ray Pace, author of *Hemmingway in Hawai'i*.

Experience rafting while staying dry! I've never been to the Grand Canyon but reading this book gave me a sense of the adventure of rafting through it. The descriptions of the landscape put me right there. Love this book.
—Laura Rink, poet

Share the river experience: I rafted the Colorado/Grand Canyon several years ago, and this delightful book spoke to my heart as it describes the river experience so well. I will read it again and again!
—CB Waissman

Five stars on Amazon

CPSIA information can be obtained
at www.ICGtesting.com
Printed in the USA
BVHW042351020623
665283BV00002B/376